IT'S NEVER TOO LATE

IT'S NEVER TOO LATE

Leading ADOLESCENTS
to Lifelong Literacy

Janet Allen

HEINEMANN
Portsmouth, NH

Heinemann
A division of Reed Elsevier Inc.
Portsmouth, NH 03801-3912
Offices and agents throughout the world

Library of Congress Cataloging-in-Publication Data
Allen, Janet, 1950–
    It's never too late : leading adolescents to lifelong literacy / Janet Allen.
        p.   cm.
    Includes bibliographical references and index.
    ISBN 0-435-08839-4 (paper)
    1. Reading (Secondary)—Language experience approach.
2. Underachievers—Psychology.   3. Motivation in education.
4. Teacher-student relationships.   I. Title.
    LB1632.A55   1995
    428.4'071'2—dc20   94-41022
                                                                CIP

Editor: Carolyn Coman
Production: J. B. Tranchemontagne
Cover design: Mary Cronin

Printed in the United States of America on acid-free paper
99 98 97 96   EB   2 3 4 5 6

Dedication

For my father, Murle Bean,
  who taught me the value of finding and celebrating
  the goodness in every individual.

For my uncommon friend, Troy Cunningham,
  who found value in me and
  taught me to believe in myself again.

and

For my student, and my teacher, Sarah Archer,
  who taught me that
  it is never too late.

Contents

sions for this Foreword, I found myself taking notes about Ms. Allen's strategies for teaching reading. I typed out passages that made philosophical and pedagogical sense. I wrote down the titles of young adult books that absorbed her students, these teenagers whose literacy futures school had so dimly viewed.

I don't know Janet Allen personally, but I hope to meet her some day. I came to know her thoroughly, however, through the readable words and compelling stories of her book. Not a bad way, I think, to meet someone. You'll like getting to know her, too. And your teaching, I believe, will be the better for it.

Tom Romano

Acknowledgments

Although many people contributed to the success of my classroom research and to my sanity while I was writing, the following individuals helped make the idea a reality. I want to thank them for their patience, suggestions, energy, and support.

My students at Presque Isle High School spent many hours being interviewed, collecting samples of their work, and explaining to me what I thought I was seeing. They were not only wonderful students, but also insightful teachers.

Four of my colleagues gave much of their time listening to me talk through both the research and the writing: Paul Carlsen, Barbara Frick, Gail Gibson, and Connie Piper. Connie spent many days reading samples and listening to stories as well as creating opportunities for our classes to work together. Barbara worked with my students during playwriting and creative dramatics as well as conducted a year-end debriefing video with the class. Paul spent untold hours proving to my students that their artistic language was as significant as their oral language. Gail was there not only to interview students, but also to listen to each chapter as it was written. These colleagues are thoughtful friends who care about children and learning as I do.

Brenda Power was the cheerleader every teacher-researcher needs. Her knowledge of and love for teacher-research made me believe that my work was important and meaningful. Each time I heard her say, "I loved this part!" it made me want to write more.

My new students at the University of Central Florida have given me support by asking daily if I have finished yet and eagerly reading each of my latest writings. My graduate assistants, Jennifer Miller-Norton and Alescia Fleming, have spent many hours checking citations and running interference so that I could finish on schedule.

As in all consuming projects, there are those who make the process work because of their support. Three of my new colleagues in Florida, Donna Camp, Judith Johnson, and Joanne Ratliffe, have provided friendship and professional connections for my writing. My network of literacy colleagues in Maine and in Florida helped me see my classroom in a broader context than I might otherwise have viewed it. The enthusiasm teachers and students have shown as I shared my research has helped me to continue writing when other work might have taken precedence.

I have been blessed to have Dawn Boyer as my first editor. Each time we met or talked on the telephone, Dawn assured me that my teaching and my writing would make a difference. She always left me with a feeling of renewal and inspiration. When Dawn's work took her away from this project, Carolyn Coman quickly moved this book along. She, too, gave positive, constructive help for all the finishing touches. Joanne Tranchemontagne has had the difficult job of actually turning my ideas into a product. She has done this task with creativity, patience, and kindness.

Last, but in no way least, my family and friends helped from beginning to end. My parents believed in and taught me the importance of education and although my father never lived to see this day, he anticipated it from my first day of school. My sister, Paula Carson, believed in the importance of my work long before it became part of my degree or my book. Aaron Nelson, my principal for thirteen years, helped set high expectations and then moved out of the way so that teachers could find success. Sandra Leighton kept me from quitting in those early days of teaching when it seemed that almost any job would have been easier. She told me every day that I was a great teacher, even the days when I know I wasn't. Chuk Estey has been the friend in charge of sunsets and leaving the turmoil behind. Those have been times of renewal that helped me get back to my writing. Micky Lewin was the kind of friend who was always there. She worked on the bibliography, lent moral and emotional support, and made countless tuna casseroles. Mary Giard has been and continues to be in charge of life's celebrations. She has celebrated rough drafts and final drafts, contracts and awards. She gave me not only the concrete model of a classroom with a new role for the teacher and students but also a friendship that sustained me when I felt like quitting. Finally, Troy Cunningham has believed in me until I could once again believe in myself. He has cheered my successes and added perspective to my failures. He has been and continues to be "an uncommon friend."

I appreciate these friends and give them the greatest compliment I know: for me, each of you has been a TEACHER, and I thank you for it.

Introduction

I suspect that many books have a moment when the author decides that a person or an event has had such an impact on her life, it must be shared. Although every day in my classroom yielded significant moments, the event that made me want to write a book occurred halfway through my first year of post–graduate school teaching. Barb Frick had led my students through several creative dramatics activities, and Sarah had been the "star" on these days. After that, she was consumed with my role as assistant drama director. Could she come to the rehearsals? How did those kids get to be in the play? Each day brought new questions and increased interest in our drama department. Finally, I asked Sarah why she hadn't tried out for our latest production. She seemed to love the theater and she was certainly dramatic. Her response immediately brought tears to my eyes, "When they had tryouts, I thought I couldn't read and so couldn't have learned my lines. But, now that I can read, I can do anything."

I wrote this book to recount my year with students who could not, or would not, read. Although many of these students had rich lives, their academic lives were ones of daily risk. In addition, many of these students excluded themselves from participation in and enjoyment of school activities, which seemed to require "good reading." It would be wonderful if there were some magic potion that could turn all these students into readers, but there isn't. And I certainly have no illusions that this book is that magic potion. In spite of the detailed strategies I recount here, this is not intended to be a recipe book for working with at-risk students. It is instead the story of our year together and, as in all stories, many days and many details are left out. I could rewrite this book several times, using events or practices that I chose not to include, but for now this is how I remember our year.

I know that once a book is finished the author has to let it go, but there are things that I hope stay with you long after the book is on your shelf. I hope that you have a desire to research and write about the "epiphanies" that come from the teaching and learning in your own classroom. I hope that you see each student as a unique gift. And I hope you believe that it is never too late to help someone experience the joy of reading.

1

The View in the Rearview Mirror

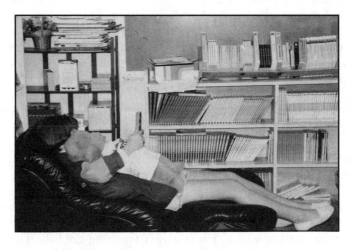

There was no reason for me to be steering; I let go of the wheel. There was no reason to sit where I was; I moved to the opposite seat. I stared at the empty driver's seat. I could see the sheen where I'd sat for years. We continued to move across the desert.

Barry Lopez, *Desert Notes*

Since teaching and researching are both reflective processes, I couldn't begin my research story without looking back at the path that brought me to this time and place. As I reflect on those last twenty years as a classroom teacher, it occurs to me that I can't think of anyone who would ever have labeled me traditional. Initially, however, it wasn't because I chose to be different. When I got my first teaching job in 1972, I was like all of the other recently graduated English majors—armed with college notes, critical texts of Shakespeare's works, and noble schemes for making students find British literature as exciting as the recently published *Love Story* (Segal, 1970). I entered my classroom that August filled with youthful illusions and delusions about teaching; images of students controlled by competition, GPAs, and research papers; and a love of literature. In the end, it would be the love of literature that would save me and my students from the mold of English teaching that had been set long before.

I know those first disillusioning days of school are something I'll never forget. They were filled with a kind of educational schizophrenia: I was thrilled that I could finally say I was a teacher but devastated by what teaching entailed. I had been a student in advanced English classes, majored in English, and student taught with a department chair who was only assigned college-bound students. This background hardly prepared me for students who didn't read Shakespeare—or anything else. Five classes of General English I, II, III; thirty students in every class. I remember thinking, "What is general English?" I don't know if I would have been comforted to be told that no one else knew what it was either. There were no textbooks, no curriculum guides, no supplementary materials.

Somehow I managed to get through that first day, and after school I found myself asking the vice principal what I was supposed to do with all those students and no texts. His reply? "Do whatever you want, just keep them in the room." Keep them? I wasn't even sure what they were! They certainly weren't the students who had surrounded me in my high school English classes, and that was only four years ago. My friends and I had talked about literature and complained that we spent too much time on the Victorians and not enough on the Romantics. Relevance was never an issue; the works we read were relevant because we needed to read them in order to get into a university, or so we thought. Some of my students were fighting, some smelled of stale smoke; some sat quietly tolerating the noise, and others stared into space surrounded by the sweet smell of newly smoked pot. I didn't know what to call it, but it wasn't teaching English. That was the day I put up a calendar to mark off the days until I could resign.

In retrospect, I had been given a gift that classroom teachers today actively seek. I wasn't tied to an anthology; I had none. I wasn't fighting with the administration to change an outdated curriculum; there was no curriculum. Academic freedom? I was free to do anything I wanted as long as I kept the students in the room. In those laissez-faire days of the 1970s, with open campus and stereo-filled study halls, the first trick was getting the kids inside the classroom. What could we possibly do in a required English class that would compete with the fun of hanging out with friends, listening to music, and getting high? No, in those first tentative days of being a teacher, that lack of direction didn't seem like much of a gift. Yet in terms of my professional growth, it was probably the best thing that could have happened—for me and for my students. Without texts, curriculum guides, materials, or administrative direction, only two things remained in my classroom: students and a teacher. Although at the time I saw these as two separate groups, the lines and roles began to change as I experienced my interpretation of what Meek (1991) refers to as "epiphanies of the ordinary."

Epiphanies of the Ordinary

As I work with secondary teachers today in an inservice capacity, I see how difficult it is for many of them to separate themselves and their teaching from the trappings of education: the curriculum guides, the canon of literature, the anthologies, and the tradition. My own separation process didn't take long. My quest to teach the way I had been taught led me to a veteran English teacher's classroom, and I was able to cajole some textbooks from her. I remember her comments still: "I can lend you these books, but you have to promise to take care of them. *Those students of yours* (not to be confused with the college-bound students of the more experienced teachers) are so irresponsible. I don't want these books returned with marks and things on them." Not wanting to imagine the kinds of things my "irresponsible" students might deposit on the books, I took them across the hall and planned a lesson. At last, I would be a teacher. I would have a lesson plan: silent reading, questions at the end of the story, and a grade in my new grade book. I was finally able to do what I thought English teachers did.

Although I gave fleeting thoughts to the fact that I planned to use the same text in all three levels of English, I wasn't too concerned, since no one cared what I did anyway. The next day I distributed the books, assigned a story and the questions following that story, and sat confidently behind my desk. It worked! Books were open, the students were quiet, and there would be marks in my grade book at the end of that day. Long before Sizer's (1984) indictment, I had learned to participate in the conspiracy: "The agreement between teacher and students to exhibit a facade of orderly purposefulness is a conspiracy for the Least, the least hassle for anyone" (p. 156).

But my newly found success lasted only a day. At the end of that first day, I walked around my classroom gathering up the books from the dark recesses of the ancient, top-lifting student desks. As I went from desk to desk lifting the books from the clutter the students had amassed in just a few days of school, I was able to get a picture of the kinds of "things" they might do to the revered texts. As I lifted one desktop, I was filled with horror to see that the hardbound cover of the text had been bent back and forth until it could be ripped in half. Nothing in my preparation for becoming a teacher, and certainly nothing in my personal experience with books, had prepared me for that sight. Admittedly, my first feelings of horror revolved around returning this book to the veteran teacher, but I was equally horrified at such an attitude toward books. It surprises me even today to think of the impact of that one experience on my teaching. I returned the books, minus one, to the teacher across the hall. Somehow I knew that if textbooks could create those kinds of feelings in students, there had to be something better. I also knew that if I could make it to the annual harvest break, when students left school to work in the potato harvest, it would be the perfect time to resign. But that still left me with one month, one hundred and fifty students, and no idea about what to do in the classroom. Four weeks of chaos loomed before me!

Looking back, it seems as though my students and I came upon the "somethings" that were better almost by accident. I spent days scrounging in cabinets and storage areas looking for anything that could be used to teach English. It seemed that everywhere I looked there were copies of Shakespeare's plays but not much else. I found some outdated copies of *Reader's Digest* magazine, which our senior English teacher used with his general classes, and some tattered vocabulary books. Although these materials didn't seem too exciting to me, at least they vaguely resembled English materials I had seen.

And then we hit pay dirt: we found several copies of *Mr. and Mrs. Bo Jo Jones* (Head, 1967) and *Bless the Beasts and the Children* (Swarthout, 1967) in a cabinet in the storage area. I had never read or heard of either of these books or authors, but the covers certainly looked more appealing than *Reader's Digest* or *Hamlet*. The department chair had no idea where the books came from and didn't care if I took them. But then I was left with another dilemma; I had no idea what to do with them. There weren't enough copies for every student. There weren't even enough copies for one entire class.

As I sat trying to figure out what to do, I remembered my childhood days when listening to stories come alive was the only thing that kept me out of trouble. My mother often told friends and relatives that when she hired a babysitter the only thing she made sure of was whether they liked to read out loud. If it worked for me, maybe it would work with these students! Nothing in my academic preparation for teaching had told me that reading aloud was an option for high school students. I had never heard of *English Journal,* and I had no idea that others were struggling with the same curricular issues. These two books became the texts for my first read aloud, not because I had carefully chosen them to meet the needs of the students in the class, but because they were all I could find.

Although many students thought being read to was stupid, as the stories of rebellious kids taking control of the system and of teenagers grappling with love and sexuality began to unfold, they gradually decided that perhaps they weren't too old to enjoy hearing a good story. I learned that reading aloud was a risk-free way to turn many individuals into one group and share literature with students who believed they hated to read. The questions I asked during and after the reading might have sounded very similar to the end-of-story questions I had experienced, but the texts were at least relevant to these students' lives.

I think this was the first time it ever occurred to me that I could really do whatever I wanted in this classroom. Curriculum didn't have to come from a textbook. It could be built from whatever we chose. I know that if I had been teaching college preparatory classes, I might not have come to that knowledge as quickly because there was an established curriculum there that would have felt familiar and matched my university classes. These general students, however, didn't fit that mold and most educators I knew had yet to create a new mold. With my new definition of curriculum came a sense of freedom—freedom to create, experiment, throw away, and start again.

I met with a local bookseller who gave us outdated magazines and newspapers. I tore pictures out of the magazines, laminated them, and put them in a creative writing box. These, along with weekly Letters to the Editor and interclass Dear Abby notes, became the beginnings of our writing program. And no one could convince me either then or now that garage sales didn't come into existence solely to help me become a better teacher.

Each Saturday was a flurry of garage sale adventures that produced paper-back books, bookcases, posters, and comfortable furniture for the room. A fifteen dollar record player was used to play records of songs whose lyrics students brought in and typed; these lyrics became our language curriculum. I bought a game of Scrabble and we played games that began early in the morning when the buses arrived and lasted through lunch breaks and after school. Soon we needed multiple games as the Zs, Qs, and Xs of the Scrabble game began to disappear. We found an aquarium and copied information from encyclopedias and science books on how to care for the fish. The wall was covered with collages and newspaper articles, poetry and photographs. Advocates of a sequential, linear curriculum would have had difficulty in our classes—we built our language and learning activities around whatever we could find. In fact, one wall of our classroom said, "The world is our textbook."

It would be the 1980s before secondary educators would talk in earnest about the need for publishing student work, but student work was every-where in our classroom because everything we did was student work. Al-though outsiders might have said there seemed to be no "rhyme or reason" to what we were doing, still there was a rhythm to our days. The students felt secure enough to begin taking risks, and I began to feel that it was my role to support those risks. It wasn't until I was in a master's program that I heard of Vygotsky's (1962) "zone of proximal development," but I didn't need to know the term to know that what these students needed was a place to begin again—a place built on success, not failure. Although I wasn't always sure where we were going or where we would end up, at least we weren't sitting still.

Atwell (1987) refers to herself as a "creationist" during her early days of teaching. "The first day of every school year I created; for the next thirty-six weeks I maintained my creation. My curriculum. From behind my big desk I set it in motion, managed and maintained it all year long" (p. 3). I guess I would have to call myself a survivalist during those first days; I had no plan, I just wanted to survive as I ticked the days off on my calendar. But in the course of those survival days, I discovered some truths about teaching and learning, or at least truths for my learning at that time. I discovered that students will read when they are given the time and opportunity to read. I discovered that students will write when they are allowed to write about what is important to them. I discovered that they could be responsible, for themselves and each other, if given the opportu-nity. I also discovered that by the time the sixty days had gone by, my colleague and friend across the hall had been right—I was meant to be a teacher. Actually, I couldn't imagine myself being anything else. Once students started coming into my classes and staying to enjoy the freedom of creating a curriculum, we were on our way.

The room began to fill with books, but as students turned into readers it seemed that there were never enough new books to go around. One day as I was trying to figure out how I could get more books, I thought of having a contest. Students in each of the five classes would bring in any books they wanted to donate to our classroom library, and the class contributing the most books would have a party (paid for by me, of course). The students were enthusiastic when they realized there was a party at stake. One of the boys, who lived on a potato farm, brought in five potato barrels, numbered each one to represent a class, and lined them up along the front of the classroom. Several students made posters for each class, which included each person's name and a row of empty boxes so we could record their contributions. The competition between classes was fierce and the potato barrels filled quickly as students begged and "borrowed" books from every imaginable source.

When the contest ended, our classroom walls were lined with books. Our vocational students made bookcases to house our newly found wealth. Books were sorted and those that didn't fit were taken to local buy and swap stores to exchange for books that met our needs. The more students read, the more they wrote. Graphic arts students began taking the other students' writings and art and creating bulletin boards. The room and the class had taken on a life of their own, although I was never quite sure how it happened.

With spring came new contracts and the long-awaited new teaching assignments, but I had been so "successful" with my students that I was once again given all general classes. And I guess if success is measured by changed lives, then I had been successful. Many of my students had changed their attitudes about reading and writing, and I had changed my idea of what it really meant to be a teacher.

If the first year of teaching was the beginning of learning how to be a teacher, then the second year was learning how to be a professional. Prior to that year of teaching, I had assumed that I had learned in college whatever I needed to know in order to be a teacher. The idea that new research could have an impact on the content and methodology of teaching never occurred to me. And, why would it? I had seen the same books and teaching at the university that I had encountered in high school, and I assumed that once I learned the symbolism and the real meaning of all of the classic works of literature, I wouldn't need anything else. My first year of teaching had taught me otherwise, but I still didn't know where to turn for help with what I was doing in my classroom. I wasn't aware of the fact that there were journals and conferences where people grappled with the same issues I was confronting.

Then we added an English teacher to our staff during that following year. Brenda had just finished a year helping put together a National Council Teachers of English conference. She was a writer and a reader. She was "from away," which could be anything from southern Maine to California for those of us who lived in rural, northern Maine. Most important, she brought a professionalism to our English department that we hardly knew existed.

Fortunately, the New England Association of Teachers of English was going to have their fall conference in Maine that year, and Brenda managed to get five of us excited enough to beg our new principal to let us attend. It was a totally new world for all of us. Every workshop presenter gave us armloads of handouts: Women in Literature, Public Doublespeak, How to

Motivate Reluctant Readers—the list was endless. Textbook publishers had just moved away from textbook series as the sole vehicle for teaching English and offered kits and workbooks, study guides and free paperbacks. It was like Christmas.

At night, back in our motel rooms near the turnpike, we would share our cache. I met Anne Dodd there, who gave me an autographed copy of her book *Write Now!* (1973). That book, and knowing a real writer, would change the way I looked at writing and the way I saw myself as a potential writer. That was also the conference at which I spent two days in a workshop with James Moffett, who had recently published *A Student-Centered Language Arts Curriculum, Grades K–13*. Here was a person who was talking about and demonstrating the kinds of learning that my students and I had been coming to during the previous year. He talked about the use of journals; the importance of reading aloud, improvisation, and classroom talk; the classroom as a workshop for writers. We experienced the power of language games and music as a language tool. We discussed the importance of the spontaneity that comes out of students' investigations and reflections.

I left that two-day session feeling validated as a teacher. The things we were discovering in my classroom might have been unusual for our high school, but they weren't unheard of in the educational community at large. During the discussions that Moffett orchestrated, I learned two important lessons: although I was from northern Maine, it didn't follow that I had nothing to contribute; the best way to learn about what works and what doesn't is from the people most affected—students. All the other participants in the workshop were waiting for Moffett to tell them what to do and why they should do it. And although his presentations made me begin to think about some things that hadn't occurred to me, much of what he said reinforced the direction my students and I had been taking for a year. Some of the things he discussed were ideas my students and I had explored, modified, expanded, discarded, or taken on as our own. Because we believed we could build a curriculum, we did.

From these early workshops I came to know that the discoveries my students and I were making together contained valuable insights for other teachers, and thus began my belief that being a professional is more than teaching, more than learning; it is collaborating and sharing. Twenty years later, the foundations for my speaking and writing are the same as they were during the early 1970s: what my students and I have learned about literacy, learning, and ourselves within the context of our classroom community.

During the 1980s I began to read the writings of the Goodmans (1986a, 1986b, 1987), Smith (1971, 1976), Burke (1988), Graves (1983), Murray (1986, 1987), and others who were looking at the processes of reading and writing, and I saw that my beliefs were rooted in what educators were calling whole language. Ken Goodman (1986) pointed us toward the idea that, whole language "is a way of bringing together a view of language; a view of learning; and a view of people, in particular two special groups of people: kids and teachers" (p. 5). My initial understanding of the philosophy of whole language, however, had not come about as a result of reading the writing of educators and researchers; rather, it evolved over time as we reflected on the key elements in our classroom, "two special groups of people: kids and teachers."

Sometimes there were specific students or situations that enlarged my understanding; sometimes it was all of us working together. But it was because we were building more than a curriculum, we were building a way to live and learn together, that reflection became such an important part of our practice. Asking students how they arrived at answers, not what the answers were; asking students to develop questions, rather than give answers; asking myself the purpose instead of the plan helped all of us look beneath the surface of our classroom and carefully examine our learning. Given the importance I place on reflection as the key to greater learning, it would be impossible for me to look at myself as a whole language teacher without looking back at some of the many students who taught me, themselves, and each other.

Candy

It's hard to remember Candy without feeling tears come to my eyes. As I write, I'm staring at Candy's journal—two sheets of blue construction paper filled with white composition paper and stapled at the top—my invitation to Candy to write. Today I buy my students more formal, more aesthetic journals, but I can't say that what is written in them is any more significant than Candy's words.

Candy came to my classroom after many scrapes with family, school, and community. She was tough and hard and defied me to make her do anything. She always wore jeans, not tapered but rolled up, and completed her wardrobe with men's cotton shirts. Overweight, her broken glasses held together with tape and anger written across her face, she was ignored by the other students. The school administration couldn't ignore her, however, because of her fights, her swearing, and her classroom explosions. My class was to be her last hope before a detention center.

When Candy first came into our classroom, the movement away from her was anything but subtle. For days she sat and glared at me and the other students. If I offered her a book, she just sat in her seat until, finally, I left the book on her desk and walked away. Conversation stopped when I made eye contact with her. She wasn't about to trust me no matter how well liked I might be by the other students. Then one day I simply stapled the "journal" together and put it on Candy's desk—no words, no instructions, no pressure. Candy began to write.

> As far back as I can remember, I fell out of the car when I was three. Dad stop the car real quick, and got out. he picked me up and put me back in. When I got in my mother was laughing at first then she started to cry . . . When I was four we moved here, that's when my mother started saying mean things to me. She say I wasnt her kid that I was my uncle and aunt's, that she just took care of me because they didn't want me. Then when my dad started making long haul trips she would beat on me I was about five and started school. I loved school because

it was a place i could go with out getting beat on . . . Then I started to like other people's stuff so i would take it. One time in kindergarten I took a radio and they kick me out and told me not to come back until next year. When I went back I wasn't too bad of a kid but I flunk first grade. Any way I treaded going home at night for when dad wasnt there I was always slapped around, and a couple of time I was forced to eat on the floor like a dog.

In the late afternoon stillness, classes and practices finished for another day and students gone to their other lives, I sat at my desk and read the journal Candy had left for me. The trauma of Candy's early life hadn't been eradicated by school. I thought of McKenzie (1977), who admonishes us to think about the role of schooling for our children: "It is a salutary thought that, in general, the children who are least successful in school, in terms of becoming literate, are those who are most dependent on what the school offers in the way of instruction" (p. 315). Candy was dependent on the school for far more than instruction, but instead of meeting her needs the school forced her to spend an additional year in the environment that was causing her problems.

Candy's behavior quickly formed a pattern: she would sit alone and write during class and leave her journal for me at night. Eventually she revealed the source of her anger, her fighting, her suicide attempts.

I remember once I was bad, I cant remember what I did But any way mum held my hands behind me and let my older brothers and sisters punch me in the gut and slap me. One time I had to stand in a corner on my knees with my head tip all the way back all night long. When I fell asleep mum would poor water over my head so that I would stay awake. So around Christmas I stole a radio. I did if for the sole purpose to get away from my mother.

It was from Candy that I learned that every person has a story. When she came into my classroom, I was told that she could barely read and write, and that, combined with her behavior, caused her severe problems in the classroom. Candy taught me that literacy is not taught in isolation from life. When Candy discovered that she was in a classroom where someone cared about her as a person and a learner, she was able to tell her story. All along, Candy had a story to tell, but it wasn't a story that would fit into the blanks on a worksheet page. Candy could write, and if she could write, she could read. Did we live happily ever after? Did the lessons Candy taught me end there? No, it was only a matter of days before Candy tried to commit suicide again. In response to Candy's journal, I had told her to remember that I cared what happened to her, and if I cared, others would also. I asked her if she needed help from someone.

Dear Janet,
The answer is no. You are all the help I need right now. You've help me alot really it just doesn't show someday I'll set down and tell you everything that's bugging me.

But, I wasn't a therapist and Candy did need help. With her next suicide attempt, she took herself to the hospital. It was from there that I received the rest of Candy's story with a note saying, "I tried to kill myself last night and then I remembered what you wrote in my journal. You said you cared about me and that I should too. So I came to the hospital. I've been writing in my journal now you can see whats wrong with me." Candy's journal described beatings and foster homes, pregnancy and the subsequent "stealing" of her baby, as well as the violence and betrayal she had learned from childhood.

It was from Candy that I learned the power of words—hers and mine. She had learned a way to tell a story and quickly moved from that to reading the stories of others. I learned that if I wanted students to see themselves as writers, they had to write. When I last heard of Candy, she was continuing to write as a writer/editor of a newspaper connected with her job. Literacy learning and growth occurred for Candy when she had a real purpose and a real audience. The skills worksheets on which her reading failure had been measured were an insult to the real words Candy had inside her—words just waiting for someone who would listen.

Carla

Carla found my classroom in much the same manner as Candy: It was her last stop before she was removed from her home and school. It was one of those cold, dreary, fall days when nothing seems to be going right that the vice-principal came into my classroom. "I need a favor." Those words had become his entree for getting my help with the ever-increasing numbers of students who were in trouble at our school. Although my head was screaming that I couldn't take one more problem student, I knew that I wouldn't be able to refuse. Where else would she go?

"This one is trouble and I don't expect you to take anything from her. This is it for her. I'll pick her up at home each morning and bring her to your classroom. Keep her as long as you can, and if she manages to stay for a ranking period, we'll figure out the credits then. When you've kept her as long as you can stand her every day, send someone to the office and I'll take her home. I don't want to pressure you, but this is her last chance—if she can't make it with you, then the juvenile authorities are going to put her downstate." No pressure—just a life.

Carla arrived the next day looking as though she'd like to kill either the vice-principal, who was holding her arm, or me for accepting her in my class. Although I had never talked to Carla before, she had maintained a visible profile at our school. For example, there was the day just a week before when Carla had been in the girls' room washing her hair during third period. The cooking teacher had gone in to the bathroom and dragged Carla to the office. I can't remember if it was Carla's screams or the flying shampoo that first caught my attention as the pair went careening past my open classroom door. And there was the recent guest speaker at our school who was stopped midsentence as Carla clomped across the gym floor in her tight jeans and cowboy boots to retrieve a quarter that had rolled just in front of the podium. Carla—swearing, yelling, fighting with teachers and other students—was a common sight in the hallway leading to the main office. But she wasn't in the hallway now. She was in our classroom and I knew we would have to work together to figure out a way to tear down the walls Carla had built. I had no idea where to begin.

"Where d'ya want me?" Defiant eyes dared me to say, "Anywhere but here."

"Sit wherever you'd like."

"You've got to be kidding! You don't even have a seating chart?"

"I want students to sit where they're comfortable."

Although Carla's look of disgust told me clearly that she believed I should be the one in danger of being locked up, she moved away from us, knocking over a trash can and a shelf of books before slamming her body into the first empty seat. The vice-principal, anticipating that I might soon change my mind, hurried out of the room, leaving the two of us locked in a somewhat uneasy truce. The rest of the class sat waiting for Carla's next explosion and my reaction. For them it was a dramatic version of the book we were reading aloud. Knowing that Carla's problems wouldn't be solved in one day and not really knowing how to begin to solve them, I returned to our reading of *Lovey: A Very Special Child* (MacCracken, 1976).

When I chose this book, I wasn't quite sure it would work with these kids. I knew that the true story of a teacher working with a group of emotionally disturbed children might seem far away from their real life problems. As a teacher, I knew that although these students weren't so problematic that they would be in classes like MacCracken's, they did have problems relating to others both in and out of school. I also knew that my students typically saw the rest of the world as out of step, rather than themselves. That was one of the things I was enjoying about these students; they were making me look at the "norms" of the world through different eyes.

As the story unfolded, it began to seem that some tension might arise from the fact that the stories of MacCracken's students might be all too close to their own, especially in Carla's case. Our class had already settled in, students either celebrating or tolerating each other in the unique way teenagers have when they feel comfortable. And because they were comfortable, I could be more at ease with them. I didn't have to stay on guard for potential problems; students had taken charge of their own behavior, not wanting to disturb one of the first peaceful places they had found in the high school. Our reading aloud had helped us become a family of sorts. Desks no longer stayed in rows; rather, kids would move them to be closer to my reading desk while others came and sat on the window sills and bookcases that were close to me. They didn't do well with interruptions. Carla, angry and mistrustful, was going to be just that. She quickly proved the accuracy of their initial apprehensions.

Maniacal laughter preceded her response to kids moving around my desk. "You're reading out loud? What do you think we are—a bunch of six year olds?" It had taken weeks for me to encourage and support students in the sheer joy of reading a good book out loud. In seconds Carla was able to shake their confidence in that. It didn't take long for one of the boys to tell her to shut up so they could hear the story. Several students pointed out that she didn't have to stay if she didn't want to, and Carla settled down in her seat as if sentenced to some horrible torture.

Weeks passed and Carla not only settled into that class, she began staying for longer and longer periods of time. Long after the class had moved on to another book, Carla spent her time sitting in my classroom, reading other MacCracken books as well as books about children in trouble. She began to write—her poetry found a place on our walls and her short stories filled our class anthologies. Her characters were troubled, misunderstood children whose already horrendous lives were made more miserable by school. And so Carla discovered the power of language. She developed friendships in the class based not on the necessity to be the school clown but on her ability to create, to write, to illustrate, and to share.

Soon the vice-principal would be checking to see if Carla had escaped his daily delivery service only to find her curled up in the corner reading and writing. Sadly, busy days kept me from reflecting as much as I should have when Carla was in my class. As I watched her walk down the aisle at graduation, still tripping and causing people to laugh, but proudly carrying a rose her mother had given her, I thought of the power of the right book for the right person at the right time. She would go on to succeed at a university and in business, while I stayed in my classroom, but I'm sure Carla taught me as much as I taught her.

When people asked what I did to turn her around, I honestly couldn't tell them. There hadn't been one moment when I could say, "From this point she'll be a different person." But I do know that it was from Carla that I learned to listen, to wait, to be patient. When she led, I responded. I learned to respect her silence as much as I did her words when they finally came. I learned the reality of reader response (Rosenblatt, 1976) when Carla didn't see herself as the struggling, angry Lovey in MacCracken's book, as I would have expected. Instead she saw herself as a Mary MacCracken, with the ability to help others tear down their walls. As Carla worked in graphic arts to publish our anthologies, she did just that—she helped give voices to an entire school population who had always been seen but never heard. But, it was Carla's voice at the end of the year in her evaluation that led me to create a new class at our school: "It's too bad everyone couldn't have a class like what I had. I could come in and stay for more than just one period. I could stay and just read what I wanted and write what I wanted without anyone telling me what to do. When I finished one book you just helped me find another one."

While I was thinking about her words, it occurred to me that it was too bad that Carla had had to end up almost in reform school in order to be allowed to read and write what she wanted. It also occurred to me that I might have turned Carla away. I might have been too involved in my curriculum to take a chance that she would ruin it. It was because of her and others like her that in 1976 I initiated a class that was extremely new for our school, a two-period block called Home Base in which students could do just that what they wanted, as long as what they wanted was reading and writing. I might have helped save Carla, but her voice helped many others: she gave me the idea for a class based on students' questions about reading and writing, learning and life; a class that started where each person was and not where he or she should be; a class that gave room and support for growth toward individual goals, not those of a scope and sequence chart.

Tony

A few years later, Tony came crashing into my life and our classroom like a wild horse just out of the chute. Weighing no more than a hundred pounds, with several pounds of that weight in grease on his clothing, Tony arrived with school supplies consisting of a bag of Wise Potato Chips and a large Coke. Although this was grade 11 Basic English III, he quickly reminded me of why I thought I hadn't wanted to teach junior high. He had stolen well-prepared April's pencil case, upset his Coke, and dived under a table before we knew what had hit us. Tony's fame at skipping school had preceded him, and I could see why some teachers were looking the other way rather than trying to find him!

On that first day I despaired that I would find anything to keep Tony from driving us all crazy. I didn't, but he did. I had developed the habit of keeping projects students had done in previous classes on the walls and cabinets around the room. Tony began investigating the various replicas of colonial punishments he found there. Initially, I thought he was seeing these as artifacts from a chamber of horrors, but with his words, "I can weld something like this," I knew we had found our first literature unit.

Although some teachers in our English department ignored the classics with the basic students, I had chosen some that seemed to have relevance for them and worked with the kids to make those works come alive. *The Crucible* (Miller, 1955) was one of those texts. The previous class had written their own take-off called, *Hey, Freak*, which depicted students from the 1970s getting high and being transported to the days of the Salem witch trials. I knew it would be the perfect beginning for studying not only the play and colonial times but also the idea of standing against the crowd. We read *The Crucible*, visited Kings' Landing, and interviewed the settlers there. We read *Constance* (Clapp, 1968), kept colonial journals, and built a replica of the early Plymouth settlement. We wrote a *Colonial Gazette* and built projects that represented the colonial vision of justice.

On the last day of our unit, we had planned a traditional Thanksgiving feast. When I arrived at school at 7:00 A.M., I found Tony standing at my door complaining about how late I was. He and a friend were standing there holding a turkey they had killed, plucked, and cooked for our feast. The other students arrived within minutes of each other and our cafeteria was quickly transformed into a colonial museum/Thanksgiving celebration. Copies of the *Colonial Gazette* were given to each visitor after a tour through the stocks and pillory. Although invited guests were stunned by the enthusiasm and total participation of the class, I was most amazed with Tony. He had orchestrated the event down to the killing of the turkey (I worried that perhaps it was his favorite part), and in his Iron Maiden jacket he was a polite, though unusual, host. But equally as impressive was the fact that Tony had not missed a single day of class all year.

Watching students offer tours and food to teachers and administrators when months ago they would have run from them taught me that when students are allowed to structure learning, rewarded for their work, and given responsibility, they will be motivated. Motivation had not been something I did to them; it was something that happened when I moved out of the way. I had also learned that self-esteem is not separate from content; the students felt good about themselves as individuals when they completed something that made them proud.

Our early success had not kept us from having a traumatic year. Our class of fifteen changed as Leon went off to jail, Mindy ended up pregnant and began missing school, and Andy's girlfriend became pregnant and they decided to marry. In early winter Tony, Gilman, and Gilman's car had ended up in the river. Making fun of the pair for their foolishness became common ground for the rest of the class. In addition, the pregnancies and upcoming marriage had caused daily disagreements as battle lines were drawn over real love, not to be confused with make-believe love, and loyalty. The students had been like a family, but they hadn't quite learned how to overcome their need to gossip, and this caused lots of problems in our group. I decided to read *Of Mice and Men* (Steinbeck, 1937) in hopes that the students might come to some deeper understanding of friendship. Although I worried a bit about the bad language, I decided that the story's beauty could carry it through any censorship issue. In any case, there still didn't seem to be anyone who cared what I did with these students.

Tony was immediately entranced. He was so like George and Gilman so like Lennie that their arguments began to fade. The others quickly followed suit as the ring leaders stopped fighting and began to live the life of drifters during the 1930s. Prior to this, I had been worried because Tony still wasn't choosing to read when given time to read independently. Because of the wide variety of reading I did orally, most of the others had found books that met their reading interests; Tony still tended to agitate on those days. During our reading of *Of Mice and Men*, however, the other students were barely allowed to breathe; the slightest interruption would bring on Tony's wrath. He sat as close to my desk as possible and didn't miss a word. When we finished the book, Tony leaned back in his chair, put his feet up on the desk, and said, "It's like I always said—there's nothing that can beat a good book." Although I'm sure some in the class would have liked to strangle Tony for the many times he had ruined their reading of good books, there was so much truth in his statement that we couldn't be angry. My teaching and learning with Tony, however, was not to end with this success.

During that year, I was reminded of the statement I had heard so often from other teachers: we should be giving these kids *skills*, not wasting their time with reading. After all, they are never going to *use* the classics. Although I had not heard of Mooney at that time, today I refer to her text

Developing Life-Long Readers to look at criteria for choosing good books. She tells us that when we are selecting books we should ask ourselves if the story has "charm, magic, impact, and appeal" (1988, p. 4). It seems to me these are a much better criteria than asking ourselves if the students will ever "use it." I knew instinctively that I could never figure out what these students might need, given that so many of them had such a late start in feeling successful. I only knew that it was important that our time together be spent with books that were meaningful, made a lasting impression, and were worthy of rereading. Classic or not, *Of Mice and Men* fit those criteria. That same thought occurred to me when I finally heard from Tony again.

I had left teaching at the end of that year to enter a doctoral program and after two years away, I returned to the classroom. It was during those years that I heard from Tony again. This time he was writing from prison.

> I heard you were back and I wanted to write and pay my respects to one of the best teachers. I made some stupid mistakes and I'm paying for them (I bet you thought I had already made my share of mistakes when you knew me). I've been in prison for three years and believe me I have lots of time to read now. But, I want you to know that *Of Mice and Men* is still my favorite book. Do you think you could tell me about some more books like that?

No, we can't possibly imagine what our students will need to know in the future. But Tony reaffirmed for me the fact that if we can teach kids to love reading, it will always be with them—even in a prison cell.

Ron

If Tony taught me not to try to anticipate what students might need at some future time in their lives, it is Ron who comes to mind when I think about the importance of being the best teacher we can be for all of our students. Tradition has often placed the newest, most vulnerable teachers with the kids who have tested the system to its limits. Veteran teachers often get the "plum assignments" of AP and college-prep English, while the lower-tracked students end up with either new teachers or those teachers who have failed to challenge the college-bound. Although not a trouble-maker, Ron's lack of motivation and boredom had landed him in one of those tracks.

I had never failed with college-track students because I hadn't taught them, but I was still relatively new when Ron was in my class. Ron was in a General English class, which meant that traditionally he would have received either a watered-down version of American literature or a skills curriculum consisting of letter writing, grammar, and short stories with follow-up questions from a literature anthology. Students and teachers both suffer in those situations: students are given material that seems worthless and teachers try to teach a curriculum to students who refuse to play school. I decided to use my budget money that year to buy class sets of adolescent novels so that we could base our entire curriculum on shared and independent reading of these novels.

One novel I chose was *No Promises in the Wind* (Hunt, 1970). The text and context reminded me of one of the times I had most enjoyed teaching. My students had done their own Foxfire-type local heritage project in the mid-1970s and their perspectives changed drastically as they learned about lives and times that were so different from, and yet so like, their own. When I read *No Promises in the Wind*, I thought it had the same potential. In addition, my juniors complained bitterly about their hatred of American history, and I thought that the historical connections this young adult novel offered might make them more successful in that class. Besides all of that, the book had a great story, and I wanted a great story to start our year together. So we began our year with *No Promises in the Wind*. I read the book aloud to them while they followed the text and the story. As we read together, we visualized the places and times Josh and Joey experienced. Natural extensions of this story led students to interview family and community members about changes over time. This led to many demonstrations by community members, showing us how to craft a variety of products: potato baskets, soap and poor-man's stew. Students truly experienced a piece of the time period being studied. Eventually students produced their own Twenties and Thirties fashion show and historical museum. Together, we actively read and wrote, researching everything from the origin of the game of Monopoly to rum running. The art teacher worked with us to create "Hobo Art," and students learned about Depression glass. Students not only enjoyed reading and writing, they also experienced interviewing, art, craft, and history. This book became the model for many others we shared together that year as well as some of the reading and writing students did independently.

By late fall, Ron had become a reader. No matter what was going on in our classroom, Ron could be found sitting in the corner with a book. When it came time for our midyear exam Ron commented, "You know, we've done more reading than my friends in College English. I had to show one of them how to use the card catalog in the library the other day and I'm in the dumb class." I've thought about that comment many times as I have struggled with the subtle and not-so-subtle messages we give to kids about their futures when we track them. It did please me, however, that Ron could feel proud of all the learning that had taken place during our time together.

I never saw Ron again after he graduated, but in 1988 I received a letter from him. "It's been four years since last we spoke, so I figured I would write and let you know that at least one of your students had finally made it. You'll never guess what I have become! A TEACHER!" Ron went on to talk about moving after high school, losing his father to cancer during those first years away, and then finding that he also had cancer. After having his stomach muscles removed and learning to walk again, Ron decided to become a teacher. He had written the letter at the end of his first day of school.

I just wanted to write and tell you that when you start feeling like you are not getting anything accomplished, to look ahead a few years and maybe try to think what some of your kids will be making of themselves. I know for myself you were a big motivator to accomplish things during my high school years . . . I can remember your teaching as very sincere. There aren't many teachers that will read a literature book to her class and get so involved in the reading that she will cry. I will never forget what you did for me intellectually. You may not be able to tell by my writing or spelling, and definitely not by my form, but I did learn a lot. Even about life. I've learned that nothing is free, unless you are giving someone something. Never volunteer unless you want to be taken advantage of and that there is something called love but it is so rare as to be almost non-existent. I couldn't get you off my mind as I prepared for this year of school. I've learned that this is more than just an 8–5 job. I know how you feel now. Especially when you finally see that look of understanding cross that young face.

Ron's words taught me that authentic literacy events do stay with students long after we think they've moved on to other things, that students change track for themselves in spite of us. He reminded me that all students and all learning have value. Huck (1987) talks about the transforming power of literature: "Literature has the power to take us out of ourselves and return us to ourselves, a changed self" (p. 69). For Ron and many others, literature helped them see and experience other worlds, and that vision had changed their own. Ron's letter reminded me that as English teachers we have the opportunity to give students that power every day in our classrooms. Today, I have come to agree with Badger's words in *Crow and Weasel:*

> "Remember only this one thing," said Badger. "The stories people tell have a way of taking care of them. If stories come to you, care for them. And learn to give them away where they are needed. Sometimes a person needs a story more than food to stay alive. That is why we put these stories in each other's memory. This is how people care for themselves." (Lopez, 1990, p. 48)

Candy, Carla, Tony, Ron, and hundreds of other students over the past twenty years have given me their stories. I have faithfully cared for them and given them to other teachers who needed something "more than food." These students and their stories have been my informants in learning that each student is unique, as unique as each reader's literacy experience. They have taught me the real meaning of student-centered classrooms and the importance of reflection in our growth as readers, writers, and learners. They have taught me that if I wanted students to enjoy reading and writing, they have to see me enjoying reading and writing. They have taught me that students still have questions and will search for answers. They have taught me that every moment with every student has value. The trick is reclaiming the value in each of those moments.

The importance of their teaching and my learning was brought home to me when I read Fletcher's *Walking Trees* (1991):

> A man I know, the father of a close friend, has this philosophy about life: "When you take away all the worthless jobs and errands and chores we do during the day, there's probably only about one minute each day when we do something even remotely important." Think of it: one minute. In fact, if you get right down to it, there's maybe only one minute in your whole life when you ever do something really important, something that really matters. The trick is to be ready for that minute when it comes. (p. 190)

When I first read that, it struck me that perhaps as a teacher I have been given more minutes than others. Today I know that by listening to, valuing, and reflecting on our time together, I can always be ready for that "one minute" when I will be able to make a difference. And because I have been a teacher-researcher, I will have recorded the memories of many of those precious minutes—minutes that will become stories—stories that will remind me that it is never too late.

2

New Understanding—Same Challenges

Dreams sometimes come true.
But not without something just like work.

Sylvia Ashton-Warner, *Teacher*

I left the Candy's, Carla's, Tony's and Ron's in 1987 in order to go to graduate school and returned two years later with a renewed fervor to make a difference. I hadn't taught ninth-grade students since my first year of teaching, but when I tried to think of an area where I could clearly make an impact, it was at that level. For years I had been appalled not only by the lack of success, in terms of interest and skills, of the ninth-grade students who were assigned to remedial reading, but also by their lack of progress out of remedial reading. Once labeled and placed in remedial programs, most students stayed there for their entire high school career, the most troublesome dropping out and the others left to survive in a program where "remediation consisted primarily of students completing skill lessons in workbook or worksheet activities with the teacher serving as a manager" (Allington et al., 1986, p. 15).

At our high school, this form of reading instruction had been offered to—and required of—students who were reading significantly below grade level since 1971. Traditionally, incoming ninth-grade students who were reading at least two years below reading grade level on the Nelson-Denny Reading Test were required to take a reading class (Efficiency Reading) in addition to their regularly scheduled English class (English I or Basic English I). Instruction in this class had traditionally focused on diagnosing reading

deficiencies and offering individual and group instruction designed to remediate those skills. A great deal of class time was spent completing worksheets
and workbooks designed to remediate individual deficiencies. For the past
several years there had been two sections of this class, each with fifteen to
twenty students. I decided that I wanted to teach one of those classes.
(There would be many days that followed when I would question my
judgment.)

When I asked the principal if I could be assigned the Basic English I
class and one of the reading lab classes, he was excited by the idea. In
addition to my two sections of Directed Studies in English, I would have
one class entitled Reading and Writing Workshop.

We decided to put these two classes back-to-back so that I would have
the same students for ninety minutes rather than forty-five in a class called
Reading Writing Workshop. On paper this could have been a reality; in
terms of scheduling, it just didn't work. There were students in my Basic
English I class who weren't allowed to stay in my reading class because I
hadn't been "approved" by the Special Education Director. They had to be
placed in the reading specialist's section of the class because the learning
disabilities teacher had worked out a system of monitoring the labeled
students for that period of her day. In addition, some students couldn't be
placed in both classes because of scheduling problems. As it turned out, I
had a group of students for period four; some stayed with me for period five,
while others left to go to a different class; then, some of those period five
students stayed with me for period six English. I had encountered the first
glitch in secondary school: trying to find sustained time with students.
Needless to say, even if the scheduling had not worked, that was no reason
to admit failure, right? After all, it was only August and I did have all the
"new" theory and practice in which I had immersed myself for two years. I
reminded myself that I had certainly overcome similar difficulties in past
years and had managed to help most of my students become readers and
writers. I also believed, somewhat smugly perhaps, that being a teacher-
researcher was going to reveal all the wonderful things I did to help students
in this process. As my journal indicates, I could not have been more wrong.

> 8/15 Today is my first day back in the classroom after two years of
> being "somewhere" else. It's hard not to wonder if I made the right
> decision in coming back. I look at these kids sitting here and wonder
> if my expectations are too high for them (or is that possible?). I've
> seen how much every student needs these basic communication skills
> in order to succeed and I'm really feeling a responsibility to move them
> along the way to communicate within their group and with others.

A friend wrote on my board:

—YOU *WILL* LEARN HERE
—YOU *WILL* GROW HERE
—YOU *WILL* AMAZE YOURSELVES HERE

At first I felt as though that seemed a little like brainwashing and then I realized that perhaps that's what I'm doing—attempting to wash away the negatives that have accumulated and replace them with some positives. Some kids came in, read the message and whispered, "I thought you said she was nice. We're going to have to work in here." Amazing that they see those as mutually exclusive.

Our year together had begun. For better or worse, I was back. I had decided that one way for me to help students see how they changed over time was to have them do a writing sample right away, so that would be my plan for tomorrow. I bought enough journals so each student could have two: an academic journal for recording and responding to class work and a personal journal for communicating with me and getting their thoughts on paper. First days are always confusing. I soothed my worries with the notion that things were bound to get better over the next few days as we all became more comfortable with each other. I moved the desks out of yesterday's thoughtfully arranged pairs and into a semicircle spreading out from around my desk, thinking that this arrangement would provide a great way for us to share writing.

8/16 I read, "To laugh is to risk . . ." and some students seemed to understand what I read. The initial comment, however, was "Is there supposed to be a point in this?" I tried to be patient and not be sarcastic. It is so hard to remember where they've been and how little people seem to have expected from them. I told them they had to write for 15 minutes and they seemed overwhelmed.

There are eleven boys and 7 girls in this class. Five minutes into the writing assignment, noted activity of students: 1 student tapping his pencil; 9 students writing; 5 students staring into space; 1 student laughing and looking around; and 1 student sorting through his notebook. All of the students seemed lost with the idea of writing without a given length for the paper. They seem to feel they've finished with the issue as soon as they have something on paper. I'm debating whether or not to use this as the beginning of a process lesson. How should I match them up? It is 11:10 and 2 people are still writing. I think I'll have them count off by 6's and then read their pieces within the groups. Focus should be on 1. Something I liked; 2. Something I don't understand; and 3. A way you could improve.

Chaos! or at least it seemed that way. Several kids were offended that they had to be with someone they didn't know. Others were offended that they were asked to share something and I didn't tell them ahead of time (*mistake). I did finally manage to get around to each group and help them with the process. Some actually seemed to learn something from it.

My ideas of what would work were so far from where the students were, I had no idea that this activity involved so much emotion. These students were attending a new school, combined with students from another middle school, and were assigned to a class in which the teacher was asking them to participate in activities that were totally foreign to them. I hadn't even taken the time to get to know them, nor had I modeled the activities and behaviors I was expecting. Today, my journal notes are a haunting reflection of a year begun with no professional respect for who students were as learners. The ensuing battles were brought on as much by my lack of knowledge about how to help the students engage with each other and with the curriculum as by their limited backgrounds in reading and writing. At the end of each day, I felt as if I had been run over by a truck, and the classroom looked as if that truck accident had taken place there.

At the end of the third day, I wrote down a comment made by one of the students: "I thought this was supposed to be reading. Why are we writing?" I responded with some platitudes about the reading-writing connection, but I still did not understand that the solution was there in his comment. The days continued, varying between chaos and apathy; at 3:00 P.M., I was never sure which I preferred. This was not the image of "active learners" I had imagined! I changed the seats in that classroom every single day during those first three weeks of school. It became the joke of the English department. Each day teachers came to view my room to see how the seats were rearranged. I tried the student desks in a circle, in pairs, in small groups, facing inward, facing the windows; I put my desk in every possible position in that classroom. The next step would have been to move with my desk out into the hall and leave the students to fight it out. As anger-filled days followed one after the other, that option looked better all the time.

It didn't take me long to see why these students had always been given worksheets and individual assignments; any attempt to get them to work together or discuss a book ended in commotion. I really did want to keep things whole, but the students were quickly tearing them apart. As I write today I can feel the muscles in the back of my neck tightening as I flash back to those difficult August days. Becky and Trisha spent their lunchtime with some older guys and came back to class drunk. Daniel decided he didn't like Melanie's decision to close the window and threw a desk across the room at her. Peter, a student with cerebral palsy who had been harassed over his entire academic career, came into the classroom each day swearing loudly. It was chaos. I shuddered to think what would happen if all the students had been there at the same time.

Peter came infrequently; he had killed his sister the year before and hadn't attended school much since then. Denny came to class more frequently, but her drinking problem kept her from really being there. Although Steffie usually came to class, she was called to the office every day during our class period because she wasn't attending any other classes. Since administrators knew they could find Steffie in my class, they dealt with her discipline problems then; thus, she missed the only class she wanted to attend.

The days wore on and I despaired. I could feel the critical eyes of those who had been amused at my new way of teaching reading. The principal teased me by telling me I had forgotten how to teach, and most days I believed him. After all, the reading class next door was quiet.

Interestingly enough, the reading specialist had met me at the door on that first day of school and informed me that she no longer used *Action Library* (Scholastic) because she was now a whole language teacher. When I asked her what she meant by that, she said she now used a new testing program that pointed to deficiencies in the reader. The student could then read a booklet and complete the exercises to remediate the problem. I had to agree with Goodman (1986a), "Whole language is clearly a lot of things to a lot of people" (p. 5). Isolated standardized testing programs and controlled reading had no place in my definition of the philosophy of whole language. On the other hand, I wasn't sure that what was happening in my classroom would fit my understanding of whole language either.

I had returned to the classroom with an even stronger belief that students will become readers when they are allowed the time and given the support to read. Although our beginning was a bit shaky, I still agreed with Weaver's (1990) statement that "the meaningful and enduring learning occurs most readily as the result of an active process of meaning-making, rather than a passive process of filling in blanks or repeating or recopying information presented by the teacher or the text" (p. 8). I also knew that if I wanted to help students take ownership of their own learning, I had to adopt a different role. Tradition may have dictated that the essence of a teacher's job is the transmission of information, but as long as I created a classroom environment in which students were supposed to listen to, write down, and give back information at the appropriate time, I was still in control. But how was I supposed to help students become active learners and support them in taking responsibility for their learning when I couldn't keep them from fighting?

Fortunately, I finally went back to the early entries in my journal: "I thought this was supposed to be reading. Why are we writing?" I remembered my first reading of *The Lottery Rose* (Hunt, 1976) and the impact of that book on an unsettled class of the past. That memory encouraged me to try the same book with these students, and as soon as I began reading *The Lottery Rose* aloud, they began to settle down, listen, and follow the text. Their arguments now focused on how they might kill Georgie's teacher if they were Georgie (I saw it as a step forward—still violent but at least focused on a text!). On days set aside for independent reading, students asked for books like *The Lottery Rose*. Gradually, things began to change. Meek's (1982) advice had been proven true: "No adolescent learns to read in a vacuum, with artificial reading matter and no purpose of his own. He needs real books, real intentions and real help and he ought to have all of these" (p. 210).

The year passed so quickly that even I was shocked when colleagues started to say, "You must be so proud of those kids. Look at them read. What did you do to them?" Once again it hit me that I had only a vague notion of what had gone on in that classroom. My great plans for research had flown out the window (perhaps just after the hurled student desk). I had managed to keep exactly eight pages of a field journal and collect several samples of writing. That was it! My last journal entry is dated August 30: "In spite of the fact that the extra credit folders are filled with worksheets, they are successful. **Write more about this later."

Later never arrived. My journal ceased to exist as I spent every minute of every day trying to help students find joy and confidence in reading and writing, and balance in their personal lives. I really didn't know exactly which things had worked because I hadn't kept any accurate field notes. I was beginning to see why Stephens (1991) would find that "there are holes in the documentation and understanding of whole language classrooms and of the students" (p. 20), at least at the secondary level. I considered myself to be a teacher with a whole language belief system, but I knew that I would never be able to answer the question "What did you do?" until I had studied my classroom practice and the students' change over time.

A research project was staring me in the face, but at this point I was too tired to stare back. It had taken all my energy just to survive in the classroom. I was ready to quit teaching, but decided to take the summer to immerse myself in professional literature, reflect on my teaching practice, and define some clear research strategies before beginning again. I realized that I was also in need of remediation. Next year I hoped to have a teaching plan *and* a research plan. I wasn't sure I had either that first year back in the classroom. This is where my year as a teacher-researcher begins.

3
Creating a Literate Environment

I thought about Indians
on wild vision quests
As the teacher scolded
and passed out the tests.
I watched a pink turtle
walk across her desk
It gave me a smile
and laid down to rest.
As I smiled back happily,
the teacher gave that dirty look to me.
She snatched away my book
and told me to listen
to her talking about vocab
synonyms and prepositions.
I snatched the book back and said,
"I can learn my lessons right in here,
better than anything you've taught
to me all year."
At this, the buffalo wallowed
the pink turtle woke,
The quest was finally over
Earthmother spoke.   Jasmine

Jasmine's poem is taped to my desk as I sit in my classroom wondering how to start getting ready for another year, new students, and a research project. The hot summer days were unusual for northern Maine and they had left the room airless and closed in. I wanted to throw open the windows and let the fresh air clear the room and my mind. I had hoped to begin this year full of excitement about my research project, but the summer had passed quickly with a house renovation that was still consuming much of my time and all of my mental space. Rather than returning to my classroom with anticipation, I was feeling overwhelmed.

I had intended to file away last year's "pieces worth saving" long before this, but the days had slipped away and now, rather than imagining the students who might walk through the door next week, I was facing reminders of students from last year whom I had grown to cherish. Perhaps part of the problem was in letting go: Everyone who has ever had a good year teaching knows the feeling. By June your students are able to look at themselves and their learning in ways you never thought possible at the beginning of the year. There's something heartbreaking about losing those students and starting all over again. Then it occurred to me that my difficulty wasn't coming from the pictures and letters stacked on my desk reminding me of last year's successes; it was focused on remembering what those students were like the preceding August.

My mind flashed back to those days that had tried my patience to the limit. Every day seemed to bring something new that would cause a commotion: the freshman baseball player whose new "Pump It Up" sneakers had the girls hysterical and the boys anywhere but in an English class; the unusually hot, September weather that had two of the girls wearing tight, short skirts, which ultimately caused more commotion than the sneakers; April's pregnancy and her fights in the halls; and Tanya's inability to keep from getting hysterical and screaming obscenities at anyone who disagreed with her. Was I ready to begin all of that again?

Then I started looking at the pictures—smiling faces, students curled up on the black chair reading books, the writing wall, book projects. Fortunately, I could begin again *before* the students arrived and reflect on what worked for those students. I didn't have to start where I started last year; I had all our collective knowledge from that time as the basis for this new beginning. I knew that rereading the letters and self-evaluations on my desk today would help me reflect on what it was that had eventually made our classroom a good place to be.

"Being in this class has made me realize that there are things that I cannot do, but reading and writing I can, maybe not as good as others, but I'm pretty proud of what I can do. In fact, I think I'm pretty darn good." Feeling proud, feeling good about what you're doing, does make an unbelievable difference. Denise had come into my classroom beaten down by years of "special" classes. She believed she couldn't spell, so she thought she couldn't write. Her reading was slower than some others' when the entire class was reading a novel, so she thought she couldn't read. For students who really believe that they're not very good at spelling, writing, and reading, the opportunities to feel proud in English class are often limited.

In spite of that, Denise talked about being proud in her end-of-the-year reflections.

Perhaps what made the difference in this class for Denise was what Nancy talked about in her reflections: "The main reason I was able to achieve so much this year was because of the structure, or lack thereof, of this class. It was a class in which you never had to worry about what you were doing wrong, or if others were doing better than you. Yes, I think that was one thing this class lacked—competition. That made it easier for everyone to co-exist."

Denise didn't have to feel stupid in this class because she was able to choose her own work—work on which she could always feel successful. She had moved from taped books to independent reading of as many of Gary Paulsen's novels as I could find: *The Cook Camp* (1991), *The Crossing* (1987), *Dancing Carl* (1983), *Dogsong* (1985), *Hatchet* (1987), *The Madonna Stories* (1989), *Murphy* (1987), *Murphy's Gold* (1988), *Popcorn Days and Buttermilk Nights* (1983), *The Night the White Deer Died* (1978), *The River* (1991), *Sentries* (1986), *Tiltawhirl John* (1977), *Tracker* (1984), *The Winter Room* (1989) *and Woodsong* (1990). I can still remember the look of pride on her face and her words, "I never wrote a poem before," when she finished one response to Paulsen's books.

The Thought
It's weird
After I finish one of his books
I'm off in nowhere
Just thinking about the book.
Sometimes I put my myself in the book
—making bows to fish
—tracking the birds
—coming face to face with the bear
—going down the river on a raft
—or maybe across Alaska on a dog sled
To read his books makes me smile inside
The joy
The pleasure he gives me
His thoughts
His imagination sets me to dreamin'
Oh, how I wish I could just once
Live in his thoughts
To go on those adventures.

Denise had every right to feel "pretty darn good" about herself as a reader and a writer, and I needed to remember that as I worked with a new group of students to make sure they were involved in authentic tasks that made them feel proud when they were finished. But what had it taken to get Denise to this point?

Students' reflections were filled with comments about the classroom: Denise called it "a compatible place." I liked that! As I looked around the room and at the pictures of last year's classes, I knew what she meant. She wasn't talking about the way students managed to get along, although students did see that as important; she was talking about the actual class-room environment. One student paper referred to the changing posters that were constantly on our door: "I always stop outside to see what the poster says today. You probably think no one even looks at those." But I didn't think that. It wasn't by accident that the poster on my door said, "Open the door to your dreams." I had built the classroom environment carefully, in much the same way a writer chooses words to create an effect. An outsider might see that effect as chaotic, but many of my students had come to cherish it. Just recently, I received a paper from a student who had been in my class for two years. Her memory piece was a reminder of the unbe-lievable importance of establishing a literate classroom environment:

> Janet Allen's room was one of a kind. I don't believe that there was or ever will be one like it again. To me the room was filled with everything you could dream of. There was posters, pictures, papers, drawings, writings, and books. Books, everywhere you would look there would be books looking back at you. If you were an outsider coming in, I think that all you would see is a room with stuff on the wall, but if you would look closer, you would find a message. The message would not be right out in the open, you would have to read into whatever was on the wall. And when I started finding those little messages, I felt proud of myself and a lot better about myself. I mean, everywhere you would look the room would be telling you to keep going, don't stop, try harder, reach for your dreams, and many other things that would tell you things that would lift your spirits. And not only was the room inspirational, it was beautiful and it was made by us, the young adults. A lot of us were dreamers, I still am, and in Room 130 I could find my dreams, and in seeing them I would try harder to reach my dreams.

Atwell (1987) talks about needing to let go of her finely crafted bulletin boards in turning the classroom over to her students. That had never been a problem for me because I could never create those bulletin boards in the first place. Each year I was totally honest with my students and told them that the walls were theirs, not only because I wanted them to see the space as theirs, but because my efforts would not be too pleasing! I've always felt that the kids think I'm giving up something, but in reality their collective abilities at creating places for their works are much better than mine. That makes sense to me. It is their work; it should be displayed in the way they choose. But there are spaces that remain mine, where students look when they come into the room.

The bulletin board nearest the chalkboard is always filled with pictures students have given me. As each new class picture is handed to me, the student waits to see me put it up on the board. There are gifts there too: a Christmas angel made in craft class; a painted rock that was created after a reading of Baylor's (1974) *Everybody Needs a Rock*; a poem entitled "Dear

Bulletin Board

Mrs. Allen"; a snake postcard from a trip to Texas. The space is mine, but I fill it with my students.

My desk is prey to the same community ownership. The messiness is a joke with students and teachers alike. Each year I attempt another grand scheme for keeping it all organized, but then the lateness of the day, a talk with a student, or a box of new books initiates a new arrangement. I often spend Sunday afternoons in my classroom, returning books to the shelves and students' writing to folders, putting notes in students' files, and bringing order to my desk. But by Monday afternoon, it has once again escaped the boundaries. My own global view of life adds to the confusion, but the fact that students use my desk as their collective desk also contributes. The two drawers on the right side of the desk keep special books: new books chosen but waiting to be read, books and messages from a reader in period one to a reader in period four, and books I am currently reading, which often become the book of choice for someone in each class. Even my desk space isn't really mine.

A foreign exchange student's reflections make me realize once again the impact of our orchestrated chaos: "I don't know how exactly English class at the high school is but the reading class is wonderful. Everyone can just sit all period and read a book. If a book is not interesting, a student can change on a different one. If somebody don't want to sit at the desk all the time, they can read on the little couches or chairs. I never saw something like this, but I think that a reading class have very good influence on the students. I just want to say that reading class is a wonderful class and we should have something like this in Poland. Some students in Poland almost never read a book so reading class maybe would be very helpful for them to start read, like and understand books." Maybe I'm looking at this process wrong; maybe I should see this as just another Sunday getting ready for my students to begin again, to "start read, like and understand books."

Atwell (1984) also talks about her classroom as a literate environment. She describes that environment as "a place where people read, write, and talk about reading and writing, where everybody can be student and teacher, where everybody can come inside" (p. 240). That is the atmosphere and pattern I've always tried to create at the beginning of each year in my classroom. Although much of that environment is created with the students as we read and write, some aspects are there before the students walk into the room. It is important that they see room for them in this place, that they see spaces that will always be theirs. But, it is also important that they see the consistencies in resources that will always be theirs: hundreds of books, art supplies, computers, tape players, and diverse resource materials. I remember all too well returning from graduate school and beginning school with an empty classroom. It took me far longer that year to help students see themselves as readers and writers and I believe that was due, in part, to the fact that the classroom did not help establish that expectation on the very first day of school. This year, I won't repeat that mistake. So, I begin the process of establishing the "literate environment" my students will walk into when they enter Room 130 in the fall of 1992.

Creating a Compatible Place

> Storying . . . very quickly becomes the means whereby we enter into a shared world, which is continually broadened and enriched by the exchange of stories with others. In this sense, the reality each one of us inhabits is to a very great extent a distillation of the stories that we have shared."
>
> Gordon Wells, *The Meaning Makers*

I've taped these words to the top of my desk. In this classroom, books are definitely the first item in our literate environment. I spend a great deal of time reading children's, young adult, and adult literature. I'm a reader. I admit it. I'm one of those people who stand in front of the hand dryer in public bathrooms and for the thousandth time read the instructions—because they are there. I once heard Jim Trelease (personal communication, September, 1987) say that if parents wanted to contribute two things to the reading habits of their children, they should never remove reading materials from the dining room table or the bathroom. His contention was that in keeping books in these two places, parents have put print materials in front of their children in a way that invites them to read. Intuitively, I know that's true. Just think of how many times we have all read the product information on a box of corn flakes! We read the print because it is there. In a way, that is what I try to do in my classroom. I know that if I want my students to read, there must be a large number of books available right in the room.

So I begin getting ready for my students by turning the classroom into a print-rich environment.

By putting two book racks on top of a bookcase just inside the classroom door I immediately signal that this will be a room filled with books. Near the doorway I want books that will catch the interest of the largest number of students, and my experience tells me that horror and suspense stories do that. I fill the racks with young adult authors like R. L. Stine, Christopher Pike, Lois Duncan, Ritchie Tankersly Cusick; contemporary authors like Stephen King, Dean Koontz, Mary Higgins Clark; and classic authors like Poe, Bierce, Hitchcock, and Stevenson. I put baskets beside the racks and fill them with sets of suspense books that have multiple copies: *Ransom* (Duncan, 1966); *When the Phone Rang* (Mazer, 1985); *Killing Mr. Griffin* (Duncan, 1978). One basket is reserved for books that have audio tapes for shared reading, like *More Scary Stories* (Schwartz, 1984). With books arranged this way, students are able to find a variety of titles if they are interested in horror and suspense. Several books in this genre are available in multiple copies, so several students can decide to read the same book and perhaps work together in book groups, read aloud, or write in their journals. Students who may not see themselves as readers, but who are still interested in horror and suspense have the opportunity to read the books that are on tape. This shared reading experience, defined by New Zealand educators as "eyes past print with voice support" offers *all* students access to the books in this classroom.

Next to these books, I put a bookcase that houses a variety of reference books. In this way, students who might not otherwise look at these types of books see them almost by accident as they stand scanning the horror and suspense books. Students who want or need these reference books know where to find them. Over the years, students have contributed their own reference books to the reference collection: driver education manuals, pamphlets on birth control; hunting and fishing license guides; and consumer information on trucks, snowmobiles, and motorcycles. There are traditional reference books here: encyclopedias, thesauruses, English handbooks, dictionaries, almanacs, and atlases. But there are also many other kinds of reference books: *The Way Things Work* (Macaulay, 1988); *The Big Book of American Humor* (Novak and Waldoks, 1990); *Cvltvre Made Stvpid* (Weller, 1987); *The Wabanakis of Maine and the Maritimes* (American Friends, 1989); *The Imperial Way by Rail from Peshawar to Chittagong* (Theroux, 1981); *The Portfolios of Ansel Adams* (1981); *America* (Cooke, 1984); *A First Dictionary of Cultural Literacy* (Hirsch, 1989); *Whale Nation* (Williams, 1989); *Christmas Customs and Traditions* (Miles, 1976); *The Art of Maurice Sendak* (Lanes, 1980). As I continue to find reference books, I add them to the collection, never knowing which book will capture a student's spirit of inquiry.

A black lab table with an Apple and a Tandy computer sits along the wall. Computer programs are lined up in small, student-made book racks on the table between the two computers with the MECC (Maine Education Computer Consortium) software available for the Apple. Since our middle schools have these same programs, I know that as the ninth-grade students find familiar programs there it will help them feel at ease. There are SAT preparation programs, *Intellectual Software* (1984) and *Microzine* (1989) disks with a variety of interdisciplinary reading, social studies, science, and language arts programs. In addition, the Tandy has *Jeopardy* (1988) and *Classic Concentration* (1989), which have always lured students in during the early mornings and late afternoons. If past experience is true, I know these games will create lots of risk-free time for me with my new students. When I returned from graduate school, this computer with these two programs saved me from complete despair. The first few weeks of school were so filled with chaos and anger, I didn't think I would *ever* be able to work with these students. Then our computer coordinator found this computer, I purchased these two programs, and the students started coming into my classroom before school, spending their lunchtime there, and staying long after classes ended for the day to play the two games. Not only did their language skills improve, but they also learned that they had to get along, since I didn't have to let them stay in the room if they were fighting. In just a few weeks, that behavior carried over into our class. In retrospect, I think the students felt they owed me some respect because I let them spend so much time in the room, and that respect carried over into their commitment to reading and writing. The computers were definitely an asset both during class and outside of class time.

As I walk around the room, I check the racks of books. A large circular rack near the corner displays a variety of books, and variety is extremely important. As Meek (1982) tells us, "No exercise, however well ordered, will have the effect of a genuine reading task that encourages the reader to learn what he wants to know as a result of his own initiative" (p. 207). Self-selection of texts has been a critical aspect of my teaching since 1973. There have been times when I've thought I allowed students too much independence and not given them enough structure in their reading. I usually experience these pangs when someone says, "But how do you compare a student who reads three hundred pages with someone who reads fifty?" Today, however, I feel supported by the research when I say, "I don't compare them." I have often considered putting all the books in genre groupings but then decided it was more important that students see all types of books than be able to find books quickly. I know that if students who like to read fantasy come into the room and see all of the fantasy books together, this is essentially where they will look when they want a new book. So, except for the horror/suspense rack near the door, I mix the books up so that students will run across new titles as they search for familiar books and authors. When I check the racks, I stop at each of the shelves and take out books that are torn and mangled. For years I had a difficult time doing this, because it took me so long to build a classroom library. Now I realize that I'm actually making a statement about books by having shelves filled with titles that are in fairly good condition.

My tour brings me to an area that has been the center of my classroom for many years—student files. As I clear out scraps of paper from the students' "cubbies," I think how strange that term seems for a high school class. Students have been calling them that ever since they heard the term in *Lovey* (MacCracken, 1976) and decided to build the storage area. I smile to myself thinking of the students who made this wonderful rack years ago so they would have someplace to keep all their belongings. This two-tier, horizontal rack with three-inch openings has allowed hundreds of students to keep their writing folders, books, pens, and projects-in-progress in a space of their own. This rack has long been the envy of the other teachers in the English department, and I wonder who will claim it if I should leave. I'm reminded as I look at some leftover name tags that I have to check the label maker to see that I have enough tape for this year's students to make labels for their individual boxes. If they are anything like those of the past, a few will see this as childish, and some will make extra labels with such mottos as "Don and Kristi 4-ever," but most will be eager to put their names on their spaces. Sometimes I wonder if this space is so important to them because they have so little ownership of their learning and the classroom, especially at this level. This is one thing that clearly separates this classroom from many of the others they will encounter during the day, and I want them to understand that here, everyone has a place.

Two four-foot bookcases, each taking up an entire wall, house sets of books for shared reading. Most of the English teachers keep their class sets of novels in storage cabinets so there will be a sufficient number when they are ready to do a thematic unit focusing on a particular book, but for the past couple of years, I've kept them out on these open shelves. Students who want to read one of them independently are usually careful to put them back with the right set. In any case, I like the idea that all these books are available to students. The "cubbies rack" sits on top of one of the bookcases and on the other one, many smaller racks, which store books that have accompanying audiotapes.

I know how important the shared reading with audiotapes will be for students who don't like to read or who can't read well enough to try the books that interest them. One chore that takes constant monitoring is checking the boxes of tapes to make sure each of the over fifty books shelved here has the right tape. As I place the books next to the matching tapes, I'm once again reminded of the impact these taped books have on the reading attitudes and abilities of my students. *The Outsiders* (Hinton, 1967), *From the Mixed-Up Files of Mrs. Basil E. Frankweiler* (Konigsburg, 1973), *Stone Fox* (Gardner, 1980), *A Day No Pigs Would Die* (Peck, 1972), *The Chocolate War* (Cormier, 1974); and all the others have been in almost constant demand since I started buying tapes. The audiotapes I've made by reading books aloud are among the most popular with students who have been in my classes before because they enjoy listening to a familiar voice. For new students, the purchased tapes, which appear to be more professional, will be the first they choose.

The tapes remind me that I also need to check the file cabinet where tape players and headphones are stored. The tape players are used so much they have almost become consumables, and just as I expect, several of the old ones aren't working very well. A battery recharger and rechargeable batteries have become classroom staples, much the way grammar books were during my high school days. (I have learned not to buy tape players with radios; the few extra dollars required to get one without a radio are well worth it to save hours of nagging students who want to listen to the radio instead of reading.)

The IBM computer on a table behind my desk is dusty, and I clean the screen knowing that this will be one of the last times it will be dusty all year. The nearby trays of disks contain several that belong to me and some belonging to former students, who will be returning for another year—a testimony to the use of this computer. The computers have given many students a confidence in writing that surprises even them. Samples of writing from one student's folder illustrate the difference, not only in length but also in fluency, from September to April.

(9/12) John's Response to *The Pistachio Prescription* (Danziger, 1988)

> Dear Mrs Allen there is a girl and she likes to eat pestasios and her mother thinks that Jelly Beans will care her. where on chapter 6 we Read 3 chapters. The guil that likes to eat pistaci oes she think it will cure her.

(4/3) John's Response to *Panther Peak* (Wallace, 1987)
When I started to read this book I didn't think that it would be any good. But, I stuck with it and it turned out to be a real good book.

It was about this boy and his family. They moved in with his grandfather and he was so bored he didn't even know what to do with him self. One day he was going for a walk and he went up on the little mountian about a mile from the farm. While he was climbing one of the hills he heared a voice saying that he was stupid to come up that way. he looked all around and he saw a boy standing their shaking his head. Well after a while they started to fight. They did that for a quite a while, when they each had to go home. When tom got home his mother was going to kill him for taring his clothes up like that. Well the next time they met they went hunting, fishing, and even swimming up on those mountains. They got bored doing that so Tom taught Justin how to play chess. They were tired of all that so they went out to the barn. Tom had a rope hanging down from the sealing. They played on that for a little while.

One morning tom woke up and it was so quiet. He knew something was roung. He went down stairs and went out to the barn. His grandfather was milking the cows. Tom went back in the house and he was expecting to have some breakfast, but their weren't even a fire going. He ran up stairs and he was haullering for his mother and father. His father came to the stairs and told him to be quiet because his sister was real sick. They took her to the hospital and she had a pusted appendix.

The next afternoon was real cold and it was haleing real bad. They 55 were going to milk the cows when his grandfather came over to the cow Tom was milking. It had a cut on it's milk bag. He told Tom to get the medicine for the cows. Tom went to get it and while his grandfather was putting it on he kicked him. It knocked his grandfather out. It almost killed him. He dragged his grandfather out to the house on the sled. Tom was going to get some help. Tom got on his horse and was heading out of the barn. He was going to go through Panther Peak. The horse Tom was riding collapsed out from under him. At first Tom thought that she was hurt but he saw that what was the matter with her was she was going to have a baby. Tom made a shelter for the two horses. When Tom was about to leave the two horses alone and go for help he sensed that their was somebody their with him. He knew what it was, it was the panther. He missed the panther the first time he shot at it. he was angry at himself for not bringing for shells for the shotgun. He had to get it the second time or he would be killed by the panther. He heared something behind him. he turned around and then he saw the panther coming for him. The panther jumped up in the air and Tom pulled the trieger on the shotgun. It hit the panther but it tore at his sholder and got his tooth and caught the side of his cheek. Tom's father was haullering for him. He was standing right over him. Tom dozed off. When he awoke he was in the hospital then he passed out again. When he woke again he saw that everyone in his family was their even his grandfather who was in the same room with him the hole time. The horses were fine. They all wanted to know how he managed to kill the panther. But he didn't say anything.

The increased fluency is undoubtedly associated with the fact that John has become a reader, but the length of the writing is due, at least in part, to his access to computers. It was because we saw results like these that we made computers so readily available to all the students. Each incoming freshman will receive a new disk on the first day of school to use for his or her writing, not only in English class, but in all the content areas. In this way, I am able to see samples of the writing students do for science, health, or social studies, which gives me a much broader view of their writing development. Although most students enjoy writing with the computers, I still maintain writing folders for each of them, so they can have access to their writing at all times. In the past, students have often taken their folders and sat down to read over their writing. It seems an affirmation of all they have accomplished, which a tiny disk can hardly say in the same way.

Deciding what to do with the furniture is easier because all the books, bookcases, magazine holders, files, computers, and file cabinets fill up the space around the perimeter of the room. I put the desks in pairs angled away from the teacher's desk, but no matter how they are arranged, they probably won't stay that way long. I have found that on that first day students seem to need some kind of familiar structure, although it won't take long before they sit where they're most comfortable. I've saved as many solitary places as possible for individual chairs and couches: one chair sits in the corner next to the door, a padded bench goes under the windows, a couch is sandwiched between the bookcase and the outside door, the favorite black chair is nestled in the corner between the two long bookcases. The couch and chair were "borrowed" from the prop room after a school production of Chekov's *The Cherry Orchard,* and that somehow makes them very appealing to the students, who need comfortable places to curl up and read. When I read at home, I don't sit in a straight chair with my feet firmly on the floor, I find the most comfortable spot I can. Although I'm not always convinced that administrators agree with my room arrangement, they have difficulty arguing with the fact that students do seem to enjoy reading and writing here. Rachel's writing about the black chair is testimony to the quiet escape it was for her.

> In the corner of the room is where I sat my freshman year. The chair was well broke in so when you sat in it you were almost sitting on the floor, but it was still very comfortable. To sit in the chair you had to be talented. If you sat in it the wrong way you would slide off the chair and end up on the floor. The buttons were all torn off the black vinyl chair and it had a little black foot cushion to match. I grew very fond of that little corner. There was nothing really neat about that one particular corner. It had no refreshment stand, no view of the outside, or anything of that matter. It was just out of the way. When I sat there I found myself getting lost in my book and forgetting where I was. Sometimes I was a princess fighting the evil Empire, or falling in love with a no good smuggler, or on an island all by myself with only my dog and my new found animal friends to keep me company. One time I was very powerful; I could create fires just by thinking about it. I had some of the best adventures in my life right there is Ms. Allen's room. You may or may not believe this, but when the bell would ring and when I would have to snap back to reality I would get disappointed, sometimes I wouldn't want to come back, my nonexistent world was better than my existent world. I had a lot of good and bad times that corner. So that corner had a lot of my memories and I would guess the memories of others as well.

As important as places for solitude are, places for conversation are also important. I've surrounded my desk with several small tables, since I know that students will want to move up to talk with me when I'm sitting at my desk or to confer with each other when I'm not. I've placed another small table in a corner away from most of the books so students can have yet another place to confer about their writing, reading, and projects. Movable stools are scattered randomly around the room so that students can sit on them while working together, conferring, or talking to me. These stools are easy for me to pick up and move when I want to sit beside a student to talk.

As I check my cabinet of supplies, I'm reminded of the fact that each year the list seems longer. Scissors, three-hole punchers, rulers, colored pencils, paints, construction paper, stencils, and graph paper are the "stuff" of the writing and the projects that help students make the room their own. I think again, as I do each year, how convenient a rolling cart to house all these supplies would be and wonder who could make one for me. If this year is like most others, I'm sure some students will be eager to design and construct the perfect storage area. My room is filled with such gifts, left by students to make the space more comfortable.

I always leave the walls bare except for the inspirational posters on the two longer walls up near the ceiling over the windows, the bulletin boards, and the chalkboard. When I look around, I wonder if I'm overloading students with print, and then I remember the student who said, "There's no place to hide from reading in here. Even if I lean back in my seat to stare at the ceiling, I'm surrounded by words." I decide to leave the posters, at least for today, as my contribution. Very soon the walls will reflect the students' vision of how the room should look.

I'm starting to anticipate what this new year and these new students might bring. The room, at least, is ready. But that is the easy part. The difficult part is making sure that I am ready—to be a teacher and a researcher. I know the decisions I make about our time together on the first day of school will affect everything I try to do with these students for the rest of the year. I tape a quote from Gibran (1986) to the cover of my grade book: "If he is indeed wise, he does not bid you enter the house of his wisdom, but rather leads you to the threshold of your own mind" (p. 51). As I sit in the empty room, I feel flutters in my stomach; I've never managed to get over those first-day-of-school nerves. I always feel that I'm opening Pandora's box and never sure if I'm ready for what I'll find there. Perhaps the fact that I'm awaiting the new students with that kind of anticipation means that I am ready to begin once again.

As I get ready to leave, I think of some words of Sylvia Ashton-Warner (1963):

> To the extent that a teacher is an artist, and according to Plato there should be no distinction, his inner eye has the native power, unatrophied, to hold the work he means to do. And in the places where he can't see, he has a trust in himself that he will see it, either in time for the occasion or eventually. (p. 89)

Trust. I need to trust myself and my students to know how best to create a learning environment for all of us. After all, isn't trust what responsive teaching and responsible researching is all about?

4

Meeting the Students Where They Are

I have to act the way I am now before I can become something else.

   Hugh Prather, *I Touch the Earth, the Earth Touches Me*

The students' silence on the first day of school is always unsettling. I keep waiting for an explosion, and usually my expectations are met fairly quickly. This year was no exception. Most of the students were seated quietly, waiting for yet another teacher to give them classroom rules, when this year's explosion arrived at the door. I heard her before I saw her. A shrill scream and uncontrollable giggles preceded the petite blonde named Tammy. "Is this stupid class where I'm supposed to be?" Maybe I was already in my researcher mode because I found myself watching the other students' reactions, rather than Tammy's. Sure enough, none of them was watching Tammy's antics; they were all staring at me for my reaction. Now, at least, I didn't have to wonder how to break the first-day silence that had worried me, I just had to worry about how to get Tammy to settle down enough so that we could *all* feel comfortable.

   Smiling, I said, "This is your class and now that you have us all awake, maybe we can get started." She smiled and sat down, not quite sure if she had accomplished what she intended. I sensed that Tammy needed our attention, and the easiest route to follow on that first day was to give her that attention. "Since you're not shy, Tammy, will you be our scribe and take notes while we develop our classroom rules?"

   "Will I be your what?"

As I explained to the class what a scribe was and what role that person would play in making a class memory of our ideas, all the students stared at me as if I were speaking a foreign language. I guess I was. Tammy, however, was not about to miss her opportunity to be a key player in the activities. In retrospect, I probably shouldn't have given in to her demands for attention so easily; I had allowed her to establish an expectation I wasn't willing to live up to for an entire school year by allowing her to demand and receive attention at the expense of others. But I wanted our year to begin smoothly, and at the time the only strategy I knew for keeping the peace was to make Tammy feel important because of her contributions to the class, not her unruly behavior.

I knew I had only a short time to hook these students as readers. That became my top priority. Our school district has a somewhat unusual schedule in that classes begin in mid-August and break in mid-September for potato harvest. Students don't return to school until mid-October, a break that causes many students, who are already at risk, to fall even further behind. Those who see work as more important than school miss extra days before and after the break in order to earn extra money. In classes where tasks are cumulative, these students often are unable to catch up with the rest of the class. The benefits and shortcomings of the potato harvest break have been debated for as long as I can remember, but while the debate continues, the students who most need to be in school are not there. I wanted our class to be so exciting by mid-September that students would hesitate to miss the extra days. Perhaps that was a bit optimistic, but what are beginnings for if not for optimism? With Vygotsky's (1962) words echoing in my head, "What a child can do in cooperation today, he can do alone tomorrow" (p. 104), I began trying to move these students from being passive, angry, and defeated to being independent lifelong learners.

Making the Classroom Ours

Peterson (1992) points out that, "with the exception of a few students, it's usually not easy for even the most experienced teachers to bring students to want to care for the classroom environment" (p. 62). One problem I've encountered often in my years of teaching is getting all the students involved in the community effort of building the classroom environment by organizing the space and the activities. If we established the routines of the classroom in our first days together, perhaps they would become just that—routine—and require none of our thinking or planning time. Developing the classroom rules as a group seemed a good way to establish the routine of building consensus. At least it seemed a good way to me; the students had other ideas.

I explained why I wanted to develop our classroom rules together: they would be our rules, not mine; they would help create a place where everyone could be productive; they would make our classroom a safe place to be. The students looked at me with blank, tolerant stares. Although this wasn't the first time I had encountered this kind of passivity, I was newly shocked by it. They were waiting for me to do the work. I practiced my wait time until it seemed as if everyone had stopped breathing. Then it occurred to me that, although I had planned this activity for weeks, this was the first time these students had heard about it. I had rehearsed this wonderful, community-building scenario, but for these students it was as far from their collective frame of reference as the beaches of California. Stop. Take a step back. Let the students catch up. I wonder how many times we plan activities for our students from where we are, not from where they are? If my goal was to involve them in building our classroom rules by deciding what could work for all of us, I needed to find a way to get them to look realistically at what works and what doesn't when a group of people live and work together. I needed to give them thinking and writing time to help all of us get into the same field of experience.

"Now that you know what our goal for the end of this class period is, maybe we can start by writing in our journals about previous school experiences we remember. They can be positive or negative, but they should be important to you and relate somehow to the way you think our class should run." With that direction, I introduced students to the practice of reflection, one on which we would base many of our curricular and community decisions throughout the year.

"Okay, if everyone has had time to write down at least some ideas, let's have each person say one thing. After everybody has had a chance, we can come back to those who may have more than one thing to say." This was one of the facilitation skills I remembered from my years of observation in Mary Giard's first-grade classroom. In the past I would have asked the class for general input. In fact, I remembered once saying to a principal that I didn't like putting artificial constraints on the spontaneity of the group: raising their hands, taking turns, going around the circle. But I've learned that although those organizational strategies can make the climate more structured, they also have the benefit of allowing everyone's words to be valued. I wanted students to see on this first day that everyone has something to say and that our group body of knowledge is incomplete without each person's contributions.

"Sixth and seventh grades went by slow and boring."

"Second grade was the worst. I stayed back because of the old bag teacher."

"I feel mixed-up because I don't know where anything is."

"I hate school."

"I never know what to write, but I guess that's what I'm doing now."

"The only thing I DO like about school is that you can see your friends. I DON'T like homework, teachers (most of them), and classes are usually BORING."

"When you're in junior high, the time goes so slow."

"The best thing about school is getting out. The worst is homework."

"My favorite class in school was shop. I liked it because I learned how things work."

"I don't like English to be two periods long."

"I didn't like my 6th grade teacher because he always hollered at kids."

By this time everyone felt comfortable sharing ideas; in fact, the difficulty was getting them to focus on establishing our classroom rules. As valuable as their comments were in terms of their own school histories, it would take some stretching to pull those comments into any list of rules. I could see that I needed to rethink the general nature of the writing prompts I gave students if I had a specific goal in mind. I needed to remind myself that for students whose academic careers have been filled with worksheets and programmed learning, more initial structure and thus more support is necessary if they are to move away from this fill-in-the-blank model. Then it occurred to me that I shouldn't see this list as an end product; that was a piece of my thinking that had to change. As secondary teachers having students for only forty-five minutes a day, I think we are often programmed to see each activity as leading to a product. We finish one and begin another activity that leads to another product. I could see this list as an end product of our journal writing or I could see this as a beginning I could use to go back to the students and expand our thinking. As Peterson (1992) says, "In holism, there is no destination or schedule. There is only thinking, doing, imagining what might be, and trying again" (p. 8).

"Okay, we have this great list. Now let's look at the list and let each person write three words in his or her journal that could have something to do with classroom rules." The students chose three rule-related words as most significant:

homework
boring
hollering

Thus, we decided to begin our list of classroom rules by focusing on our three key words:

1. *Homework:* We will do homework two days a week. We will choose the days. The homework must be something that is halfway interesting.
2. *Boring:* Work in class should not be boring. We need to tell you if we are bored. What's boring for one person might be interesting for somebody else, so we will give everything and everyone a chance. We will all try *not* to be bored.
3. *Hollering:* The teacher won't holler at us. We won't holler at each other (or the teacher). We won't do things that would make someone want to holler at us (we know what those things are).

Although my own "rules agenda" might have included things like respect, active listening, and putting things back after use, the students had built a framework that could encompass all of those and more. I knew that sometimes it would be a stretch to fit a problem into one of those categories, but in general these were rules we could always come back to when we needed to bring things back together. Students who have found so much joy in breaking rules don't need a list of *don'ts*. They probably already have those lists permanently in their heads: *Don't* chew gum. *Don't* write notes. *Don't* hit. All things for the students *not* to do. The list included things for all of us; in fact, the students saw the "boring" part as more for me than for them!

By the end of the year, I could remember many times when someone had gotten out of control, but before I could say anything another student might say, "Now that's something that would make someone want to holler at you." Usually it made the student smile and the activity would change. Notice that I said "usually." If only classroom life were really this easy! Although I do find that these kinds of community-building, standards-setting activities are most tolerated on the first day of school, it is never easy to help students see that ultimately, they are in control of and responsible for their own actions. However, once they were established and posted, the first-day rules did give us a place to come back to during the year when we need to refocus our energies or our activities.

I had three more goals for that first day of school: I wanted students to know what books and other resources were available in the classroom; I wanted them to choose a book for independent reading; and I wanted to establish read aloud as a critical part of our time together. In the past, I had always walked around the room pointing out the various areas in the classroom and the books or supplies that were contained in each. Although students were generally attentive while I did my tour, the very next day they might ask, "Where are the tape players?" This year I decided to try something new. I would put students in groups and ask each group to draw a map of our classroom, labeling what each area contained (see figure 4-1). Sound simple? As my students would say, *"not!"* The task, however, was not the problem; grouping turned out to be the major issue.

"I'm not sitting with that geek."

"I didn't speak to that slut all through junior high. I'm not talking to her now!"

"Terri and I are working together and we don't want anyone else in our group."

Once again I had completely ignored the fact that students in this class came from two different middle schools, which had been seen as rivals for the past three years. Now I wanted them to start working together, and it wasn't going to be easy. In his *Life in a Crowded Place*, Peterson (1992) states that "life in classrooms is an intense social experience." In the past teachers and administrators have attempted to curtail that intensity with rules. Traditionally, we have "managed to cope with the crowded conditions by restricting everything we could think of. Movement. Talk. Note passing. Even handwriting style" (p. 1). In my attempt to help the students gain ownership of the class I had taken away some of the artificial barriers, barriers that had served in place of respect and self-control. When those

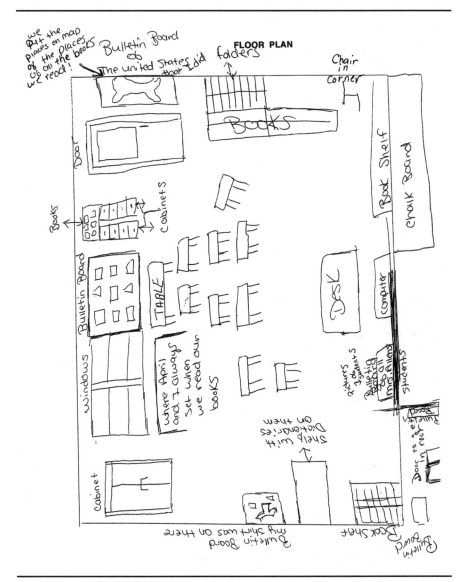

Figure 4-1. Floor plan

were gone, students felt free to be who they were and say what they wanted, even on the first day of school.

Again I had not met students where they were, nor had I given them enough support to move from where they were to a new place. With students who had previously had no part in the design or substance of their learning, I had directed them to an incoherent place. Since our time was limited, and I could see that this would not be a five-minute process, I told them to think about one other person they would like to work with and we would begin our class tomorrow with that activity. I didn't want students to leave with angry comments ringing in their ears; I wanted them to leave eager to come back tomorrow.

One of the keys to making students want to come to class had always been my reading aloud; I hoped it wouldn't fail me now. I have always agreed with Huck (Twain, 1962) that literature makes us more human by helping "us develop compassion and insight into the behavior of ourselves and others" (p. 69). After only an hour with these students, I decided that I needed to choose a book that would capture their interest and make them want more. I've often started the year with *The Lottery Rose* (Hunt, 1976), but after being with these students for just a short period of time, I decided that this group needed something with lots of action and suspense that was closer to their age and interest levels, at least for a beginning book. The book had to have a hook and lots of opportunity for prediction. I decided on *I Know What You Did Last Summer* (Duncan, 1973).

In his discussion of the importance of reading aloud to teenagers, Matthews (1987) points out that "somebody has to pick the right book and present it in an exciting fashion" (p. 410). This isn't always easy given the negative attitudes these students have toward books. I knew from past experience that if I billed something as exciting and suspenseful and students found it predictable, it would take me weeks to rebuild their trust. But I had read this book aloud before and it had never failed to get students involved, not only in the action of the story but in the moral dilemmas of the characters. In addition, this book would be perfect for looking at prediction as a reading strategy within the context of meaningful text.

I asked students to begin by looking at the cover and writing down the title and author in their academic journals. As I wandered around the room I was once again amazed at their lack of experience with books. Of the fourteen students in the room on that first day, six asked me where they could find the author's name. I quietly pointed it out and continued walking. When I got to the other side of the room, I said, "Now that we have that information, let's each look at the cover and make one prediction. What do you think the book will be about?" Students looked at the front and back covers and then wrote their predictions in their journals. When everyone had one to share, I wrote them on the board. The following quotations from students' written predictions show the class range for this important reading strategy:

> **Terri:** Somebody did something wrong and somebody knows what they did.
> **Angel:** It's all about four kids who all got in trouble last summer and what people found out what they did and they don't tell them. They keep it a secret. And probably at the end of the book they come out with what they did.
> **Peter:** Someone trying to black male Someone else.
> **Karen:** A girl did something really bad over the summer and did not tell anyone. But somehow someone found out and is using it against her.
> **Jennifer:** Didn't make a prediction because she "didn't understand what you wanted."

Sam: Didn't make a prediction because he started looking through the book.

Amy: I think it would be something about these guys killed or raped some girl and another girl knows about it and she's threatening to tell the police or something and they try to kill her.

Jeff: Someone knows something someone else did wrong.

Danny: Someone might of hit a little boy on his bike and left him somewhere.

Derek: There's a boy and he's scared someone found out what he did.

When everyone had contributed I said, "These are great predictions. Now I'd like you to take just a few minutes and write down what you saw on the cover of the book that helped you make that prediction." Although this seemed a small task, I felt that it was important to establish the necessity of going back to the text *and* back to our thinking process to support our answers. Their supporting ideas stayed in their academic journals and their predictions stayed on the board. I told them I would ask them to come back to these predictions as I read the book so that we could confirm or reject them. Lynch (1986), who supports the practice of writing and leaving children's thoughts on the board, explains: "As the book is read, their predictions and suggestions will receive confirmation, which will build their confidence" (p. 3). In terms of predictability, this is one of the best aspects of the book: almost every student is able to predict some piece of the plot by looking at the cover. This activity would ensure that everyone who tried would feel success on the very first day.

As I began reading the book out loud, the students settled in. All except Corey and Derek were following along. Some had inched their desks closer to mine. Others had looked furtively at me, then moved from their desks to the comfortable chairs and couches. I continued reading as if that were exactly what I expected them to do. It has long been my personal belief that a bond is created during a read aloud that is unrivaled in terms of literacy. I also believe that until students experience that stage of their literacy growth, they can't move forward in their development. I wanted this time each day to be analogous to a lap reading experience: a time when everyone is comfortable, shares in the creation of meaning, and experiences a life apart from, yet connected to, his or her own. As the bell rang, students put their books away and left quietly. I felt good about the way the class had come together and all I had learned about the students in that short period of time. As Jennifer walked past my desk she said, "I understood what you meant by prediction, I just didn't want you to write what I said on the board. I don't want my name up there. I don't want to be here and I don't want anyone to know I'm in here."

In a class where students did worksheets and independent assignments, Jennifer could easily have been invisible. My good feelings were gone. If the stigma about being in a "special class" was this great, would we ever make any progress? This was a not-so-gentle reminder that I needed to get to know my learners as individuals as quickly as possible so I wouldn't repeat my first day's mistakes. I wasn't so naive that I thought I wouldn't make other mistakes, but at least I could learn from what my students had tried to teach me on that first day.

Knowing My Learners

Part of knowing my learners was sensing immediately that it was not only ethical to bring students into my research, it was critical in terms of their learning. Vygotsky (1962) emphasizes the importance of students' understanding of and involvement in their learning processes when he says that understanding of a function is necessary in order to control the function. In spite of the importance of understanding learning, my students essentially had no idea what it would take to help them become readers, individually or collectively. As Figure 4-2 indicates, when students were asked "What could I do to help you become a better reader?" over half of them didn't have any idea.

Their lack of knowledge about reading—what reading entails, how they could become readers, or what they could do to improve their reading—had left them disenfranchised. They had sat for so long waiting for someone to give them "work," then doing the work and still not being any better at reading, that they had lost (if they had ever had) control of their learning. If I hoped to help these students become better readers and writers, I had to show them how to get access to the system. In terms of literacy, I believed that access would come with seeing themselves as learners and sharing in the control of their learning. Thus, it was important that I explain my research and solicit their involvement. With this act, I was aware that I was bringing them in as co-researchers, which was my inten-

Figure 4-2. Data from "Helping Become"

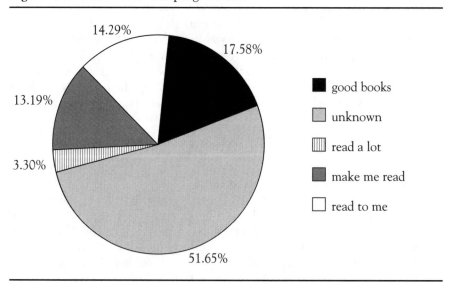

tion. I think this alone made a statement to the students about how I viewed them. I didn't see them as incapable of making decisions or taking responsibility for those decisions, and that alone seemed to make them more decisive and responsible—at least some of them some of the time.

In 1902 Dewey admonished readers that "it is he [the child] and not the subject-matter which determines both the quality and quantity of learning" (p. 9). In my opinion, nowhere is that distinction more critical than when working with students the system has failed. I think Rachel emphasized this point with her comments about what had contributed to her success during the year:

> Just tell them my story. I hated to read, and now, in time I want to read just about everything I can get my hands on. I want to be in the plays, I write poems and read short stories. And the only things that got me into reading was the encouragement, and a teacher who really cares about what we do. Not just as a class, but to each and every one of us. I think that is all that we need, is to have some of the teachers come down to our level and think like us.

What helped Rachel come to a place where she could articulate these insights into her learning was my acknowledgment and understanding of her as a person and as a learner. I wanted students to see that as much as I loved reading, the books we read were intended as vehicles for us to know ourselves and others better. Our discussions of books and the topics these books brought to the surface gave me one kind of information. Informal events—such as listening to and talking with students when they came into my room during their free time—contributed more, helping me get to know them as individuals. It was the somewhat "formal" assessments I asked of students, however, that provided the additional background knowledge I needed in order to choose content, design activities, and understand as well as support their learning.

During those first weeks of school, I asked students to complete several surveys or writings so that I could get to know them. In addition, the initial fall survey (see Appendix B), provided valuable background and experience data for the class that helped me come to know the class and the individuals within the group.

Knowing the Class

Their History with Conferences

Although most students reported a history of individual conferences about goals and classes, fewer reported conferences in which they discussed themselves as individuals. My first reaction was that perhaps, in the process of discussing students' goals and classes, counselors and teachers were also discussing those characteristics that made them unique and valuable, but so subtly that the students were lumping it with conferences about selecting classes. As I interviewed individual students, however, I found that this was not the case. I was brought back to Rachel's comment: "A teacher who really cares about what we do. Not just as a class, but to each and every one of us."

My initial interviews with students also clarified some of my questions about the conferences they reported (see Figure 4-3). Later in the year when I talked with them in individual interviews about conferences related to their writing and referred them back to their fall surveys, several students said, "I thought you meant when somebody told us what we got for a grade." Other students reported that conferences were a time when "the teacher told us what she wrote on our papers because we couldn't keep them." Their interpretation of a reading conference was any kind of discussion, or even answering questions about a book. But none of them had actually sat down and discussed a book he or she was reading in any depth. During that first week of school, I did a reading interview with Tammy that helped me understand the students' definition of conference.

> **J.A.:** Now you've talked a lot about what happened to the boyfriend. Do you really think he's dead?
> **Tammy:** Yeah.
> **J.A.:** What is there in the book that makes you think that?
> **Tammy:** What do you mean?
> **J.A.:** What words or actions make you think that he is dead?
> **Tammy:** Oh, I see what you mean. Here, where it says, "He's history."
> **J.A.:** Good for you for being able to support your opinion.
> **Tammy:** I thought you just wanted an answer.
> **J.A.:** Didn't you have to support your opinions in your conferences about the books you were reading?

Figure 4-3. Data from "History with Conferencing"

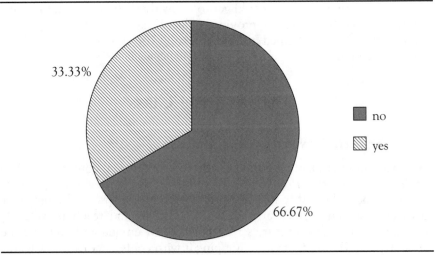

Tammy: We had different conferences. The teacher asked us the questions about the books and we told her the answers and she checked them in the answer book.

It was my role as researcher that had sent me back to the students for further information, but the impact of what I learned on my teaching was dramatic. If I had taken the fall survey results at face value, I would have thought that students were quite familiar with conferences and therefore able and ready to confer with me and with each other. The results of this data collection, my reflection, and my subsequent discussions with students, however, confirmed for me the veracity of Martin's (1987) statement: "Classroom teachers are in the best position to ask questions about learning, to accumulate data, and to take up teaching directions based on the learning patterns that emerge" (p. 220).

Attitudes Toward School

The self-reported data from the fall survey indicated that most of the students enjoyed gym, vocational classes, lunch, and study hall and disliked math, science, English, and social studies. Disliked subjects fell into the category of academics, while classes they enjoyed fell into the category of "extras." (Actually, I think students saw these subjects as the substance of school; it is teachers who have sometimes seen them as extras.) In addition, two students reported disliking everything about school, including the social aspects. This did not surprise me, but as I compiled the results I was once again reminded of the importance of taking information back to students for debriefing and further clarification. When I chose an individual subject many of them had reported as one they disliked (such as English), through further questioning I was able to pinpoint some of the perceptions that made English objectionable and some of the things that might have made it better.

I Dislike English Because . . .
1. It means work and work and work.
2. It means being in a special room.
3. It means reading out loud.
4. We have to read, and write, and do journals.
5. It's boring.

6. The grades are stupid.
7. The teacher is boring.
8. We have to read in front of the class.

It Would Have Been Better If . . .
1. We had less homework.

2. I could have been in a regular room.
3. I hadn't been embarrassed.
4. We could do things that have nothing to do with English.
5. We did something fun for a change.
6. The grades were fair.
7. We had a better teacher.
8. We could do stuff alone.

Although most of the students said they disliked English, or at least that it wasn't their favorite class, our discussions and the survey results did bring out some activities they had enjoyed: projects, working in groups, and reading silently. In addition, not only did they feel that the teacher made the difference, they were able to articulate the qualities of a "good" teacher.

Good Teachers . . .
listen
have brains
respect the student
are patient
have a good personality
don't give kids a hard time
understand students
help you when you need it
are nice
teach skills

Feeling sure that sainthood would be just around the corner if I could do and be all of these for each student, I was pleased that they had been able to pinpoint so clearly what it was they needed from me. Their ability to do that seemed based on trust, and I wasn't quite sure what I had done to earn their trust so quickly. Or maybe they had just decided that, since I was asking for a wish list, they would give me their ideal teacher. In any case, it helped me to understand what they saw as important.

Understanding Themselves as Learners

In spite of all the recent research indicating how important it is for students not only to see themselves as learners but to understand their individual learning processes, much classroom practice remains more focused on answering than on questioning. The results of the fall survey indicated that these students had very little idea of what had happened to their reading. Most knew they had been placed in a "special" class because they couldn't read well, but they seemed to have no idea why.

As Flavell (1979) points out, metacognitive awareness leads to efficient reasoning. An inability to reason in terms of their own learning is a common characteristic of at-risk students. In fact, when I looked at the results of this survey, I did not think these students were aware that their learning was anything they could understand, let alone control. Although most of the class saw reading as important, all rated themselves as average or below average in their reading. In addition, ten students out of fourteen rated themselves as equally good in both reading and writing. If students considered reading and writing important, yet felt that they were not very good at either, I didn't have to ponder long to understand their negative attitude toward English.

Using the Burke Reading Interview (1988, p. 171), I found that fewer than half of the students said they knew someone they considered a "good" reader: four listed family members and two listed students they knew. When I asked what in their opinion made that person a good reader, nearly half of them said reading a lot. The characteristic traits of a good reader included pro-

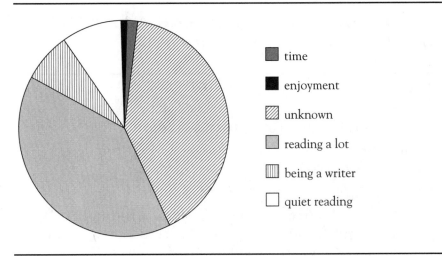

Figure 4-4. Data from "Making a Reader"

nouncing big words, reading quickly and smoothly, not making mistakes and reading hard books. The data from this survey are summarized in Figure 4-4.

Students seemed to believe that reading a lot would help them, and I certainly believed that, so we agreed on at least one aspect of classroom practice. In fact, eleven of fourteen students said that the way I could help them become better readers was to "give them time just to sit and read." Perhaps they did understand their learning better than I had originally thought, and I simply needed to build the curriculum around their knowledge of what it would take to help them improve. Traditional techniques for teaching reading had certainly failed with these students, and since I agreed that one thing that would help them become better readers was actually reading, it seemed natural that we would plan to spend much of our time reading. In order to accomplish this I knew I had to understand what would make students want to read (see Figure 4-5).

At a conference in 1991, I heard Carolyn Burke say, "You can't learn about anything you're not already in the process of doing." If I wanted students to understand reading and themselves as readers, they had to be actively involved in the process of reading. Our primary focus had to be on reading, because I felt that students' writing would improve as they began seeing models of good writing through their reading and feeling that they too had legitimate and valuable stories to tell. Whenever I hear teachers say that students don't have anything to write about (or that students *say* they don't have anything to write about), I am reminded of Burke's words: "It isn't that students don't have anything to write about, it is that they think that what they have to write about isn't legitimate for school" (personal communication, April 1991). This was certainly the case with these students. When I asked students whether they considered writing important, all but one agreed that it was important or extremely important, but, at the same time, they didn't see themselves as writers. Yet when I asked them to make lists of things they had written in the past six months,

Things that make me want to Read or write.	Things that make me not Read or write...
Choosing your own books.	Writting something long.
Reading books.	Sammaries
Reading fun things to read	Reading dramas
Doing fun things	Working by yourself
making things	Not doing fun things
having art	Reports
having parteners	Watching boring movies
or working in groups	Rdg too much by yourself
having people come in	Rdg w/ the guys
presentations	When Mrs Allen never w/ us
watching good movies	When Im in a bad mood
group discussions	boreing books.
Mrs Allen Rdg to us	not picking your own books
going in the Rdg center	when the teacher makes you read a certain book you hate
Playing games	Rdg books having to do w/ kidnapping
Writting letters to Mrs Allen	Rdg books that start off real boreing
Writting in our personal journals	loong books
Having a nice teacher	Having a mean teacher
a teacher that you like	teacher that hates u.

Figure 4-5. "Things that make me . . ."

many listed letters to friends, personal journals or diaries, poems, short stories, and lyrics for songs. As important as the class-generated data was for my planning and practice, I knew that real changes would occur only when I came to know the individuals within the group (I thought of Rachel's words: "not just as a class, but to each and every one of us"). I knew their writing and their voices were the key to my knowing them as individuals. I also knew that I would have to hear and celebrate those individual voices if they were ever going to see this as *our* (and not *my*) classroom.

Knowing the Individual

Each day of those first weeks added another piece to the fifteen human puzzles I found in our classroom. Just when I thought I had figured out what was going on, new information would show up in their writing or in an interview that would make me reexamine my assumptions. On our first visit to the computer lab, I asked students to write about their best and worst experiences. I had borrowed this practice from MacCracken's *Lovey* (1976), in which she used the children's discussion of a best and a worst as a way of helping them get past negative experiences and build on the positive aspects of their lives. From their initial responses, I knew it was going to take some work to convince students that learning can be fun.

Terri: I did bad in school that year. That was because my cousin was in my class and we always got in trouble. In first grade I stayed back. That was because I couldn't stand the teacher and she couldn't stand me. She was a real bag. She wore lots of make-up and she thought she was queen of the world.

Peter: The first day of high school I did not like. I did not go the day before school, so when I went to school the next day I did not know where anything was. So I asked my friend where the freshmen lockers were so he showed me. But after my first class I could not find my locker if I bumped into it. But any way my schedule was mest up and I got more lost. I did not know where lunch was or anything. So when i went to see my consler he made a new schedule but that was wrong too. he sent me to a algebra 1 class, but there was a problem, it was an all girls class. I was imbarris. I went back and told him and he apulliged. I had to drop one class and add another. So this last Tuesday they call me down to the office and said I was absident for Health that day. But I do not have Health until the last two quarters. Today they called me back down to the office and said I was absident for Health class again. But I don't have Health until the last two quarters. So what a start for High School.

Jennifer: The first day of school was horrible. My first class I hated the teacher plus there were some of the students who were seniors. That's all right. Next was the class I hated to think about because all of the dumb students or as you could say low students are in. If you ask me there are no girls in here that are not skums except for Casey and me. All the boys are ugly and don't talk. I do like the teachers. But I would like to drop the class.

The students' writing was filled with negative experiences from the past as well as new feelings of failure, although they had only been in high school for a few days. All their problems were important background for me, but it was comments like Jennifer's that concerned me the most. Given the active dislike many of them felt for each other, our class, and school in general, I knew this was going to be another difficult year.

5

Voices Within and Without

If he is indeed wise, he does not bid you enter the house of his wisdom, but rather leads you to the threshold of your own mind.   Kahlil Gibran, *The Prophet*

And so our year together began. The disagreement over forming groups on that first day remained one of the critical issues in the class. Tammy quickly took more and more control of the class, and her aggressive behavior became problematic as most of the boys and a couple of the girls actually seemed intimidated by her. I could understand that. If I were a new teacher, I think even I would have been intimidated by her constant need to be in control.

On the positive side, students had responded well to both their independent reading time and our shared reading. Each day as I wrote in my journal, I realized that my words sounded like a teacher's version of Charlip's (1980) *Fortunately, Unfortunately!* That's exactly how it felt to be with those students. Within a forty-five minute period, I felt the tears in my eyes when Derek said, "This is the first book I've ever read!" and when Jennifer said, "I never knew there were strategies for figuring out the words."

Within minutes, however, I found myself losing hope as Tammy caused yet another fight and Wayne was called to the office for skipping science class. There were days when I despaired that they would ever be able to change because of the personal and academic failure they had experienced. But there were also days when I felt that I was watching flowers blossom now that they finally had the right mixture of sunlight and water. One of those days came after I watched Terri surreptitiously hand a folded note to Tammy. She looked up guiltily when she realized I saw her and then a defiant look came over her face. "So what if I wrote a note?"

I realized at that point that I could either make the negative attitude escalate or I could try to use the situation to help me establish a relationship with Terri. I chose the latter. "I don't have a problem with the note, I'm just always amazed at the way you fold those notes into such little pieces. I could never do that."

"That's easy. I could teach you that in five minutes."

I laughed. "Don't be too sure. I'm terrible at crafts and building things."

That afternoon Terri came down during my seventh period planning which was also her study hall. The wall was gone as she brought a chair up close to mine and began folding a note. "See, you just do this, and then do this and then fold it here, and that's it."

After several attempts, my folded notes still resembled the snowflakes we used to fold and cut to decorate our classroom windows at Christmas. At that time the teacher used to say, "That's just fine, Janet, we want them all to be unique." My folded notes were certainly unique. Terri was more than patient. She went over the method again and again as I fumbled along.

Finally, in an unimagined display of warmth, Terri put her arm around my shoulder. "I'll tell you what, Ms. A., why don't you just give me any of the notes you want folded and I'll fold them for you." As I smiled thankfully at her, she said, "Don't feel bad. There are things I'm not that good at either." One wall down—fourteen to go.

Listening to Their Voices

So, In spite of the difficult times, we established a routine together, not in the negative sense of the word, but in the comfortable sense that comes from consistency. The students had chosen Mondays and Fridays as the days when they would read independently. Although I didn't initially stress writing in the way I did reading, I knew that in time I would encourage and support students' writing in the same way. During those first days, however, I thought they needed to establish the pattern and expectation of silent, independent reading.

When I started reading *When the Phone Rang* (Mazer, 1985) during independent reading, Tammy, Tori, and Anne decided to read it too. I've always been amazed at the impact of my reading choice on students' choices. During the ten years we've had sustained, silent reading at our high school, I have had to push some teachers to read while their students are reading. I've always tried not to do anything else during that time, since I want to

Classroom Environment

make a statement to students about the power and importance of reading. It has also been my experience that if there is one sure way to get students to read, it is by saying, "This is what I'm reading. If you want to borrow it you can, but don't lose my place." Two drawers in my desk are full of books I've started, which students appropriate for their own independent reading. Each day when they return the books to the drawer, they check to see if I'm still ahead of them or if they have caught up to me. Near the end of the year, when Jennifer said to me, "You're my competition," I realized that many students in special classes don't want to be compared with the other students in the class; they want to get to the point where they are reading with me, both literally and figuratively.

Within two weeks, most students came into the room expecting to read. In fact, I'm sure they would not have tolerated doing anything else. For some, I think it was the fact that on those two days they were free to make all the choices. Others, however, had actually found a book that interested them and were actively reading. During the third week of classes, after everyone had started reading, I took the time to watch them and make notes in my journal.

> Melvin has finally found a book with an accompanying tape, *If I Had a Hammer* (Vance, 1991), and seems really interested in the book. He has been one that hasn't seemed too interested in this whole reading business. One day last week I noticed that he was looking at baseball cards during our reading time and that made me think that perhaps he'd like this book about a baseball player. Derek also has broken down

and is reading *Tales of Mystery and Suspense* (Potter, 1976). Although this would not be the kind of reading I would choose for him, the one-page stories with accompanying questions seem to feel comfortable for him. He came in today clearly happy that he had a book and a plan. I think I'll just give him some time and some space and see if he stays with this kind of format. Jennifer didn't want to read because she was too upset when she came into the class. I quietly asked her if she would like to write instead of read and she spent all period writing in her journal. Anne and Tori started a new book, *Funhouse* (Hoh, 1990); reading the same book motivates both of them to read more, I think. Wayne is engrossed with *The Outsiders* (Hinton, 1967). Some of the students were complaining that they'd already "done" that book in junior high. Wayne responded emphatically, "Shut up. I only read pieces then, but now I'm really reading it." It made me wonder how much kids get out of what they *have* to read. Trish is really into *The Boyfriend* (Stine, 1990). Others are at various stages of reading or pretending to read. *But* they aren't fighting and they do have books they've chosen. One step at a time. The bell is ringing and over half the class is still sitting reading, oblivious to the time. Success!

Did that one moment of success happen overnight? How did I get the students to this point and how could we sustain and build on where we were? It would have been rewarding if I thought we had broken the cycle of failure so easily for these students. I'd like to be able say that from this point it was a smooth path to the end of the year and fifteen success stories. I'd like to say it because I wish it were true. But our year together was more like a ride on the pothole-riddled roads of Maine in the springtime than a ride on an expressway that gets you to your destination with the least amount of effort and in a minimum amount of time! I also know that I learned more from the disequilibrium I experienced on those "pothole" days than I did on the days when we moved from point A to point B with few problems. Intuitively, I agreed with Gillespie (1992), "When we do our own teacher research, when we collect stories from our own classrooms, we must be careful to see the whole story, to notice and describe the problems and exceptions as well as the triumphs" (p. 17). As I looked at the stories and the artifacts, the words and the silences of our days, I thought it was important to begin by letting the students' words choose the significant themes of our year.

On the last two days of the school year, I asked two colleagues to do videos with my students. I wanted someone to facilitate discussion so students could talk about their year of learning together. The entire class participated in the first video, and three students continued the dialogue with another teacher in the second video. In the course of these ninety minutes, and in their writing reflections, students pointed to the themes they saw as significant during the year: reading aloud, choice and independent reading, a teacher who listens and who is supportive, learning reading strategies, the classroom environment, and comparisons between this class and previous classes. In order to establish the context of our year together, I shall look at the way in which each of these themes came to be significant for the students and for me.

Reading Aloud

Jan Duncan, a New Zealand educator, talks about New Zealand teachers' responsibilities with what they call "ten book children," children who come to school having had few or no experiences with books. These teachers consider it their responsibility to fill this gap by seeing that students experience a great number and variety of books. In working with students such as the ones in my Reading and Writing Workshop, I see my responsibility in the same way.

In her book *Reading to, with and by Children,* Mooney (1990) defines and illustrates diverse experiences with reading that help students become lifelong readers. I have grouped our reading activities within these same categories in order to look at my role within each. A case in point: most agree that read aloud is one way for students to see themselves as readers, to have the background knowledge that comes with wide reading, and to feel successful with books in a short time. But the term "read aloud" can have many connotations. When my students talked about reading aloud, they were actually referring to several different activities that occurred consistently in our classroom: my reading aloud to them, their participation in shared reading, and their own reading aloud. Although these three activities share an oral reading component, in our classroom each had its own distinct purpose.

Reading to Students

I read aloud to my students when they did not follow along in the text in order to give them pleasure and information. The selections I chose varied from picture books to poetry, from articles on killer bees to "Dear Abby" letters. Mooney (1988) regards this as a time when "the teacher acts on behalf of the author, presenting the writing with as much enthusiasm and commitment as if it were his or her own" (p. 24). I used this time to introduce students to a variety of texts and genres as well as simply to share the pleasure of words. After I read one of the Oompa Loompa's poems, which began, "Augustus Gloop, Augustus Gloop, you great big greedy nincompoop" (Dahl, 1964, p. 82), I often heard students repeating the rhyme. It is important to provide occasions for students to experience the magic of language. Students who have not had that experience as children and who have been in classes where reading aloud was not the focus have never had that opportunity. If students are to see reading as an activity they want to do, it is my responsibility to demonstrate the magic they will find in books.

Reading to students is also a key ingredient in creating a risk-free environment. They know that their only responsibility during this time is to listen. They don't have to worry about issues like pronouncing words correctly, so their stress level decreases considerably. After my reading of *Alexander and the Terrible, Horrible, No Good, Very Bad Day* (Viorst, 1972), a number of students wrote about horrible days they'd had. A reading of Maya Angelou's poem, "No Losers, No Weepers" (1989, p. 9), prompted writing about stolen boyfriends and girlfriends. Terri's letter, for example, indicates not only the degree of her reader response but also the safety she felt in sharing her feelings with me. She handed me a folded note with these words, "I knew just what that Myron guy was talking about in that poem you read us yesterday."

> Dear Ms. A,
> Hi, what's up? Everything is fine here. Well, not really. I am so mad at Steve. I can't believe he broke up with me for that slut after we had been date for over a year. Everybody in the school knows what a whore she is. They even call her Electrolux because she has F———— the entire Electricity class.

Although Terri's note was a little unconventional, I didn't need to wonder if she had connected with my read aloud the previous day. In the past I might have used those readings as a prompt for everyone to write about horrible days and lost loves. Today I simply put the model out there, so that students can decide whether to pursue more reading by the same author, to reread this text, or to write using this reading as a prompt. Reading aloud allows me to introduce students to a variety of good writing in a short amount of time, a variety that can serve as a model, in either content or style, for their own writing. It is always my plan, and my hope, to read something that will inspire the same kind of strong connection Terri experienced with "No Losers, No Weepers."

Reading aloud also helps build community. In a read aloud situation, everyone has equal access to the text and can participate in the discussion. A "Dear Abby" letter about drinking and driving prompts an involved discussion in which nearly everyone participates; an article about killer bees allows students to connect this new information with things they've heard in science and seen on television. These activities might seem insignificant to some, but for students who have not experienced curricular conversations, either at home or in school, it is critical. These students need to find their own voices if they are going to share in the voices of others. Reading to students thus became a significant part of building our community: sharing the beauty of language, meeting new authors and texts, and exploring a variety of writing styles.

At the end of the year, as students discussed what worked for them in the classroom, they referred to the conversations, curricular and otherwise, and the ultimate impact of those conversations on their literacy.

Interviewer: Is this room kind of special?
Several respond: Yeah. It's comfortable. You can sit and read.

Sam: This class is more sociable than others.

Interviewer: You talk more?

Sam: Yeah, we talk a lot about what we're doing and not just in here either. I mean, now I know most of these people. I know a lot about them—not just in this area, but personally. You just get to know each other.

Jennifer: In my other classes I don't even know people's names.

Anne: And if you're reading out loud, it's easier to read with people you know than others—people who believe in you.

It will be the talk that so many of these students remember. Long after my reading of a poem, a letter, a short story, or an editorial has faded from their memories, the talk and the comfort associated with that talk will linger.

Reading with Students

The shared reading experience, in which I read aloud and each reader follows in an individual copy of the text, was one of the most critical components in helping students become readers. At the beginning of our year together, we accomplished this in two ways: I read aloud to students while they followed the text, and students independently listened to recorded books on tapes and followed the text. The two activities, one within the larger community and one independent, shared a common purpose: assisting students as they assumed increasing responsibility for their reading. For many of these students, this was their first enjoyable experience of someone reading to them.

From past experience, I know that reading aloud must be carried out with even more preparation than one would put into many other classroom activities.

I also know that a read aloud can be critical instructional time if the teacher has prepared with as much energy as it deserves. The preparation is undoubtedly different for each teacher, but I have identified several areas to attend to in the process of choosing and carrying out a read aloud that truly is also quality instruction. I focus on defining my purpose; establishing a positive reading environment; preparing myself and my students for oral reading, and knowing the text well enough to be able to choose places to begin and end as well as places to wonder at and question (Allen et al., 1991).

Barton (1986) reminds would-be readers that, without the proper preparation for reading aloud, both readers and listeners will have a joyless experience. Students intuitively, or perhaps experientially, know this to be true. Rachel gave me some indication of what was missing from her previous read aloud experiences.

If they read to us, they'd usually read a book—you know, like a textbook—with something that was kind of boring. I remember once we read *Tom Sawyer* or something like that in school and we'd have to follow along. I would never follow along because I didn't think it was exciting. I guess maybe it was the book—I wasn't really enthused with *Tom Sawyer*. It didn't catch my attention or nothing, but like when I got up in high school in your classes, maybe it's the books or something, the books I've paid right attention to. That's it. I think after *The Lottery Rose* that I kind of liked it. Because most books they read, the ones they give us at school, was always "great literature" like *Tom Sawyer*, but the books you give us are more something I'd have to deal with today. I thought that was pretty cool. Like when you were reading the books out loud, you'd read it and stop and I'd want you to read more. I was dying for the next day to come. When we wouldn't have reading periods, I'd just sit there and stare at the book and think, "I want to read some more."

She points to several things I consider in preparing for a shared reading experience:

Is this the right book to meet the needs of these students at this time?

This year, when I reviewed students' fall surveys, I discovered that many of them were interested in horror and suspense. Given their problems with school and reading, I wanted something that would hook them right away, so I began the year with *I Know What You Did Last Summer* (Duncan, 1973), a book that offers an interesting, suspenseful story. Within that context I would be able to assess some of their reading strategies—predicting, connecting with background knowledge, and making logical deductions. This did not mean that I didn't eventually read some "great literature" aloud—at the end of the year, many students said the book they enjoyed the most was *Of Mice and Men* (Steinbeck, 1937)—I just did not read that book as the first one of the year. How did I choose the books I read? As Derek said in the debriefing video, "She's read enough books so she kind of knows just which books will capture our interest."

Can I read this book in such a way that students won't see it as "boring?"

Not all books lend themselves to reading aloud; in fact, many excellent books do not provide optimal read aloud experiences. In selecting books for this class, I knew that, especially initially, I had to choose titles that were long on excitement and short on description. Terri said, "She reads a book and it's like you're seeing a TV." That's what I hoped for. These students did not come to my classroom with a history of varied and positive reading experiences that would help them construct meaning from a complicated text. I needed books with a strong plot line and lots of dialogue so the story would come alive for them. Read aloud was like a performance. I made sure that I had practiced enough to give the characters distinctive voices. I found it is the characters' voices that bring students into *Of Mice and Men* (Steinbeck, 1937) so quickly. As one student said, "I remember *Of Mice and Men* really good. She read George kind of typical, but then when she read Lennie, she kind of took the character. Looking at the book and hearing her voice, I could see a man not emotionally stable. It really made a difference. Class would be over and I'd still be sitting with the book in my hand."

Is this a book I enjoy?

In *Tell Me Another,* Barton (1986) reminds readers that we have to be able to bring all of the elements and emotions of the story to life. This is easier to do if the story is one with which the reader personally connects. I know from experience that I can't do this unless I am reading a book I have really enjoyed. I chose many of the books we read together during the year—*Lovey* (MacCracken, 1976), *The Lottery Rose* (Hunt, 1976), *Jemmy* (Hassler, 1980), *Of Mice and Men* (Steinbeck, 1937), *Ask Me If I Care* (Gilmour, 1985) and *That Was Then, This Is Now* (Hinton, 1980)—for that reason. All had characters with whom I could empathize, which in turn helped me read so that students could be drawn into the book through the characters' voices and actions, their hopes and dreams.

Does this book meet my instructional purposes?

Although it may seem that I chose the books for our shared reading randomly, I actually put a great deal of thought into what I selected for shared reading. Although one consideration was logistical (having sufficient copies of the text), my main questions centered on which text would meet my instructional purposes. Although the list that follows is only a beginning, it guided my selections.

1. Show students that words can be fun.
2. Demonstrate a genre and its characteristics.
3. Model a writing style.
4. Meet the social problems we encountered as a community.
5. Introduce another text or unit.
6. Stimulate curricular conversations.
7. Build community.
8. Give everyone access to books with "charm, magic, impact, and appeal."
9. Help students think critically.

It might seem that I was doing all the work, but that was not the case. I made it clear from our first reading together that this was a time when all of us would be active readers; I would be speaking the words, but they would share responsibility in their role as readers. During the year as I held individual conferences with students, I asked what they did while I was reading. Their responses indicate the level of their commitment to the shared reading experience and their involvement in it.

1. I follow along and pay attention to the words. You could follow along and be thinking about something else, but I follow along and concentrate on the book. I put myself in that book. Like, I put myself as a character in the book so when the character goes through emotional phases, I feel like I'm going through them with her.
2. I pay attention to what's happening in front of me and not everywhere else.

3. I read along with you to try and keep up and see if I'm right in what I think the words will be.
4. I focus on the words as I listen, to remember that word and what it sounds like.
5. I make mental images because seeing the images helps me remember.
6. I try to keep it [the reading] in my head and then put it in with all the other thoughts and keep it.

At the end of the year, I asked students to comment on the practice of reading novels out loud by citing its pros and cons. Students mentioned only one "con," the times when I stopped reading for some reason and asked a volunteer to read. Many of them did not like it, perhaps for the reason Rachel gave: "I got used to each different voice you had for a different character so I only had to read the important words, not who said it." The "pros" were more numerous.

Pros
1. We all got to read the same book.
2. It was more interesting to read out loud.
3. I learned better reading skills by hearing it and stopping to talk about things.
4. I learned a lot of new words.
5. I learned to concentrate.
6. I read faster as I kept up with your reading.
7. I could read *and* relax.
8. I could hear what I was reading and I could remember the story.

From my perspective, reading aloud to learners during shared reading allowed me to model reading strategies I employed when I came to unknown words, concepts or inconsiderate sentences; show excitement as well as sadness in my appreciation of the characters' lives and problems; encourage discussions in which everyone could participate, extend the story to our lives and build community background knowledge; and demonstrate ways in which readers question themselves, the text, and the author in order to make the experience personally meaningful.

For many students, a read aloud or a shared reading experience was enough to help them become independent readers of self-selected texts. These students were more alliterate than illiterate, since they had previously seen no purpose in reading. When they encountered a large variety of interesting books, they were able to find titles that met both their interest and their ability levels. For many others however, the problems were more significant. Days given to independent reading time meant pretending to read or getting in trouble. In order to cope with that problem, I tried to find a way in which the success of the shared reading experience could be continued into independent reading time. The solution to our problem: books, unabridged tapes, and Walkmans.

After searching catalogs and local bookstores, I was able to find a large number of tapes to accompany books I knew students would like to read. Then I purchased several Walkman tape players, a battery recharger, and rechargeable batteries. The tape players allowed students to follow someone else's reading inconspicuously until they were ready to read independently. This transitional period at the beginning of the year made these tapes a prized commodity. The tapes allowed everyone to have equal—and enjoyable—access to the literature. Students who wished to could even read the same novels and plays that were being read in the higher-tracked courses, and for many students that was very important. Students could hear and follow along as Steven King read *The Gunslinger* (1988) or Gary Paulsen read *Woodsong* (1991). If a student still wanted or needed the tapes and the chosen book was unavailable on tape, I often took the book home and read it aloud, taping as I read. This not only broadened the scope of available books, it also allowed me to meet students' individual needs. As a group, however, we had to establish rules for using these materials: no listening to the radio; no Metallica tapes to replace *The Outsiders* (Hinton, 1967); and returning tapes, batteries, and books to the storage area so they were available for the next person. The rules helped ensure that students would use their independent reading time well by having all the materials ready and staying on task. Students learn to read by reading, and this shared reading experience encouraged many students to become readers during our year together.

Most students eventually stopped using the books on tape, but they had served a purpose. As Jennifer remarked, "At the beginning, if we didn't want to read, we could be read to on those cassettes, which helped a lot. Because that's what a lot of the guys did. We always used to fight over those things, but none of us want them anymore." When questioned about the reasons for making the transition from the taped books to independent reading, Jennifer replied, "I'd rather read to myself than listen to someone else now. I can go at my own pace and put more emotion into it."

Some students never used the tapes, and several, Derek and Melvin, were still using them at the end of the year, Derek only on days when he "just felt like being read to" and Melvin as he worked through *The War on Villa Street* (Mazer, 1978) and the accompanying reading guides I had prepared to help him acquire some reading strategies he was missing.

Shared reading with taped books provided a great deal of flexibility in meeting the individual needs of students while maintaining the quiet that others required in order to sustain their independent reading. I have heard other teachers talk about allowing students to move around and talk quietly during independent reading time. There were days and times when the students and I agreed that they could choose their reading and writing, and a variety of literacy-related activities would be going on at the same time. On Mondays and Fridays, however, we had sustained silent reading, which meant no interruptions. Jennifer reminded me of the importance of those times: "I've always been really easily distracted, but in here we had days when everyone read at the same time so I was able to concentrate on my reading." Although some students could read if the building collapsed, I found many more who needed quiet in order to concentrate. For most, silent reading was a new activity—and one that needed uninterrupted attention.

Reading With and To Others

Eventually, many students felt comfortable enough and competent enough to read out loud and wanted time to do just that. We initiated a number of activities for which students could volunteer: reading ghost stories they had practiced to the class at Halloween; small group reading of a common novel; sharing their writing; reading plays; and participating in paired reading with a group of first graders. All the girls eventually decided that they liked to read out loud and clamored loudly to do so as often as possible. Mac and Derek also enjoyed oral reading by the end of the third quarter. Melvin, Wayne, Dean, and Peter, however, preferred not to read out loud right through the year, although Melvin and Peter both chose to participate in the paired reading with first graders, which required them to read aloud, and both seemed to enjoy it. Wayne and Dean might choose to read a line or two in a class play, but otherwise they were content to read independently and silently. Reading orally had more negative significance for them than I might have imagined. Once they started telling me why they hated to read, I was pleased that I had followed their lead and had not forced the issue. For most of them, their initial dislike of reading was associated with the embarrassment of being forced to read in front of the class or in reading groups. The fact that I didn't believe in the traditional round robin reading and never forced students to read aloud in front of the group allowed them to come to that practice when and if they felt comfortable.

The various activities related to oral reading became the cornerstone of our reading. I recently heard a teacher say, "I don't read aloud to students because I'm never sure what they're getting." I have never felt that I had to be sure what students were getting. I have always been confident that they were getting something because I could see their attitude and level of involvement change each day. I prefer to endorse the thinking of Vacca, Vacca, and Gove in *Reading and Learning to Read* (1987), who find no reason for teachers to know every single thing a reader is taking from a text. If we have carefully chosen our texts, and if we really believe that reading is an active, meaning-constructing process in which each reader takes from the text in proportion to what he or she brings to it (Rosenblatt, 1976), then we must support our students in many and varied reading opportunities. Reading aloud is one way to give students the freedom to respond to texts without worrying over pronunciation, inflection, and those around you.

As the year progressed, we spent more and more time reading aloud. *I Know What You Did Last Summer* (Duncan, 1973) became our first shared novel. We continued this practice on Tuesdays, Wednesdays, and Thursdays throughout the entire year. This novel became the introduction to a larger unit on mystery and suspense, which led to our shared reading of *Teacher's Pet* (Cusick, 1990). Although I read the novels aloud, the students were also reading aloud: they practiced and read ghost stories, and we read plays and scary poems together. With each reading experience, students knew more about the world, about books, and about what it really means to be a lifelong reader, writer, and learner.

6

The World Is Our Textbook

I planned to leave that door open, weather permitting, to be a reminder that this classroom, and the students' words and pictures, could lead to an awareness of the world around us, what Maxine Greene calls "wide-awakeness."

Karen Ernst, *Picturing Learning*

Early in the year I asked students to complete some open-ended responses to prompts I gave them (see Appendix B: Sentence Completion). Two of the prompts were: "When I have to read, I _____" and "To me, books _____." These two simple sentence starters elicited important information. It also told me that if I planned to get kids excited about reading and writing, I needed to have lots of books to get them involved. A room full of books was a beginning, but that would not give them the broad picture of how enjoyable and informative words could be.

When I Have To Read, I . . .	To Me, Books . . .
feel like nothing	are fun
skim it	are horrible
read	stink
sleep	mostly stink
do it	are sometimes okay
hate it	are good
listen	are good to read
think it's lousy	are for boring days
read	are great
hate it	are something to read
	suck

In addition to their obvious apathy toward reading and writing, the students themselves seemed apathetic, beaten down. I'm reminded of Nehring's student in his book, *The Schools We Have, the Schools We Want,* who said:

> School is boring. I mean you know we sit in a chair for almost an hour, listening to some guy go on about stuff and we take notes and then we go to another class and we hear some other guy go on about stuff and we take more notes, and it's just all day long. Wouldn't you be bored? So, anyway, that's why students looks so tired all the time. It's not 'cause they're worn out, it's 'cause they're worn down. (1992, p. 128)

These students were definitely worn down. Although I find reading exciting, I guessed that what these students needed were more active days—physical involvement with literacy. Making the world our textbook would show them just how active literacy could be.

Creative Dramatics

We read a play together early in the year, but I knew it was really just "more reading" for these students. The most active part of the whole process had been trying to keep the girls who wanted to read all the parts from slugging the guys who didn't want to read at all! One of the successes of my previous class had been inviting the drama director in to do creative dramatics activities with the students, so I contacted her and we set up a date. Perhaps I should have given the students some warning, but I had learned that when I told them about something new ahead of time, they simply stayed home. For these students, even the "same old things" were scary; new things were just too big a risk. So one day at the end of period two, I announced, "We're going to do something different next period. Barb Frick is coming in and we're going to do creative dramatics." There were loud complaints and angry looks, but my timing had been perfect. The bell rang, and since no one wanted to miss the five-minute break, they decided to deal with me and this issue of strangers in our room on my time, not theirs.

When Barb arrived, she was met with fifteen sullen faces. Two types of body language prevailed: tense anger and fetuslike fear. She began by talking with them about body language and movement and suggested a simple exercise "just to get everyone moving." I don't think she realized what a task it would be. Students just would not get out of their seats, and I hoped I had not taken away the joy they associated with our class. But Barb was resourceful. "Okay, you're probably as tired as I am. Let's try something else first. Mrs. Allen says you are great at telling stories (a few smiles escape), so let's start with a cumulative story. Does anyone know what that is? Well, it's kind of like gossip. Each person says a line and the next person builds on that line in order to make a story. Remember, the story has to make sense. I'll begin. Once upon a time there was a teacher named Mrs. Allen . . ."

"She was my favorite teacher."
"I like her class."

"The best thing I like is that she doesn't give much homework."

"She makes me do her errands for her."

"What I don't like is that we read too much."

"I like the books she gives us to read. Class is fun."

"Not!"

Barb built on the momentum, "Great job. Now let's move into another way to tell a story. It's called improvisation. You not only have to think of one line, but you also have to keep the dialogue going. When someone has had enough, someone else can come in and keep the story line going or change it, but remember it has to make sense." I couldn't imagine that these kids would do this, but Barb pulled the shyest young man in the class up, propped him on a stool, and proceeded to fall on the floor. After the kids stopped laughing, she began to weave her spell.

"I'm tired of living in this stupid box—all curled up in here—no way to stretch out. It's cold in here and I never can find a way to get warm. Hey you, up there. Why don't you help me out? Don't just stand there! Hey!" Wayne was obviously ill at ease, soo Jennifer jumped up and took his place. I almost cried. I knew she was no more secure about this than he but sensed his pain, and it was enough to make her overcome her fears. Once up on the stool, she quickly became involved in the conversation.

"Well, why are you living in that stupid box anyway? Why don't you get a house or an apartment."

"You rich kids all think it's so easy. Let me tell you, I used to have a house. You think you're always going to have someone taking care of you—you're not, you know."

When the bell rang, the kids seemed stunned. You could see that it was almost hard for them to come back to the reality of this classroom. The city streets of New York, an old homeless woman, and the wonderful scenario they had just lived were hard for them to leave behind. Everyone had eventually been brought into the improvisation. Sometimes it was with not-so-subtle encouragement from other students, but *everyone* participated. I think it shocked them as much as it did me.

Our connection with the drama director continued to be valuable. Barb was able to get students from the drama program to come in and do readers' theater performances of books and plays that might have proven too challenging for students to read independently or as a group. We were able to attend rehearsals of student-written and -produced plays, critique them in discussion with the playwrights, and become a part of the school-based theater program. This involvement eventually led to the students' decision to write their own play, *Revenge of Minnie Mouse*. Creative dramatics proved to be a productive avenue for the students as active readers, writers, and learners, as well as critical viewers and consumers.

Picturing Reading

In *Picturing Learning*, Karen Ernst makes the important connection between pictures and written language. "Literature, as part of the artist's workshop, gave students ideas for pictures and projects and helped them decide on topics. Through reading literature . . . students learned how pictures and written language work together" (1993, p. 59). For many years I had thought about the connection between art and literature; I believe that is one of the reasons my room was always so artfully planned by the students. For us, art was an obvious extension of the words we shared together.

For the nonreaders in Reading and Writing Workshop, there was no obvious connection. Derek synthesized the feelings of all the students: "At first I thought it was stupid when we did art. It was fun, but I thought what did this have to do with English. Then when I was reading I started wondering how I would make that into a picture. Now when I read, I always see pictures in my head. If I don't, I know it's not a good book and throw it away." For students who had never expected words to make any sense, to get "pictures in my head" was a miracle.

I began this process during the reading of our second shared novel, *Teacher's Pet* (Cusick, 1990), by asking students to find a sentence or a phrase in the book they could illustrate with a magazine picture (see Figure 6-1). This simple process made students look at descriptions, figurative language, and precise words. In the passageway into our classroom, we posted e. e. cummings' words, "There is no such thing as best in a world of

Figure 6-1. Teacher's Pet

Learning a new art technique

individuals," over the students' display of their illustrated quotations. Al-though many, like Derek, wondered at the connection, they enjoyed the cut and paste nature of our project and pointed with pride to their contri-butions. It was a perfect entrée into reader response when Anne said, "Look we have the same quote, but really different pictures."

We continued to use art as a way of thinking about, extending, and demonstrating the words we were reading. Every few weeks, I took the art teacher's assigned study hall while Paul Carlsen came to our class and worked through a new art technique with the students. Prior to his visit, students would choose several pieces of personal writing, shared poetry, phrases from our read alouds, or independent reading they thought created particularly strong pictures for them. Once Paul demonstrated the tech-nique, students chose a piece that matched the technique and began their projects (see Figure 6-2). They loved these days, and, not surprisingly, the students who were unsure and unsettled when we were reading often shined on art days. That tranquillity seemed short-lived when we changed our plans one day and asked the students to go to the art room to work on a new project. Pandemonium reigned.

"I'm not going up there. Those kids are all smart and they'll make fun of us. They'll stare at us!"

But I was not going to be deterred. An open door is only useful if people feel comfortable walking through it. Several students announced that they were absolutely not leaving the classroom. I stood at the door giving them my teacher look. They left the room, but reminded me that they could easily get lost on the long walk to the art room. I thought I

Figure 6-2. Lifesaver

might only have a couple of students left by the time we got there, but all of them showed up except Wayne. They straggled in looking like hunted animals and huddled at a table in the corner. And, just as they had predicted, the students in the art class were staring at them. They gave me a look of betrayal and then stared at the table waiting for Paul.

Paul eventually got two of his art students to help with the demonstration and we were on our way. After the demonstration, Wayne came in the room, smiled at me, and sat with the others. Students quickly got into their work with the help of two Art II students. Although my students were all purposefully engaged, the other Art II students, the "smart kids," were creating chaos. They kept glancing at me for my reaction, but stayed with their projects. Jennifer asked for repeated assurance that we wouldn't put her picture on the wall. Brad was smiling for the first time in days. Anne said, "Can you believe how those kids are acting?" Mac had found his forte. He was basking in the art teacher's praise but was even more pleased with the kind words of his classmates. His antics usually brought on their anger, so I'm sure it was a refreshing change to receive their compliments. Derek said, "Do I have to do what's on the cover of the book or can I do what I see?" For many students this was the beginning: they understood that they had to see—really see—the words on the page (see Figure 6-3).

Figure 6-3. The Boyfriend

We eventually extended our picturing reading strategy as a way to learn new words. Students worked together to create Language Collection Notebooks. When they found an interesting or unknown word or a category of words in which they had a particular interest, those words became a page in the notebooks. Those who contributed the words were responsible for helping the rest of the class understand what the word(s) meant in the context they had pictured (see Figure 6-4).

The room quickly became theirs as words, pictures, and projects covered the walls and hung from the ceilings. Groups of students took responsibility for two walls in the classroom, where they created bulletin boards during their study halls and after school. "Things to Read" and "Be an Original" were their first creations and the ones they seemed to like best. After a particularly trying curricular conversation in which no one could tell one area of the United States from another, we decided to put up a map of the United States and track the settings of the stories we read together. This became a visual to which students referred all year as we talked about books, traveling, and current events. "The Writer's Wall" was also a constant in our room. It was a place where students could display an edited and/or illustrated work of which they were proud. Doing what you see; seeing what you hear. I have no numbers to support my claims, but in

Figure 6-4. Stoned Dreams and Green Dollar Sign

my heart I know that the act of picturing reading was as useful a strategy as any my students learned that year.

Bringing Voices to Books

As exciting as I hoped my read alouds were, I knew they would not compare to the excitement of having a real author read. During the fall when our district Writing Awards grants were due, another teacher and I cowrote one to bring a Maine short story writer, Sanford Phippen, and a poet, Paul Janeczko, to work with our students. We combined my Reading and Writing Workshop class with a class she was teaching and prepared for the events of our Writing Week.

My students got ready for Sanford Phippen's visit by gathering in small groups to read aloud articles about Mr. Phippen and his writing. Then they generated all the facts they could find and we built a community knowledge bank of information (see photo below). This activity helped students overcome their initial resistance to something new and also gave them the opportunity to acquire some background knowledge so that when Mr. Phippen said, "Do you have any questions for me?" they were ready. Although some of the "facts" were questionable, Sanford enjoyed the obvious preparation that had gone into his visit and was able to use some of those "facts" (see Figure 6-5) as a point of discussion and clarification. He was especially amused when they mixed up the date of college graduation and his age!

His reading and his exciting life stories stayed with the students

Sanford Phippen Chalk Board

Sanford Phippen Facts

1. From Maine
2. teacher
3. 64 years old. graduated from collage
4. The Pouce Knows everything
5. Most of stories of Maine
6. Editor
7. Graduated from the university of Maine
8. Taught first English 1987.
9. Born and named in eastern Maine village of Hancock.
10. New York Times, The Ellsworth American, Maine Alumnus, Maine life, Bangor Daily News.
11. He's an explorer of stories
12. He says he's not cool.
13. Don't Know how to play golf.
14. Don't know how to shuffle paper.
15. Geographically - and spiritually.
16. During the summer he is a librarian at the Hancock Point Library.
17. Author of a just-published collection of Down east stories, ignores the pointed firs exc...
18. He grew up in a summer resort community on the coast.
19. His relatives and neighbors from who he drew heavily in his native Hancock may never speak to him again.
20. Didn't like school
21. He doesn't read 'GIQ
22. Phippen is a native of Maine who grew up in a small town, very much like the Tauton of his stories.
23. He attended the local schools and the University of Maine.
24. He says he doesn't fit in
25. After fifteen years ~~century~~ the native returned to Maine.
26. Book editor of Maine life.
27. Is a contemorary Maine short-story master.

Figure 6-5. Sanford Phippen Facts

I thought he was very obnoctious
I didn't really enjoy the storys he
told they were pretty borring I
would rather here about something
interesting. I like to here about when
my grand parents found Indians
in there atic I dont like to
her about shoveling cow poop. I
wouldn't want to hear him again

Well today we had a guest speaker. He was a real good
guest speeker. It was fun listening to what he had to say.
He was really funny and he had the whole class laughing. He
was a real smart man and he knew alot about writing. He
likes to write about things that have happened or that is
real. He wrote alot about his family life and how he was
brought up. It was listening to his life story. It sounds
like he had a real fun life. It was funny listening to the
things that have happened to him. You wouldn't want to
beleive that they were real but they were. I thought that
he did a real good job. He did do alot of swaring but other
than that I thought that he did a good job and was really
funny.

Figure 6-6. Samples of writing

throughout the year. He brought his characters to life for them and showed
them that writers are real people who take the time to write down the
stories they have lived. Although there was some controversy over the
"swear words" he used, most students enjoyed his day with us. Whether the
reactions were positive or negative, it was a joy to see that their apathy was
gone. The samples of four students' writing (see Figure 6-6) show that
everyone had an opinion and felt free to express that opinion.

Paul Janeczko's visit was rewarding in a different way. After his open
meeting with the two classes, in which he shared his stories and his poetry,
he came to our class and helped students with their writing. My fears that
they would be too awed to write for this stranger, who was also a poet, were
quickly allayed as Paul let them see that they were writers. He began by
modeling formula poems, skinny poems, and poems with a sense of humor.
When he followed this by asking students to write poetry, they all became
quickly involved. After his visit, I found that the students had learned about
much more than poetry.

"I learned to write poems you have to be creative."

Dear Mr. Allen,

Sanford Pippen seemed like a nice guy and he was a funny one. He told a lot of good stories that people liked. I thought it was a good thing that he did use swear word, because like he said it was probably not uncommon to hese people swear all the time. In the halls I head them talking about Sanford Pippen, and they thought he was a pretty fun guy.

Mr. Sanford Phippen was very funny. I liked how he told us all the stories that what happened when he was a child. I don't think he really cares what other people think about him. He made me think about how the years have changed since he was a kid and now. How we don't have to do as many chores as he did.
What I didn't like about him was how he criticized his family and friends.

I thought he was better than Paul because he was funnier but didn't have as many books out as Paul.

I would like to see more of these speakers.

Figure 6-6. Samples of writing (*continued*)

"I liked him even if he didn't have the feeling Phippen had. I'm surprised they don't get the money when they sell one book."

"I really liked him. His poems were funny. I also liked the way he talked about how much money he makes and I liked how he taught us to write poems. I learned that I don't want to be a writer because they really don't make enough money."

"One thing I learned from this was that you can be different and be good at the same time."

"I learned that when you write a poem it doesn't have to be about what's happening, but what's in your head."

"Remember, if you write something down, then you will remember it when you want to write about it."

EXPANDING OUR VIEW OF AVAILABLE BOOKS

BEFORE ARRIVING AT THE BOOKSTORE
I. Do you have any books already in mind that you would like to purchase?
    Yes   Ⓝⓞ
    If yes, what types of books or specific authors do you already know
    which you are interested in?

2. Have you ever been to a bookstore before?   Yes   Ⓝⓞ
    If yes, which bookstores have you visited?

3. Think back to the books we read together this year. Which books did you
    like well enough to buy another book similar to those? *I liked*
    Teacher Pet the best

    Think of the books you've read during independent reading. Which books
    or authors have you enjoyed so that you would like to extend your reading
    with similar books or books by the same author? *I'm reading*
    Party line and I read the Babysitle I and 2

DURING THE BOOKSTORE VISIT
I. Name the two bookstores we visited today.
    a. *Momentos*
    b. *Paper Back*

2. In order to learn about as many new books as possible and really find books
    that you will make a commitment to read, I'm asking you to find books of
    each of the following types and then list a book/author for each type. I'm
    hoping that as you do this you might find books you never would have
    thought of reading.

    a. HISTORICAL FICTION-- *little house on the Prairie laura ingalls wilder*

    b. REALISTIC FICTION-- *S.E Hinton - taming the star Running*

    c. BIOGRAPHY/AUTOBIOGRAPHY-- *Mikhail Gorbachev -the August Coup*

    d. ADVENTURE/WAR *-The Guardians Death charge -Richard austin*

    e. FANTASY- *Shelter lives . Charles oberndore*

Figure 6-7. Expanding Our View

Seeing each student proudly displaying poetry he or she had written
was significant. Although I might have been able to get them to write poetry
eventually, the fact that Paul was a poet validated their work. Many of these
poems became the inspiration for their next art projects. As those projects
decorated the walls of our classroom, they were a constant reminder of the
many gifts these students possessed that had been buried for many years
(see Figure 6-4).

As our classroom came alive with storytellers, poets, theater produc-
tions, and artists, students came to expect the unexpected each day. Just
when they thought classroom happenings were becoming routine, I decided
it was time to take them out into the larger book community.

f. NONFICTION--

g. MYSTERY/SUSPENSE-- muder in manhatten - steve Allan

h. WESTERNS-- Ride the Rider - louis lamour

i. COLLECTIONS OF POETRY OR SHORT STORIES

j. BOOKS FROM MOVIES OR BASED ON MOVIES

AFTER YOUR BOOK SELECTION

3. When you were deciding on books to buy/read, what things affected your decision? (CIRCLE ALL THAT APPLY)
    a. cover   b. back of the book   c. title
    d. length of book   e. an author you've read and enjoyed
    f. a book someone recommended   g. type of book in which you know you have an interest
    h. size of the print/type

4. Which bookstore did you prefer? Why?
   Paper back more selaction

5. List below the three books/authors which you purchased today.
   BOOK   AUTHOR
   1. Sunset secret   Cherie Bennett
   2. Nathavie   John Saul
   3. Fiter Starter   Stephen King

6. Interview two of your friends or people in the class about the bookstore experience. Record in writing the highlights of your interviews (what they liked/disliked; kinds of books they bought; books they purchased which you might like to read, etc.).

Figure 6-7. Expanding Our View (*continued*)

Expanding Our View of Available Books

Earlier in the year, Connie Piper and I had coauthored a county grant for books and tapes that we could use with our two groups of students. We had received the grant just as the winter doldrums were at their worst, an ideal time to get our students out of school and into the local bookstores to look for new books for their independent reading and our classroom libraries. Our surveys showed that only a few students had ever been in a bookstore, so we figured that some support was going to be necessary or they would just stand around looking at key chains and highlighters.

The bookstore form (see Figure 6-7) helped students find a focus before they arrived at the two stores and reminded them of the purpose of our visit. Having a task also helped them overcome their initial discomfort as they walked into the unfamiliar bookstore settings. In filling out the form, they looked at hundreds of books they might not otherwise have considered.

When we left, the question asking them to evaluate the two stores once again helped them see themselves as critical consumers. Although no students actually completed the final interview question (#6), they discussed it on our ride back to school. The bus was alive with talk of books. That week their "Learning about Learning" reflections were filled with comments about their bookstore visits.

> **Anne:** Those [visits] were fun because we got to pick out our own books. I learned that there are so many books that you could choose from.

> **Tori:** I liked it because it was fun and we didn't have to pay. I learned to pick out good books.

> **Trish:** I liked reading the children's books more than I did the novels. I learned that books are really expensive and some bookstores have a good selection while others don't.

While many talked repeatedly about the fun of getting out of school and choosing their own books, I was reminded of how seldom students like this get to leave school or make choices about the curriculum. For many students in our school, sports events, clubs, and academic field trips away from the routine of school are a regular part of each semester. For these students, this was an entirely new adventure. As important as the books and bookstore learning were, I can't help but feel they learned something more significant: someone cared enough to plan something special "just for us." It validated their positive changes, their feelings of being part of the school community, and the trust I placed in them. This was one of the events that I believe led to Derek and Jennifer's comment at the end of the year: "She made us feel like we were worth saving."

Students as Teachers

Our bookstore visit had allowed us to spend a great deal of nonthreatening time reading children's books. I had intentionally planned this activity as a way to move into our paired reading project with a first-grade class at the elementary school near our high school. Our classroom had always been filled with children's books, and I often shared picture books during read aloud time. As Muriel Roy, the first-grade teacher, and I paired her first graders with my ninth graders in the initial pen pal stage, I once again wondered if students had enough confidence to take all they had learned about themselves as readers and writers into a new environment.

Initially, students shared pen pal letters for a couple of weeks and then we arranged for the pals to get together for their first shared reading (see Figure 6-8).

As we crossed the parking lot and the elementary school playground, students began walking slower and slower. I couldn't figure out what was

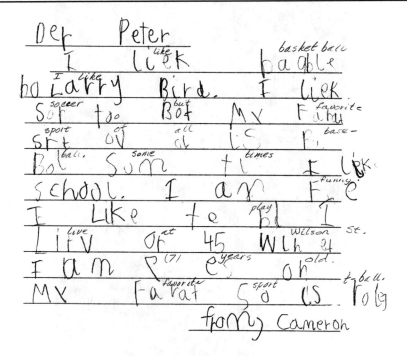

Der   Peter
        I   lick   basket ball
                              ba able
ba Larry   Bird.   I   lick.
   soccer   but   favorite
Sor   too   Bot   My   F my
   sport   of   all   base-
Srt   ov   o   is   F.
   ball.   some   times
Bol   Sum   tl   I   lick.
                              funny.
school.   I   an   F e
I   like   to   play   bl I
   live   at   Wilson   st.
Liv   or   45   Wlh   2t
                (7)   years   old.
I   am   r   e   on
                         favorite   sport   tballl.
My   Farat   So   is   roly

                from   Cameron

Dear, Cameron,

    My name is Peter. I am 16
years' old and will be turning 17 in May.
    I like sports and my favorite sport is
Basketball and I like the Boston Celtics.
Larry Bird is my favorite Basketball player.
    I like the woods a lot but I don't like
school vary much.
    I like to watch Nascar racing on Sunday
and when I get out of school I would like
to be a Nascar driver. But if not I would
not mind being a Game Warden.

                Your Friend
                Peter

Write Back Soon!!

Figure 6-8. Pen Pal letter

Students at Bookstore

going on until Derek said, "I hope they like us." I realized that my students were really nervous and said, "Listen, they're going to be glad to have someone pay attention just to them. They'll think you're great."

Once again, Wayne had refused to come. He decided at the last minute that he was sick and said he was going to the office. Sometimes I wonder if I'll ever learn just how fragile their newly found confidence can be. When I looked back and saw Wayne walking across the street to the store, I yelled, "Hey, Wayne, come here. I need your help." Kurt Hahn (1988), founder of Outward Bound, believes that honestly needing children's help is a surefire way to get them involved.

There are three ways of trying to win the young. There is persuasion, there is compulsion and there is attraction. You can preach at them, that is a hook without a worm; you can say "you must volunteer," and

T= She asked them if they have a brother or sister. She's reading real good they're listening real close. She's starting on the second book One kid asked about a picture. She's asking them about the books.

J- She's asking them what's going to happen in the book. they like the book. One girl know about the book already. they liked the book. they want her to read Grandpa.

A- She is winding questions about the kids. They liked the book she read to them. She Likes the Book and the kids like it to.

S- He is reading a book about where wild things go. He thinks the book is ok but his choice would be not to. The little tike liked the book to, thought it was cool.

Figure 6-9. Wayne's Notes

that is of the devil; and you can tell them, "you are needed," that appeal hardly ever fails.

Wayne came walking toward me and said, "What do you need?" and I knew he would stay.

"It just occurred to me that if you can just wait until lunch to go home, I could really use you to help me take notes while students are doing their shared reading."

"What do you mean?"

"Well, I told the kids that I would help them if they needed it while they read to their partners, but I have to take pictures and take notes. If you could just go and listen to one person at a time, then that would help us when we talk about what went right and what we want to do differently next week." Wayne's notes appear in figure 6-9.

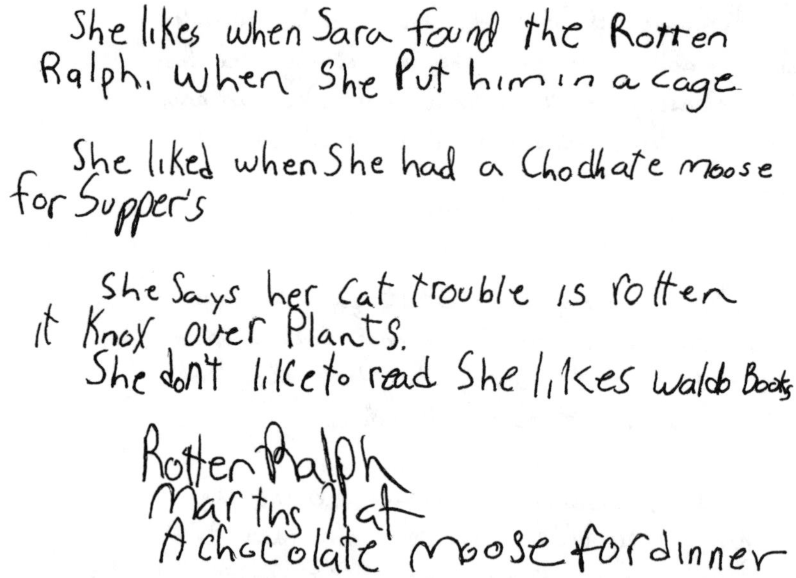

> She likes when Sara found the Rotten Ralph, when She Put him in a cage.
>
> She liked when She had a Chodhate moose for Supper's
>
> She Says her Cat trouble is rotten It Knox over Plants.
> She don't like to read She likes waldo Books
>
> Rotten Ralph
> Martns hat
> A chocolate moose for dinner

Figure 6-10. Paired reading with first graders

We spent the last month of school involved in a paired reading and writing program with the first graders (see Figure 6-10). My newly confident students planned a day at the high school for the first graders. They took them to the art room for face paintings. The greenhouse became a place for them to show the first graders all the produce being grown, and the vocational shops gave the first graders much to think and write about. When the first graders returned the next day, we all went to the computer room for students to do shared writing and teach the first graders how to use the computers.

As I watched my students and the first graders work together, it struck me how self-assured they seemed. No longer apathetic, they quickly decided what needed to be done, chose tasks, and went to work. On the last day we spent with the first graders it was like watching an entirely new group of students: Trish had a group of students sitting around her listening to a read aloud. Jennifer was sitting with a clipboard interviewing the two students with whom she had worked for her case study of her partners as readers. Melvin was lying on the floor doing an illustrated story with his partner. Derek was talking with his partner about what kind of books she now liked to read. Wayne, no longer content just to help me, was at the computer doing Word Munchers with his newly chosen partner. It was a picture of active learning I hope never to forget.

What did this project mean to the students? I think their words express it best.

I enjoyed that because we got to discuss things over. I learned that it was fun to work with others.

It was fun and I learned I can get along with a lot of different people. I learned that I might want to be a first-grade teacher.

I really liked working with the students because they were funny. And they were really enthusiastic about everything. They were also really smart. I learned that you have to be patient with kids and you can't rush them in reading. You have to take your time.

I liked it because it gave me a chance to see if I acted like that and learned as fast as they do. I didn't because sometimes they were not listening.

I liked working with those little kids. I learned that it might be fun to teach little kids.

It was fun going over there. I think it was a really great thing that we did because those little kids really looked up to us. When T—said I helped him a lot it made me feel good.

As students moved in and out of our classroom, the school and the community became a less intimidating place. The days when Jennifer was

Lying on floor illustrating story

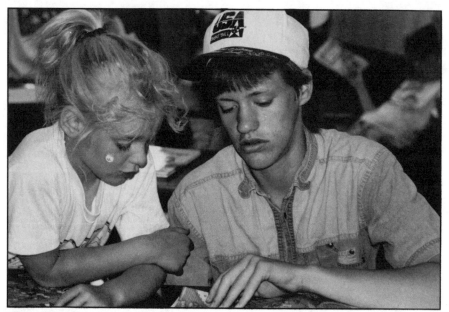

Shared Reading

Working at computer doing Word Munchers

the only one who would go into another teacher's room to get materials or leave a message were gone. Students now felt comfortable even in the principal's office. As they sat with two different teachers on the last two days of school, they talked about how they had changed and what had caused them to change: My smiles. Time. Lots of books. Making them feel special. A comfortable place. The list continued and it seemed they could barely remember the frightened, angry students they had been in August. Perhaps the selective memory of youth is a blessing. The best and the worst were still very much a part of my memory—and my field notes. Fortunately, I now had a record of that journey to help me as I made plans for other classes.

7

Supporting Real Choices

Inside classrooms, teachers and students must come to terms with each other about the extent to which the subjects they mutually confront will be taken seriously or just endured. A multitude of understandings or bargains, sometimes quite subtle, are possible to accommodate the range of preferences of both students and teachers.

Powell, Farrar, and Cohen, *The Shopping Mall High School*

It has always seemed to me that there is a fine balance between supporting choice and helping students develop both breadth and depth in their reading. In reaction to the highly structured requirements of the traditional English program, I had for many years allowed students to have complete control over their reading and writing in my Directed Studies classes. Although I didn't read Veatch's (1968) work until long after I started my Directed Studies class (formerly Home Base Learning), I must admit that the emphasis in my classes on an individualized reading program was similar to that in Veatch's suggestions. These classes had been very successful, due in part to the independence they supported, since students chose work that was meaningful and significant to them.

For several years I had been concerned about students' isolation as they pursued their interests. In addition, I worried that I was abdicating my responsibility as a teacher by leaving the acquisition of independent learning strategies to fate, luck, or the power of words. In spite of my support for and encouragement of collaboration, many students chose to work alone much of the time and therefore lost the benefit of the deeper understanding people gain when they share collective knowledge. But I didn't want to forfeit the benefits of choice in order to nurture the strengths of community. When I presented my dilemma to my students in Reading and Writing Workshop, I think they felt I had gone completely over the edge, but we did agree to the following compromise (one in which I had more initial investment than they):

1. Mondays and Fridays were days of independent literacy exploration.
2. One period on Mondays and Fridays was saved for sustained, *silent* reading. The other period could be used for any exploration that involved reading, writing, or investigation.
3. We could negotiate a third day each week for independent exploration.

I did not continue to allow independent reading to be a time when I would abdicate my responsibilities as a teacher. During sustained silent reading, I saw my task as twofold: modeling silent reading behaviors and monitoring the progress of each individual student. In my view, the success of a sustained silent reading program is directly related to seeing teachers as active, involved readers of texts they have chosen for themselves. When students were involved in their own texts, I would often take time to make notes on reading behaviors in my monitoring book. These notes I would combine with individual conferences during the independent literacy exploration period. This allowed me to share silent reading with my students and to help them develop the individual strategies they needed to become more independent. I also devised a checklist (see Figure 7.1) for each student so I would know where I should focus my attention.

For those students who seldom exhibited any of these behaviors, I still saw it as my responsibility to monitor their progress and support their next reading choices. Another checklist (see Figure 7.2) helped me keep track of positive reading behaviors so I could compliment students on their commitment to reading and their progress. In addition, I was able to remind myself of texts I needed to suggest or purchase and authors I thought might interest the students, and support risks they might take by choosing more difficult texts. This checklist was also helpful in conferences with students or their parents in discussing their strengths and the problems they might be attempting to overcome.

In addition, each day when students chose their reading, I asked them to tell me the name of the book and what page they were on. At the end of the class, I always asked them what page they stopped on. In one of the debriefing sessions, the three students who were involved commented on the positive aspects of this practice.

> **Interviewer:** Did you find that the praise you gave each other was contagious?
> **Jennifer:** Yeah. Usually when somebody has been rude, you want them to fail, but now when you see them reading and you're reading, you want everybody to read more and more.

INDEPENDENT READING BEHAVIORS
INDICATING HELP MAY BE NEEDED

_____ 1. Having difficulty selecting a book.

_____ 2. Moving around a lot in order to find a "comfortable" spot.

_____ 3. Looking up frequently from reading.

_____ 4. Checking the clock often.

_____ 5. Spending an inordinate amount of time rewinding tapes.

_____ 6. Body language indicates lack of enjoyment of the book.

_____ 7. Frequently changing book for a new book.

_____ 8. Has trouble finding ways to respond to reading.

_____ 9. Falls asleep during independent reading.

_____ 10. Tries to disrupt others during independent reading.

_____ 11. Asks if we **have** to have independent reading today.

_____ 12. Needs to go to the bathroom during reading time.

_____ 13. Tries to write notes or do things other than read during reading.

_____ 14. Lip reading.

_____ 15. Doesn't like to talk about or share the book being read.

_____ 16. Doesn't attempt to try new authors, titles or genres.

Figure 7-1. Independent Reading Behaviors checklist

Rachel: My friend Tracy and I would sometimes read the same book and we would always have a contest about who would finish it first. I thought it was fun.

Jennifer: I liked that too. She'd [Mrs. J.A.] would always ask how much we were reading and I liked that. It's like in gym—I hate running, but if we could race, I'd like it better.

Interviewer: You like the competition? What would be some ways you could do that—like keeping a list to see who's read the most books?

Derek: Every day Mrs. J.A. would ask what page number we were on. It was really kind of a competition because if somebody said 68 and you were on page 40, you'd want to get caught up or ahead of them.

Jennifer: Yeah, even if they were different books.

Interviewer: She does that every day? Is that important?

Derek: If somebody won't read a day or something, she never says anything. But, when you read the next day she says, "Boy, you really did a good job today!" And then you think, "I'd better read today because she thinks I read yesterday." (All the students laugh.)

Rachel: If you tell her you read and you didn't, she'll look at you and turn her head (*demonstrates a look I give them*). The way she looks at you like maybe she's disappointed that you didn't read, but she never says anything.

Derek: She doesn't say anything, but she knows when you're not reading. She's not stupid.

Rachel: I think that what helped me the most was when I did read something and she'd say, "Wow, that's great!"

Derek: Yeah, I knew that she'd always be proud of me for reading.

This simple method not only helped me keep track of students' reading and show my support for each step they took, it also allowed me to track

Figure 7-2. Independent Reading checklist

INDEPENDENT READING

NAME _____   DATE _____

NOVEL BEING READ _____

AUTHOR _____   GENRE _____

_____	1. Seems engrossed in the reading.
_____	2. Seldom asks to leave during reading.
_____	3. Asks about taking the book home to read independently.
_____	4. Asks for books "like this one."
_____	5. Asks what else this author has written.
_____	6. Points out words or scenes to friends.
_____	7. Asks for feedback from me or others about the book.
_____	8. Has something to say, either verbally or in writing, in response to book.
_____	9. Quickly finds a comfortable place to read.
_____	10. Has book or knows where book is when class begins.
_____	11. Asks not to be disturbed.
_____	12. Asks for help or has questions about the text.
_____	13. Doesn't want to stop reading to do other activities.
_____	14. Makes connections to life or other texts.

SUPPORT FOR STUDENT

A.   OTHER TEXTS WITH SIMILAR THEME
B.   OTHER TEXTS WITH SIMILAR STYLE
C.   OTHER TEXTS BY THE SAME AUTHOR
D.   SUGGESTED STRATEGIES

any problems they might be encountering with the text. For example, when Wayne was reading *The Outsiders* (Hinton, 1967) he could read ten to fifteen pages in one period, but when he began *Hatchet* (Paulsen, 1987), he slowed down to three pages during his first day of reading. I knew it was time for a conference. Our discussion showed that he was having difficulty getting a sense of the story because of the flashback. I took the book home, made a tape of the first chapter so he could listen to me reading it, had a short conference with him about what had happened so far and where he thought the story was going, and then he was fine. That intervention occurred during the second half of their independent literacy period and then he was able to continue reading *Hatchet* (Paulsen, 1967) independently again. In his limited reading experience, he had not encountered the flashback as a component of the author's style. Once he understood the concept and could find clues in the text, he was able to continue reading on his own. For me, the practice of knowledgeable and timely intervention was as crucial as having time for independent reading. Both helped students acquire the strategies and the practice they needed to become independent readers.

In January I asked students why they thought we were doing some of our activities, such as independent reading. All listed at least one of the following: so they could choose reading they enjoyed or liked, become better readers and practice their reading. One student suggested that perhaps it was so I would have more time to read! Although I laughed at the time, on reflection it occurred to me that they must truly be seeing how much I value reading if they thought I would orchestrate the whole school day so I could have time to read, too.

The students were ultimately responsible for choosing their independent reading on those two days, just as I was responsible for choosing mine. In the "dining room table" (Atwell, 1987) discussions that sometimes followed our independent reading, *how* we chose our books often became as much a point of discussion as *which* books we had chosen. If I had decided what books the students would read during that time, our discussions about book choice would have had little relevance. I was able to tell them that I had chosen a Nikki Giovanni book because I had read and liked an essay she had written and wanted to read more of her writing; I read *The River* (Paulsen, 1991) because I read *Hatchet* (1987) and wanted to read the sequel; I read *Ghost Girl* (Hayden, 1992) because I liked to read books about teachers who figure out how to help their students solve problems; and I read Hugh Prather books because they made me think about my life and my goals. Students not only respected my honesty, they were also able to see that what I chose to read depended on my purpose.

One day, during one of those discussions, it occurred to me that students needed to have more than a purpose for reading; they needed to know some of their options. I was able to make choices because I was a reader, and I knew about lots of books I wanted to read, lots of subjects in which I was interested, and lots of authors whose works I wanted to read more of. Because of their limited experiences with books, my students did not have those options. This discovery affected the choices I made for read alouds and shared reading, as well as the support I gave students for their independent reading.

The Student Who Was Overwhelmed

Although the students loved the wide variety of books in our classroom, for those who had never chosen a book the process was overwhelming. Derek said, "She knew what I'd like to read, and she would start picking out all of these books she thought I'd like to read. She kind of suggests according to what she knows we'll like. Usually, I would just go over to the shelf and look at the book and just find one and say, 'That looks good.' But that never worked for me. I had to find a story—not a picture."

In order to encourage that match of the right book and the right person at the right time, I absorbed all I could about each of my students from surveys, writing, class discussions, and informal eavesdropping. I also got to know the resources available in my room and in the community at large. The book that made a difference for Derek was *A Day No Pigs Would Die* (Peck, 1972). I don't think I'll ever forget his words and the look on his face when he finished: "That must be the best book ever written!" I also hope I remember the authentic voice that emerged in Derek's writing when he responded to the book.

> I like this book alot better than any other book I have ever read because I feel like Rob in the book because I live on a farm. And my dad is similar to Robs father. But it's a little unrealistic when they tell about the cow calfing because from experience you know that the feet always come first. But it doesn't matter because its still a good book. I'm not trying to put the author down but a cow doesn't choke when something is caught in its throught. They blote and they don't dye from lalk of oxagen. It's from build up of fluids in the stomach. But, A day no pigs wuld die was a good book. It was just like some of the stuff I do like when he delivered the calf. me and Brad do that alot. and when Mr. Tanner gave him a pig I remembered when my uncle gave me a baby calf and I thought it was the best calf in the world. and my dad slaughtered it when I was 8 years old and I was so sad but I got over it. and when his father got sick and started sleeping in the bar that reminded me of my cousin when his wife kicked him out of the house and when his dad died that made me think of my uncle when he died but my uncle was 85.

That book changed Derek's attitude toward reading and writing, but he would never have found it without my assistance. On the other hand, I would not have recognized the power of Derek's writing if I had given him a test when he finished the book. For Derek and for many other students, the options at the finishing stage were as critical as the options at the choice stage. "Students should have to do *something*, but they should be able to pick it themselves, you know? If they want to do a book report, let them do it. If they want to write about a story, then let them. Things like that, that's what I found important."

Our shared evaluation of their reading was based on what the students chose to demonstrate of their involvement in reading. Many students began the year by writing voiceless summaries, a form with which they were all too familiar. The following three samples of Jennifer's responses indicate the typical pattern most students followed.

Stage 1: Concise Summary of Text
8/23/91
I started a book called My Darling My Hamburger by Paul Zindel. It is about these two girls who go on a date with these two guys and they kiss.

During our shared reading, we explored many alternatives to this response that affected the kinds of responses I began seeing when they finished their independent reading. Initially, however, many shared the difficulty of actually connecting their response to the text. I began seeing responses that were certainly full of emotion, but it was impossible to tell from the response the name or specific substance of the text.

Stage 2: Authentic Response Without Text Connection
9/2/91
Dear Editor:
I think it is awful that people are so stupid that they drink in drive. I am sick and tired of these people. They drink, drink, and drink some more until they are so drunk they don't know what they are doing. I think if you kill someone because of drinking and driving then you should get the electric chair. Thanks for listening.

All the students were producing one of these two types of responses until I started modeling ways in which I might connect my response to the characters and events in the text. Through thinking aloud and writing in a language experience model, I showed them the kinds of things I ask myself as I read and respond to a text. As I read Ask Me If I Care (Gilmour, 1985), I stopped to talk about how I thought the book and the characters might have been different if the setting had been Maine rather than New York or Florida. Then I asked, "I wonder how I might have reacted if I thought my mother was choosing her new husband over me?" Using the PC-Viewer, an overhead projector attached to my PC, I wrote about the events in the book that made it seem as if Jenny's mother had made that choice. "Wait a minute," I continued, "although I was older, I did feel that way when my mother remarried after my father's death, especially when I got a divorce, and I thought she chose to go along with her new husband's anger with me, rather than to help me. I think I'll put all of that here in my response because it's kind of like what Jenny was feeling." With each example of this practice, students became more likely to connect the text and their personal responses.

Stage 3: Interwoven Text Response
3/24/92

I read Remembering a Special Student. It really touched me. I felt like crying. If I were in the parents situation, I know I would wish he didn't play football and that he would have got moved up. Also I would think the world of all the high school kids. I really don't know if someone died of sports up here if everyone would be sorry, but I don't think they would go this far! People wouldn't talk about it and if they did, I wouldn't think very highly of them.

The "I wonders" I used to help move students through these stages occurred naturally as I talked through my response to the text. As I was talking, students often spontaneously added their own questions: "Yeah, and I wondered . . ." (Some of these questions can be found in the figure, "Connecting Kids and Books.") Although I wouldn't recommend that these questions become rigid guides, they are a place to start in modeling how to get inside a text. As students become more honestly connected to their reading, they usually see a purpose for reading and want to continue. This motivation is something teachers can build on.

The Student Who Needs
Genre or Author Assistance

Once students started reading, the hook that kept them going was the possibility that there might be other books by the same author or within the same genre. I think it's the same as being hooked on television shows like *The Guiding Light* or *Knot's Landing*: it isn't that any single episode makes a significant difference in your life, it's just knowing that it's always there. Viewers get used to the language, the characters, and the dilemmas, and the consistency feels comfortable. Reading multiple books by the same author or in the same genre can have the same effect. I smile each time I remember Tex (Hinton, 1980) asking his English teacher if she was sure the same guy had written another book.

This was the case with Jennifer. After I read *The Lottery Rose* (Hunt, 1976) in shared reading, Jennifer often wrote or talked about Robin's death. It occurred to me that perhaps she would like a book I had recently read by Lurlene McDaniel. I gave it to her one Friday saying, "I just finished this and thought you might like it." When she returned on Monday, she had finished reading the book and was asking if I could get any of the others written by the same author. She had looked in the back of the book and found that McDaniel had written several other books. Fortunately, I had done the same thing before I gave her the book and had made a weekend visit to the bookstore to get other McDaniel titles! For Jennifer, getting hooked on an author had helped her. "What made the difference for me in becoming a reader was that I just read and read and read and read. That's it."

For other students, the hook was their liking for Stephen King books.

Actually, what they knew was that they liked Stephen King movies, since none of them had read his books. That told me that they would probably like R. L. Stine, Christopher Pike, Ritchie Cusick, and collections of short stories such as *More Scary Stories* (Schwartz, 1984). An excerpt from the videotaped discussion between Terri and interviewer Barb Frick hints at the fine line between support and independence in book choice.

> **Terri:** I've improved on my reading this year. I can even read faster. I never really liked to read, but this year—the books that she has—I'm more interested in things now. I don't like to have people pick books for me though.
> **Frick:** You like to pick out your own books?
> **Terri:** Well, she finds out what you're interested in and then she buys the books for you.
> **Frick:** And then you pick out what you want?
> **Terri:** We both pick.

Given the explosion of horror and suspense books over the last few years, helping students find books in that genre was relatively easy. As the students guessed, however, I did value independent reading time because it also gave me time to read books I might not otherwise have chosen. Books related to sports, Vietnam, or the Wild West have not been my top reading priority, but they had to become part of my reading repertoire if I wanted to help all the students, not just those whose reading interests I shared.

Once again, I went back to my students to check what they understand about why I asked them to take final responsibility for choosing their own reading at least two days a week. When I read their responses, I was forced to review my own assumptions as well as the curricular implications of their answers.

Why Do I Ask You to Take Responsibility?
1. Because you know maybe we don't want to read the books you choose for us.
2. So we can have fun.
3. To give us two days when we're not busy.
4. I don't know.
5. We'll be bored with something you would pick for us.
6. If we pick it, we'll be more interested.
7. So we can feel like you trust us.
8. So we won't blame you or be mad at you if we don't like the book.
9. Because something might come up and we'd do something else instead.

This self-report revealed that students had varied and divergent notions about our practice of independent reading. Certainly, they were pointing to benefits I had not imagined, but their statements also made some not-so-subtle statements to me about choosing their reading for them. When I read these responses it occurred to me for the first time that I couldn't possibly always choose the right book for each student. I had really believed that it was possible, even though I didn't always do it. I could provide the resources, support, and suggestions, but ultimately the decision had to be in their hands. I wanted my students to become lifelong readers. I wanted them to love reading in the way that Norma Fox Mazer describes: "The way we love ice cream is the way we should love reading. Passionate involvement, willingness to try all flavors, a lighting of the eyes, eating it in all seasons, a pint always in the freezer" (Gallo, 1987, p. 20). I knew I needed to provide variety and time to sample, but whether they chose to stick with vanilla or try the flavor of the month had to be their decision. I needed to be pleased that at least they were finally eating!

Developing Reading Strategies

Toward the end of the school year, Jennifer commented: "One thing I noticed with those first graders is that they don't seem to have any reading strategies. All they know how to do is try to sound it out." What a difference nine months can make! The first time I told the students I wanted each of them to develop strategies to help them make sense out of a variety of texts, they sat and stared at me. I was reminded of a colleague who had been having particular difficulty enforcing our new "No Hats in Class" rule with her Basic English class. One day, frustrated with arguing about the legitimacy of the rule, she finally yelled, "Do you have congenital hat syndrome or what?" When she related the story to me, she said the most frustrating thing was that during her whole tirade, the students just sat and stared at her. I remember saying, "Do you think they understood any word other than 'hat' in your question?" I wish I had remembered that before I said "develop strategies to help them make sense out of a variety of texts."

Clay (1979) notes that high progress readers "operate on print in an integrated way in search of meaning" (p. 7). That was the critical point for my students; they didn't expect the text to have meaning, nor did they see themselves as responsible for or capable of making the text have meaning. I knew that helping these students develop strategies or "operations" (Clay, 1979) would be critical if they were to become independent readers capable of getting information and enjoyment from reading.

Brozo and Simpson (1991) report Weinstein and Mayer's (1986) definition of strategy: "cognitive behaviors that a learner engages in during learning that are intended to influence the encoding process so as to facilitate the acquisition, integration and retrieval of new information" (p. 20). This was certainly what I wanted for my students. I wanted to find ways to help them draw on their knowledge of text structures and their own prior knowledge in order to develop strategies for learning the meaning of individual words and understanding the larger concepts within a text. For me, all of these components came together under one umbrella: wanting students to see reading as enjoyable and worthy of their time. I wanted them to share Rachel's sentiments: "Reading is a gift, like no other gift."

Guiding Readers Through Texts

Throughout the year I led *guided reading lessons* with my students individually or in a group, so they would learn how to think and talk their way through the text. My role during these lessons was that of facilitator as I guided readers to connect their personal knowledge and reading strategies to the words in the text. One of the most remarkable traits distinguishing readers from nonreaders is the ability to question themselves, the author, and the text during reading. During a discussion of reading strategies, Jennifer said, "I thought if I just learned all the sounds and the syllables and stuff, I'd be able to read. And then I would open a book and it didn't happen." Variations on this theme were quite common. Students had become firmly settled in a passive position, waiting for reading "to happen." Guided reading was a way to help students see what they needed to do to make reading "happen" for themselves.

Mooney (1990) views the role of the teacher during guided reading as threefold: being aware of a learner's interests, experiences, and competencies; being able to determine the supports (those ideas or elements in the text that help readers construct meaning) and challenges (those words, concepts, or events in a text that require additional information in order for a reader to make sense of the text); and accepting the role of supporting learning. When I explained the rationale behind our guided reading to my students, I talked about the importance for all of us of learning each other's reading strategies so that we would have lots of things to help us read no matter how difficult or incomprehensible the text. The folloiwng scenario describes a guided reading lesson with Mac. Before I decided to do this lesson, I had to determine four things: the purpose of the lesson, what I knew about Mac's interests and abilities, the supports and challenges of the text I chose, and how I could support Mac's learning in such a way that he could become a more strategic thinker. The following graphic organizer allowed me to plan and document guided reading lessons. I always tried to frame the lesson by guiding readers through three ways they could ask questions: before they started reading, while they were reading, and after they had finished reading.

Guided Reading Lesson
STUDENT(S): Mac

PURPOSE: Mac is still having difficulty making predictions and supporting his answers through either the text or his experiences. Needs guidance to understand the need to look within his experience and the text in order to have the reading make sense to him.

STUDENT INTERESTS AND EXPERIENCES: running, sports/family problems, low self-esteem, school problems

TEXT: *The War on Villa Street* (Mazer, 1978)

> **J.A.:** Mac, this is a book I'd like you to read and we can talk about some of the strategies you use as you read it. First, I'd like you to look at the book covers and tell me what you think this book might be about.
>
> **Mac:** Well, maybe a kid on the street trying to survive.
>
> **J.A.:** What's in that picture that might make you think that?
>
> **Mac:** I don't know (*long pause*). Well, I guess it looks like three against one.
>
> **J.A.:** Good for you—it does look like that, doesn't it? Have you ever been in that situation?
>
> **Mac:** (*Laughs*) Almost every day.
>
> **J.A.:** Is there anything else you see on the cover? How about the body language of the boys? Do you know what body language is?
>
> **Mac:** Like when my stomach tells me I'm hungry?
>
> **J.A.:** Well, you made a good connection—that language is communication. I guess when your stomach growls, it is communicating. But, when we say "body language" we usually mean what we can tell about a person and how they're feeling by looking at the expression on their face or the way they stand, whether they look relaxed or uptight. Can you make any guesses or predictions about this book by looking at the body language of these boys?
>
> **Mac:** Well, the three guys on the stairs look relaxed and in charge. The guy by himself looks mad—he's kind of got a fist.
>
> **J.A.:** Those are really good observations. I knew you'd be good at that because you really like art and you're good at picturing things. Okay, now how about the setting? Do you have any guesses about where the story might take place, based on the cover?
>
> **Mac:** How am I supposed to know that?
>
> **J.A.:** You're not supposed to know. I want you to see if you can find some clues there that will help you make an educated guess. For example, look at the picture again. Do you think this is a place like where we live?
>
> **Mac:** No.
>
> **J.A.:** What is there in the picture that tells you this might not be a place like our city?
>
> **Mac:** Well, it looks kind of like a big city apartment place or something. We don't have any of those kind of big buildings.
>
> **J.A.:** Great. Now I'd like you to read the first paragraph on page 1.
>
> **Mac:** I'll be collecting Medicare before we finish this book if we spend this long on each paragraph! (*We both laugh.*)
>
> **J.A.:** We won't. I just wanted you to see some things you could predict by looking at the clues from the cover. Sometimes those things help you understand what's going on in the book.

After Mac finishes reading the first page of the novel, I ask him if he can relate in some way with what he has read.

Mac: Well, he runs to school, well, home from school, every day and he isn't in good shape.

J.A.: How do you know that?

Mac: Well—

J.A.: Look back at the paragraph and see if there are words or ideas there that hint that he might not be in good shape.

Mac: Well, it says "his heart expanded" and "his chest filled."

J.A.: Those are two good examples of things that tell us that he was running hard. One observation you made that really interested me was that "he runs every day." What helped you know that?

Mac: Well, I didn't know this word (*points to "accustomed"*) but I knew this was route, 'cause of my paper route, and I sure know that's something you do every day!

J.A.: That was a great strategy you used there. You were able to figure out the meaning of a word you didn't know because you knew the meaning of the word that came after it. Why do you think Willis was running so hard?

Mac: I don't know—maybe those guys—maybe he's mad. I think it is a big city though, cause of East Broadway. We don't have streets like Broadway.

J.A.: I think that's another good prediction, Mac. Why don't you read the rest of the chapter. While you're reading I'd like you to to think about these three questions and then we'll talk again when you've finished reading that part.

I handed Mac an index card with three questions on it. The first was a literal question: (1) Why did Willis's mother make him go to the factory to see his father? The other two questions required Mac to analyze and make judgments based on his reading: (2) How do you think this made Willis feel? (3) When Willis left his father, he had $25.00. Do you think Willis considered his trip successful? Why or why not? My interaction with Mac only took six or seven minutes, and then I was able to move on to other students. He was able to read independently—or read as he listened to a tape I had made of the first chapter—before coming back to me for further discussion.

When Mac returned, we talked about his answers to the three questions, and after some prompting he was able to support his opinion that Willis would not have liked his task "because it was like begging" by pointing to a place in the text where Willis had actually said he didn't want to go. I then asked him to look at another line on the same page, "Sure! I'll make him turn over all the money, and then I'll give him a receipt" and talk about tone by asking him to tell me what tone of voice he thought Willis might use when he said those words. Mac, a wonderful mimic, quickly produced a sarcastic voice, and we continued our discussion about tone and how much more exciting a book is when we give our characters voices. At the end of our time together, I asked Mac if he had any new information that would help him understand why Willis might run. "Willis's father likes to drink and that's about 90 percent of his family's problems. I think when he's running he is just clearing out his thoughts and stuff."

Guided reading lessons on novels demanded more of me as a teacher, but it allowed students to get more involved in a text they could continue reading alone or with another student. Individual guided reading lessons were often transitional; they supplied individuals or small groups of students with specific strategy support. Since the only reading strategies students admitted to knowing at the beginning of the year were "sounding out" or "looking it up in the dictionary," I also met for guided reading lessons with the entire class as we were working through texts together.

My ultimate goal was always that students develop strategies they would use automatically in their own conversations with the text. At times I used shorter, more manageable, pieces of text, which they could later read and think through independently, for collective learning about specific strategies. Some of these strategies included developing ways to learn the multiple meanings of words; using headings and subheadings as text organizers; using visuals such as charts or maps to supplement and expand on print information; and noting author's techniques, such as bold print or italics for emphasis.

At other times, I used novels, plays, short stories, and poetry, reading aloud while each student followed along in the text. These shared reading experiences allowed me to guide students through the strategies they needed for reading longer texts. I wanted them to understand that active readers comprehend in the process of reading, not when they finish. (Years of end-of-the-story questions had that notion very firmly entrenched!)

Activating Prior Knowledge

Vygotsky (1962) advocated the practice of activating prior knowledge, connecting a new concept or word to something familiar in order to make sense of a text. One of the methods I found most effective in helping students make these connections was the use of *anticipation guides* (Readence, Bean, and Baldwin, 1985). These guides allowed individual students to reflect on and express their opinions in relation to statements that challenged or confirmed their beliefs. When students had given an initial response, they discussed their responses in small groups. Then those groups would meet together so that students could have the benefit of the collective background knowledge of the longer group. The following is an anticipation guide I created for *Ask Me If I Care* (Gilmour, 1985).

Anticipation Guide: *Ask Me If I Care*
Before we begin reading *Ask Me If I Care*, I would like each of you to read each of the following statements and decide whether you agree (A) or disagree (D) with each one. After we finish reading, I'll ask you to decide if you think the author would have agreed or disagreed with each statement and if you have changed your opinion based on the new understandings you may have developed from the book.

Before	Statement	Author	After
_____	1. Parents act more mature because they are more responsible.	_____	_____
_____	2. Life gets less complicated as you get older.	_____	_____
_____	3. Adolescents learn most of what they need to know in school.	_____	_____
_____	4. There is always a rational explanation for our problems.	_____	_____
_____	5. If you are willing to work at something, things will always turn out for the best.	_____	_____

By completing these anticipation guides, the students not only drew on their prior knowledge about relationships between parents and children and about conflict resolution, they also had a chance to see their opinions in the context of those of others in the class, the author, and the text. I asked them to save the anticipation guide and revisit it at the end of the book to look at their original opinions, describe any changes, and ask questions of both the text and the author, all critical elements in interacting with literature at more than a surface level.

Anticipation guides were only one of many ways we prepared before reading. Brainstorming about concepts that were embedded in the text, journal writing, charting related ideas, and group discussions were also common practice for each piece of literature we read together.

Word Attack Strategies

During our initial discussion of strategies, the students volunteered two ways to know a word: look it up in the dictionary or sound it out. So I gave them each a word, asked them to look it up and sound it out, and then tell me what it meant in the sentence. For example, one card read as follows:

epitome   I considered his comments the epitome of rudeness.

It took only minutes for them to realize that even those who could figure out the pronunciation of the word still could not figure out its meaning within the context of that sentence. This became an ideal lead in to the fact that words can have more than one meaning and that we could develop strategies to help us find the meaning to fit our context.

In the past, I had always considered it important to give students a list of words before beginning any new text. They seemed comfortable when they heard the word within the text, almost as if they were meeting an old friend. Then I came across a passage in *Reading in Junior Classes* that challenged my thinking: "Teaching words ahead . . . makes children unwilling to face the hazard of a new book: in short, teaching words ahead produces dependent rather than independent readers" (Simpson, 1962). I wanted to change my practice to encourage students to develop independent strategies, and yet I was continuing one that made them very dependent. I had chosen the words; I had mediated the discussion of which dictionary definition fit the context; and I had pointed to the word as I read the text aloud. I had given strong support to the notion that the only way we can figure out words we don't know is by looking them up in the dictionary. I needed to make some changes if I planned to give students processes for finding answers rather than the answers themselves.

Using *Effective Vocabulary Instruction* (Adams and Cerqui, 1989), as a resource, I developed some ways we could work together to determine the meaning of unknown words and develop a deeper understanding of words we might know peripherally. By the end of the year, when I asked students to tell me how they might go about finding the meaning of a word they needed to know in their reading, they were able to list the following strategies:

1. Look at the word in relation to the sentence.
2. Look the word up in the dictionary and see if any meanings fit the sentence.
3. Ask the teacher.
4. Sound it out.
5. Read the sentence again.
6. Look at the beginning of the sentence again.
7. Look for other key words in the sentence that might tell you the meaning.
8. Think what makes sense.
9. Ask a friend to read the sentence.
10. Read around the word and then go back again.
11. Look at the picture if there is one.
12. Skip it if you don't need to know it.

When the students finally realized that they didn't have to know all the words in a book beforehand, that everyone figured out words while they were reading, the entire process of reading became less stressful for them. I knew they were internalizing these strategies when I began reading aloud "The Origin of Tularecito" (Steinbeck, 1974) one day in class. The second sentence in the story read, "Once every three months, Pancho took his savings and drove into Monterey to confess his sins, to do his penance, and be shriven and to get drunk, in the order named." As I read that aloud I said, "I wonder what it means to be 'shriven.'"

Melvin said, "You should know what it means. You're the teacher."

Jennifer responded, "Nobody knows what every word means." This surely was one of the elusive "teachable moments" for which we all wait. A lively discussion followed as students talked about what penance was and the kinds of things you might do that would require penance. As some figured out the meaning of penance, it was fairly easy for them to see the cyclical action in the context of the sentence: sinning, penance, absolution, and sinning again. By then, Melvin had gotten the dictionary and found the word: "'To listen to a confession and give something as a priest does.' That's what's wrong with looking the words up in the stupid dictionary. You can't figure out the meaning without looking up a bunch of other words."

Most students felt they understood the word better by using the strategies we tried. They were pleased that they had been able to figure out a definition that at least made sense. Others thought that, for some words, it would be good to check a dictionary after you thought you knew a meaning. It was at this point that I realized that they were not only internalizing the strategies, they were making them their own by adapting them. When students talked about strategies in our end-of-the-year interviews, it was clear that they had developed their own strategies based on those I had demonstrated in class or in individual reading conferences.

> **Derek:** One way I used was to read one book by the same author and then it's easy to read the second one because they use the same words. Well, not the same, but they use the same kind of words, the same text, so it's kind of the same.

> **Rachel:** I like to read quietly because then if I see a word and I'm not sure of the meaning, I can just skim over it and get the meaning from the whole sentence, not just one word.

> **Jennifer:** At the beginning I like to put all the characters down and words about what they're like. That helps me with words they say.

> **Jennifer:** What I try to do is when I come on a word and I don't know the meaning, I ask. Once I know the meaning, I try to associate it with something I already know and that helps.

> **Derek:** When I was reading this book [*Charlie and the Chocolate Factory*], I formed all kinds of pictures in my head—like rivers of chocolate. That helped me picture some of the other words. And I asked questions like I wondered how they get all those little things to work for them in the book—the little bolts, nuts, and other things.

I knew that these students were well on the way to becoming independent readers if they could make strategies like these work for them in reading unfamiliar texts. But these "bolts, nuts, and other things" were just that without the context students saw as the most critical: what worked for them in our classroom environment that had been missing for them before.

8

Going Around the Edges

Learning how to not-learn is an intellectual and social chal-
lenge; sometimes you have to work very hard at it. It consists
of an active, often ingenious, willful rejection of even the most
compassionate and well-designed teaching. It subverts attempts
at remediation as much as it rejects learning in the first place.
Kohl, *I Won't Learn from You*

After listening to my students for only a few days, I wondered what kept them in school. Their writing and their conversation were full of their dislike of schools, teachers, and books. Perhaps Terri's first journal entry is as close as we might get to understanding why, other than being too young to drop out legally, students stay in school: "The only thing I DO like about school is that you can see your friends. I DON'T like homework, teachers (most of them) and classes are usually BORING." School had become a social place in response, perhaps, to the minutes, days, and years of academic and personal failure.

Although at times I was overwhelmed by the barriers we had to confront in breaking that cycle of failure, I did believe that each one of these students could be—and would be—successful. I agreed with Smith's comment that "children learn constantly, and so do adults—when they have not become persuaded that they can't learn" (1986, p. ix). Comments I heard from some educators, who referred to these students as "in-school dropouts," told me where these students had been persuaded that they couldn't learn. "Counseling," like that given to Derek, tells students exactly what we see for them in the future:

I failed math for three years and I got Ds and Es in English. They always blamed it on my hearing before and then last year they said, my counselor said, "You'll probably never change, you know."

How many of us would continue to return to a place where we were told we didn't fit, we weren't as smart as the others and never would be, and we needed "special" classes (that at times weren't all that special)? I wanted a classroom where everyone fit, everyone was smart, and everyone was successful, a far cry from what most of these students had experienced in elementary and middle school.

"Tell me about a time when you've felt successful, a time when you've felt like you worked hard for something and you were rewarded, and a time when you felt like a failure." I asked this of all the students, and their answers told me a great deal about how they had ended up in my class, feeling as though they were failures and not expecting any miracles to change that status. Since the focus of our class was reading and writing, many of their comments revolved around those aspects of their learning; those responses were the most critical for me, since I did not want to repeat any experiences they associated with past literacy failures.

Other comments, however, dealt with a sense of inadequacy related to tracking, retention, and feeling "behind the others." I knew I couldn't change what had happened in the past, but I could help students attain very different futures. In order to do that, I knew that I needed to start where the students were, while still being mindful of the individual stories of the journeys that had brought them to this place. Each day as my students put their stories before me, I knew that someday I would "give them away where they are needed" (Lopez, 1990, p. 48).

What Went Wrong

The more I listened to my students' stories, the more I realized that they were in fact telling me not only what had gone wrong for them in the past but what might help them feel more successful in the future. I could learn if I really listened. Many of these stories emerged when I requested their responses about feeling successful, rewarded, and like a failure. As Wells has remarked, "The reality each one of us inhabits is to a very great extent a distillation of the stories that we have shared." (1986, p. 196). Although I wanted to build our program on students' successes, I felt it was important to get the word *failure* out on the table so we could really look at it. Comments like Stan's told me that, in large part, the students did not see that the failure had been society's or the school's, not theirs.

Well, a long time ago, I had to go to a special teacher and at that time I didn't really like to admit it. It was just my problem and a lot of it was things that just happened and because I didn't really understand I stopped paying attention. It was my fault, I know, but still—

I knew that no matter how successful students felt in my classroom, they would consider this experience as an isolated anomaly without some discussion to somehow debunk the myth that the failure had been theirs.

Peter's story told me very quickly how firmly entrenched those beliefs were. Peter usually entered the room and sat quietly waiting for direction. I always felt that he saw this class as a punishment, one he would endure in silence. His fall survey told me that he disliked everything about school except gym, that a teacher's most important quality was the ability to "teach skills," and that he had hated previous English classes because he had to be in a "special, not a regglar, room." He reported that he liked to read, but had a hard time with it and knew that he needed to read and write a lot in order to become a better reader and writer. In spite of Peter's tolerance of the class, I still felt as though he were holding himself apart from any success he might be experiencing while here.

During the course of a reading interview with Peter, I learned that he was resistant to this class *because* it was a special class. When he was told that he would be in Reading and Writing Workshop, Peter said that he felt just like he did when he was told he had to go to the Resource Room. The Resource Room and its memories brought back many feelings that stood in the way of his ever feeling really successful.

> Yesterday when I was writing I thought of when I was in second grade with all my friends. We had to write a paragraph in school the day before and I couldn't do it. I just couldn't do it. I don't know—I just couldn't write a paragraph. I would write the, and and all of those words, but—I just put all the words together. She couldn't explain to me how to do it. I remember the next day her telling me she was going to take me out and have me put into the first grade instead of the second grade. I remember my mother, she tried to tell me not to be upset, but I'll never forget it. I cried for days. I had to leave all my friends and everybody knew. It was into the second quarter. I felt so awful I'll never forget it. I stayed back in kindergarten, too. I didn't like that either, but I remember my mom she told me that my dad stayed back too so not to feel bad, but I still did.

On the surface this is certainly a painful story of retention. With further questioning, I came to see that the more significant issue was Peter's lack of understanding of literacy. Peter told me that when he was assigned to this class his teachers told him "that it was a good reason and that I'm no different from anyone else, but it still felt bad."

For Peter, the years of special classes that had separated him from his friends had not produced any changes that were worth the pain of being labeled. He had no understanding of what the classes were trying to accomplish, nor did he see any results from his time there. He had fallen prey to the negative aspects of tracking: "Tracking can contribute to the polarization of the student body. The students in the advanced track may feel superior and look down on other students, and the students in the remedial track may feel angry and resentful" (Steinberg, 1993, p. 204).

Given those negative experiences, I was amazed that on the first day of class, Peter was able to believe he could improve. When he said the only thing that might help him as a reader and writer would be reading and writing more, I knew he had already taken the first step. It seemed sad that his experience with resource room classes did not support his understanding of what he knew he needed in order to improve.

> Well, we'd go in and set down—this would probably be like on a Monday, and we'd get a list of about 20 words. We'd have to spell those words on paper a couple of times or so and write sentences with those words. That would take the period. Tuesday we'd go to class and do some worksheets and stuff. On Wednesday we might read something and answer questions and then on Friday we'd take a test and do worksheets on those same words. It wasn't like a reading class. It was like a class where you did—well, I guess it was more like spelling than anything, but I never had another reading class—this was instead of that. We didn't really read. We just worked out of the books and stuff— workbooks—but it was a good class because I liked the teacher.

In spite of the fact that Peter did not see himself as a good communicator "because I stutter," his stories taught me a great deal about his past experiences. Peter needed to see that the work he was doing could and would result in increased literacy skills. While I couldn't go back and change the events that had marred his perceptions of himself and his ability to learn, I could see that his experiences in this class were rich literacy events that not only were relevant to his life but also resulted in improved attitudes and abilities. Peter would never feel better about his painful second-grade experience, but he would feel better about himself and his learning when he could do the things at which he had "failed" during those years.

As I became a more adept listener, I found an amazing similarity in the students' stories. Although Peter's was one of the most poignant, it was not particularly unique; many students reported backgrounds, attitudes, and educational experiences much like Peter's. For example, all the students, except one, had been retained at least once; a few had been retained twice. Very few complained about teachers in terms of personality; in fact, most reported liking many of their teachers. On the other hand, very few talked about any classroom practice that had been successful for them. It was the classroom practices related to their literacy backgrounds that were most significant to me, since it was there I felt I could make a difference.

Stan's words confirmed the importance of ensuring that all students were able to see academic changes: "They've [the students] got to be able to trust you, to know that you're just not going to be somebody else who's no help to them." Students highlighted some of the practices that had been "no help to them" and in doing so became a great help to me.

"I Never Understood Reading"

As in Peter's case, most of my students had been put in special classes in order to improve their reading, some in addition to their English/Reading classes, and others instead of their English/Reading classes. As Huck remarks, "Ironically, we frequently give this kind of time [to enjoy reading] to the better readers, while we drill remedial readers on more isolated decoding skills, thereby denying them the opportunity to develop fluency or enjoyment of reading" (1977, p. 367). Although they enjoyed the small numbers and the attention, few students said anything about improving reading ability or changed attitudes toward reading as a result of these classes. Not surprisingly, none had anything good to say about the reading opportunities or instruction they received in their mainstreamed classes. In a reading interview with Jennifer, we looked at what had happened to her reading and how it was now changing in order to see what her next steps as a reader would be.

> **Jennifer:** I was always in the low reading group and stuff like that. We did vocabulary words, little reading books—like cards, worksheets and workbooks. For me, failure was going to those classes for different—you know different—I was completely down all the time. I felt horrible. I felt that I was put down, but I don't even know if I ever learned anything or not. I guess I probably did, but I never felt it.
> **J.A.:** Can you tell me what those classes were like?
> **Jennifer:** We never read. I always did my homework or something.
> **J.A.:** You mentioned the other kids in higher reading groups. What do you think made them better readers and in that higher reading group?
> **Jennifer:** Well, what they did at home and what their parents taught them, I suppose.
> **J.A.:** So, do you read at home now?
> **Jennifer:** I read a chapter at night and I read in the morning. Sometimes I read when I first go home, depending on what I'm doing.
> **J.A.:** What kinds of reading things have we done in class that have been helpful for you?
> **Jennifer:** Reading, reading, and more reading. This is a big success for me. I enjoy it more than I did before. I feel better about myself.
> **J.A.:** What about the first graders you're working with? Do they have good strategies for figuring out words?
> **Jennifer:** No, not really. They wouldn't read the sentence over or anything like that. They just see and say one word at a time.
> **J.A.:** That's right. That's one of the things I'm hoping that you're getting from those first graders. When they do that, they sometimes miss what the story is trying to tell them.
> **Jennifer:** I know, I used to do that a lot. I didn't even know what it was talking about. I would read the word but pay attention to something way different—think about something and read. I don't know what that means, but I know when I read I think about it now. I was going to ask you. When you read, do you read the words before and then say them or do you just go along?

Jennifer was able to look at her past reading experiences with a more analytical eye because she felt successful. She actually used those experiences as the base for doing things differently when she worked with first graders in the paired reading program. Since our classroom practice was so different from what Jennifer had experienced ("we just read and read and read"), and she had been successful in that environment, she was able to understand her own reading process and begin to develop strategies that worked for her. Jennifer had not only developed a reading habit, but in asking questions of herself, the text and others, she had taken steps toward becoming an independent, lifelong reader.

Being forced to read orally, either in front of the class or in reading groups, seemed to be the practice that had the most negative impact on the students' self-esteem and attitudes toward reading. Rachel's discussions of the problems she experienced when she was forced to read aloud made me very aware of how carefully that aspect of our class had to be handled.

> **Rachel:** When I'm having trouble reading, I have a hard time pronouncing my words. I guess that's what makes me a slow reader. In my mind I can go on really clear and not really stumble across words. But when I'm reading out loud sometimes I get nervous and my voice shakes and I get really confused when I hear myself read like that.
>
> **J.A.:** When you were reading out loud today, I'm sure you noticed that you were able to go back and self-correct anything you didn't say correctly on the first reading—entirely on your own.
>
> **Rachel:** Yeah, I kind of like that because usually I would have to stop and stop and stop and now I guess I just stop every now and then. Reading out loud, even little words, I'd have a hard time pronouncing. I'd feel like that's why I didn't want to read, because I'd feel stupid. So, they'd say the word and then they'd say it again and I'd feel so stupid, you know.
>
> **J.A.:** If you knew somebody who was having trouble with reading, what advice would you give them?
>
> **Rachel:** Well, first they should read something that they like, but don't read it to a big crowd, read it to yourself a lot. You know, read it by yourself or have someone read, like you did, so they could follow along. That's what really helped me a lot because, like, when you were reading *The Lottery Rose* or *Ask Me If I Care*, you'd read and I'd go along and read like a few words ahead of you, like when you had stopped, and then wait for you to come to it and then I learned how to pronounce some of my words like that. And even spell them. Like the word *really*. I always used to spell that wrong, but now after watching you read and going along with you as you read, it's really helping my spelling and stuff. It's little words like that that I couldn't pronounce or write really well.

Rachel was able to articulate what had gone wrong for her in the past, but more important, she was also able to describe the literacy experiences that made a difference for her. Although most of my students were not able to talk about their problems and their changes in as much depth as Rachel, they all had advice for would-be teachers, advice they saw as critical so other teachers would not make the same mistakes with students that had been made with them.

Rachel: Take a book, *not* like *Tom Sawyer* or something, but something that kids can relate to. Find a book that deals with problems like falling in and out of love, drugs, pressure, stuff like that. The teacher should read out loud and the kids follow along with them.

Tori: We always read stories like out of reading books. Not good books. I like to pick out a book that sounds good and is interesting. If they aren't interesting, then I don't bother reading them.

Peter: I always thought reading was something for girls. The books were so boring and they always took so long to happen, they were like days. I guess the teacher tried to explain them to us when she gave us worksheet pages and stuff.

Anne: You have to be able to talk with them. Other than being a teacher, you have to be able to understand their feelings. Sometimes you just have to go around the edges—just go with what the kids are like. You can't yell at them all the time. You've got to let them read by themselves. I mean like maybe once or twice a week. Then do some reading all together. That's about it.

Dean: We should write when we have something to say. Sometimes if I have something to say, I can write about it. If I don't have anything to say and have to try and make up something, I'll want to put down one word but I'll put down another word because I don't know how to spell the word I want. Then it isn't really what I wanted to say.

Stan: You've got to get their trust first. You've got to be social—a friend—more than a teacher. And help, you've got to be more or less a helper and then be a teacher afterwards, after they're all set and stuff. You've got to help or people will just tune you out. Then they won't listen and they won't learn a thing.

Jennifer: Sometimes the language doesn't even make sense, like that *ph*, sometimes it sounds like *f*—or like the word *psychology*. You've got to know that it's okay to ask questions and nobody will think you're stupid.

Spend more time reading. Write when you have something to say. Don't focus on worksheets as follow-up for reading. Help students make sense of what they're doing. Make it okay to ask questions. Show students ways to improve their reading. Read out loud often and choose good books. As I read through their advice, I wondered if perhaps these students should be teaching some of our education classes in reading. They certainly knew the difference between what worked and what didn't. They not only knew good strategies for understanding text, but they had also experienced the joy of reading. They knew that literature could be one place where they could share the feelings and experiences of others. They would have no problem now being an integral part of a system that would "trust that teachers can teach and that children can learn" (Smith, 1986, p. xi), and they would see themselves as both teachers and learners.

A Special Place

"Is this room kind of special?" Barb Frick's question to the class during the debriefing video prompted a discussion of the classroom environment, both on a personal and an academic level, and how that environment affected their learning.

"This class is more sociable than others. We talk a lot about what we're doing and not just in here, either. I mean now I know most of these people. I know a lot about them—not just in this area, but personally." Stan's response reminded me again of the contrast between these involved and empowered students and the detached, apathetic faces I had encountered last August. Although I had not been sure how I could get them *all* involved, I knew that one of the most critical components of our class had to be talk.

"The Sea of Talk"

In my twenty years of teaching I had found that students in lower tracks were often relegated to classrooms that had virtually eliminated talk. I certainly understood teachers' hesitancy about involving students in discussions. I have many memories of trying to build and sustain conversation in remedial classes—experiences that haunt my dreams to this day. In seconds one comment can spark another's anger, and fists compensate for an inability to disagree with words. I also knew that if I continued a practice based on silence and worksheets, I was denying students access to a system based on one's ability to use language. Whatever it took to help students become able to carry on conversations, whether about books or life, I was willing to try and Stan's comment was testimony to the importance of our attempts. Jan Duncan, a New Zealand educator, says that in our classrooms, "Reading and writing should float on a sea of talk." Other students were quick to validate the importance of that sea of talk in our classroom.

"In other classes I don't even know people's names."

"Yeah, and if you're reading out loud, it's easier to read with people you know than others—people who believe in you."

"In here you never feel stupid. You ask questions—you trust her."

"One of the things I've noticed is that the guys who might be obnoxious in other classes were really different in here. Nobody says, 'You're stupid.' People listen."

That sea of talk, however, didn't come naturally. Because these students had been in "special" classes where much of their work was done in isolation, or in mainstreamed classes where they felt inferior, they were not accustomed to expressing their opinions, solving problems, or gaining group consensus in collaborative decision-making. I began by involving them in as many class decisions as possible. If I planned to be absent, I let them express their opinions about the work they would like to do during my absence. When we planned to start a novel, I gave book talks on several that met our purposes and let them choose the one we would read together. When we finished sustained silent reading, I would talk about the book I had read and invite others to do the same. We used the PC-viewer to compile group memories of our activities. We worked together writing a play. We talked about basketball games and the "No hats" rule. We talked about problems and the way we were feeling.

Each class began the same way. As each student entered the room, I would hear the same question: "What are we going to do today?" I always responded the same way, "What would you like to do?" As each person responded, I would say, "Hmmm, that sounds good." Most days I went through that ritual about ten times before the bell rang.

One day a colleague said, "Why don't you just put a schedule on the board so you don't have to answer each one of them every day?" In the past I had done just that. But I wanted that interaction with the students. It was our ritual and it was my way of saying to them, "Your opinions matter to me." Some days I would do whatever I had planned, which coincidentally was often what at least one of the students said in response to my question. Other days I would say something like, "Most of you said you wanted to work on our class play today. That wasn't what I had planned, but since that is what you'd like to do, why don't we do that."

I don't think the process would have been quite as successful if I hadn't acted upon their opinions once I solicited them. At the same time, I didn't let them take control of the class. If someone wanted to watch a movie, we might indeed watch a movie, but only if I had planned one that supplemented the novel we were reading. Students quickly began to see that their actions and opinions made a difference in the fabric of our days; they began to make careful choices about the opinions they expressed. In addition, we talked often so that I could ascertain their background knowledge before we started a particular reading or so that they could gain a sense of the wealth of knowledge they shared as a community. There were days when this was the most difficult thing I attempted.

One of them was the day we discussed a biographical piece about Maya Angelou's life. The piece was included in a workbook entitled *The Reading Road to Writing* (Porter, 1984, pp. 1–2). I had no plans to have students do the multiple choice questions that followed the text; I only wanted them to read the article about Angelou's life before I read them some poetry. I read the piece aloud as they followed along and then began our discussion.

J.A.: What do you think they're talking about when they say, "She did what her ancestors could only wish for?"
Melvin: She freed the slaves.
J.A.: Did we have slaves when Maya Angelou lived?
Tammy: No.
J.A.: When did we have slaves?
Mac: With Columbus.
Terri: In the 1500s.
Derek: 1700s.
Tanya: World War II

By this point I was becoming more exasperated than I wanted to admit to the students or myself. The class was in pandemonium.

> **J.A.:** Wait . . . Stop . . . What war was fought to get rid of slavery?
> **Tori:** World War II.
> **Diana:** World War I.
> **Mac:** Revolutionary War.
> **J.A.:** This is pathetic. What war was fought over slavery?
> **Melvin:** The Silver War.

This wasn't horseshoes; close was good enough.

> **J.A.:** That's close, Melvin. The Civil War. Who was president at this time?
> **Terri:** Abraham Lincoln.
> **J.A.:** Great, now we're getting somewhere. What two parts of the country were fighting?
> **Tanya:** England and the West.
> **J.A.:** Now, let's try and get these facts straight.
> **Tammy:** Just tell us if it's *a*, *b*, or *c*. It's *a*, right?
> **J.A.:** The point is not whether it's *a*, *b*, or *c*; the point is learning something. This needs to make sense.
> **Tammy:** It would make sense if we just wrote down the right answer.
> **Anne** (*disgusted*): I know the answer. The Civil War was fought between the North and the South.
> **Mac:** I thought that was the Revolution War.
> **J.A.:** What was the Revolutionary War fought for?
> **Diane:** Freedom.
> **J.A.:** For whom?
> **Tori:** Jews?
> **Melvin:** Blacks?
> **Mac:** Italians!
> **J.A.:** Arghh!

I then gave them a minispeech about goals and aspirations, that it was important that they started thinking about something other than their dates for the dance this weekend, that we all need to start thinking and come out of la-la land. Mac said, "I know that land." Sadly, he did.

With each one of those discussions, as difficult as they were, their confidence and involvement levels increased. Equally important, and even more painful, was the talk I forced and fostered between students. Many of these students came into the class not simply with a dislike of English and English teachers but with an animosity toward each other. I constantly put them in different paired and group situations so that they could complete assignments. Some days I let them choose a partner in order to collaborate on their reading, writing, or language collection notebooks. Other days, I put them in two larger groups to work on group projects. Our first, and almost our last, group project occurred in mid-September, the last day before our traditional harvest break.

For two days, the students had been meeting in groups to write questions about the book we were reading during shared reading, *Teacher's Pet* (Cusick, 1990). I decided that we should have a contest to see which team could "win" in a game that involved the questions they had written. Thinking that this activity would give them lots of time to talk through the process of creating rules as well as developing deeper understandings of the text, I told them we would begin by coming to an agreement about the rules of our game, and then we would play the game abiding by the rules they had chosen. What chaos! I should have realized that they were too competitive—too angry, too concrete—to compete for fun. It wasn't fun for me and it couldn't have been fun for them, but if my goal was classroom talk, we certainly got plenty of it. Making the assumption that all kids spent their childhoods as I did, playing everything from Uncle Wiggly to Monopoly, I thought the easiest part would be establishing the rules of the game.

"We ought to have gum!"

"We ought to have a free day!"

Variations of those themes abounded until I stood quietly for a few minutes, just waiting. Finally, Derek said, "Those aren't rules, they're prizes." Good point, Derek. With Derek in charge, they then generated the following rules.

1. Someone blurts out answer, team loses points
2. No talking
3. Spokesperson *only* for each team answer questions
4. Has to be answer on card
5. Once answer said, no changes can be made
6. Thirty-second limit

The game was on. Kids on opposing teams complained that questions were too easy, too hard, unfair. They complained that the other team was cheating. The second card brought the turmoil to a head. "Who was the author of the book?" The students in Group 1 looked at the book. Screams erupted from Group 2.

"They can't look at their books!"

I said, "Is it in the rules?"

"No, but it's not fair!"

"Let them answer this question and we'll put it in the rules if you want." The question was answered. Group 2 was angry; Group 1 was elated. Things were going downhill. Then we added rule number seven.

7. No looking at the book.

They continued to argue slightly until we came to another glitch. Group 2 asked, "What did Gideon and Kate do in the woods?"

Group 1 answered, "Kiss."

"That's not what we wrote for an answer on the back of our card. It was a French kiss." Pandemonium from the *Teacher's Pet* experts as well as the kissing experts. Finally, in spite of my decision to let them run the game, I stepped in.

"Kiss is the right answer."

"No, it was a *French* kiss."

Surely they would listen to reason. "It didn't say that in the book."

"Yes, it did!"

Before I thought to look at our posted rules, I said, "Find it in the book."

Group 1 had already been in trouble with this one. "They can't look in the book. It's rule #7!"

I learned that day that all talk is not productive talk. I also learned that if I wanted students to be collaborative, then I should not set them up to be competitive. My assumption that giving them permission to talk and make decisions would naturally make them more responsible with their words was wrong. They had too many years of practice at using words to hurt. If I wanted our room to be a safe place, I had to make sure that I modeled using words in a way that would allow us all to feel safe. Fortunately, by the end of the year, it was my supportive words that students remembered the most.

In an end-of-the-year interview with two colleagues, several students talked about the atmosphere my words created and the impact of my talk in making our classroom "a special place."

> **Derek:** One thing was when we'd read just a little bit, she'd always praise us for reading. Boy, that was so great. I mean even if you'd only read two or three pages.
>
> **Stan:** 'Cause you knew she wanted you to learn so you felt like you'd please her if you learned—if you read—because she put so much effort into trying to help us.
>
> **Derek:** She always made you feel so proud. She always had a compliment for you when you read. And that makes you feel good that someone tells you that you did good.
>
> **Jennifer:** She does so much for us. She just wants us to be a success— she wants us to be ourselves, but successful.
>
> **Derek:** That made me want to read—for her and for myself.
>
> **Jennifer:** She always had patience.
>
> **Rachel:** And she was always positive. I never heard her say anything in anger.
>
> **Derek:** All of the teachers have got to make you feel like you're not a loser, like you're something worth—you know—
>
> **Jennifer:** Worth saving.

It would be wonderful if none of our students felt they were lost and so didn't have to see themselves as needing to be saved. That certainly wasn't the case with these students. Although there were times when I completely lost patience with them, I tried hard to keep my talk full of respect and honest praise. This was another area, however, in which my role as a researcher affected my practice as a teacher. I became more aware of my words and their impact as I listened to the words come back to me on tape. Knowing that I didn't want to be one more person in their lives who said, either openly or in subtle ways, that they weren't "worth saving" made me very conscious of my contribution to the sea of talk in our classroom.

By the end of the year, when students discussed and wrote their final evaluations, the isolated events of the past months had blended together for them. They didn't particularly remember days or times when we weren't as successful as we might have been; rather, they focused on the feelings of success that had been building for many months. Tanya's final response distilled what the other students wrote:

> What makes a good reading/English class is when you have a good teacher that knows what she is doing and that is willing to help. The advice that I would give to a teacher is that you have got to know your students really well. You have got to do lots of things with your students too. Lots of reading. Read out loud, read silently. Do lots of different stuff. But have fun with your class while you are doing it. Help your class to become better readers. Sit down and help them when they need help. And by the end of the year your kids should enjoy reading. You shouldn't make them read so much that they hate it. By the end of the year the kids should talk good about your class and how well and how much fun they had and that they learned.

The story of this year would be incomplete if I focused only on the individual and collective feelings of success students experienced. Although the themes students saw as critical to the success of our program were indeed critical, they don't give an accurate picture of the daily "epiphanies of the ordinary" that moved us toward our goals. Johnston (1992) talked about "that period of quiet" in which she learned to be reflective about her practice (p. 31). The following chapter highlights excerpts from my journal notes, where I, like Johnston, told "the whole story—the discovery as well as the underside" (p. 32).

9

"It Was the Best of Times, It Was the Worst of Times . . ."

I can listen to someone without hearing him. Listening is fixing my attention only on the other person. Hearing requires that I listen inside me as I listen to him. Hearing is a rhythm whereby I shuttle between his words and my experience. It includes hearing his entire posture. It includes hearing his tone of voice and his silences. And hearing also includes attending to my reactions.
   Hugh Prather, I Touch the Earth, the Earth Touches Me

As unbelievable as it might seem, my most productive "period of quiet" occurred each day during an assigned noontime detention. When I received the duty assignment at the beginning of the year, I was not pleased. On the first day, however, Chad, one of my students from the first period Directed Studies class, had received detention between my class and lunchtime. He walked into the room still carrying the book he had chosen during first period, sat down on one of the couches, and began reading. I was sitting at my desk, writing in my journal, when the next detention victim walked into the room. He looked at Chad engrossed in a book and at me writing and said, "Can I borrow a book?" I nodded; he took a book and started reading. As others came into the quiet room filled with books and readers, each one took a book and followed the *obvious* requirement in this noon detention. Each day, those remaining from previous days, established a quiet reading pattern for newcomers.

During the previous school year, I had attempted to do a research study but could never find a consistent time in which to write and reflect. I had been worried that once I was again engulfed by the hectic schedule demanded of a teacher, department chair, and writing committee chairperson, I would have the same problem. Noon detention turned out to be the answer to that problem. Occurring directly after my Reading/Writing Workshop, the duty assignment gave me twenty-three minutes of sustained writing time each day. Most teachers would agree that twenty-three minutes of sustained time to do anything in a teacher's day would be a gift from the gods! My journal reflection experiences that could be summarized by Dickens at the beginning of A *Tale of Two Cities*: "It was the best of times, it was the worst of times, it was the age of wisdom, it was the age of foolishness . . . it was the spring of hope."

"The Best of Times"

One of our first "best of times" days occurred in late August after our first day of creative dramatics with Barb Frick. The students were already slightly apprehensive when Barb walked into the room. Two weeks of classes had made them feel fairly comfortable with my expectations, but they were sure they didn't want a new teacher in the room. An African proverb says, "It takes a whole village to raise a child." Because I believe that, one of my goals for these students was to have them feel part of the school community. Often at-risk students see themselves as apart from everything that happens at school, with the possible exception of the vice-principal's office and In-School Suspension. The sooner I could support a connection between these students and other faculty, students, and activities, the sooner they would develop a sense of their own place within the community. I had planned this day with Barb as a way to start making those connections. Although I've already written about the students' enjoyment of that day, what gave me hope was learning about the value of debriefing.

In my role as a teacher-researcher, I had sat taking notes and wishing I had thought to record the class on videotape. One of the things that struck me was that this was an excellent way to see the sense of story these students were developing. I didn't have to ask them to define the word *story* or list the elements of a story. I could see immediately that they had already developed a sense of what made a story. My purpose had been somewhat more limited: I wanted them to take risks, work together, and learn to connect their thoughts. I wondered what the students would say the purpose of this exercise had been and decided to make sure to leave time at the end of class for a debriefing.

"Why do you think we did this improvisational exercise?"

Trisha's response brought lots of laughter. "To see how stupid we are." But others stopped and thought for a few seconds. I waited quietly. As I sat watching Barb work with these students the previous day, I realized that one of the reasons she had been able to get everyone to participate was that she had given everyone time. My waiting paid dividends.

"You could see how we use our imaginations."

"To get a meaning."

"To get used to talking to other people."

"So we wouldn't get so embarrassed in front of people."

Those comments had come from Melvin, Anne, Stan, and Tanya, who seldom volunteered any thing in our discussions or group activities. The wait time had obviously given them the opportunity to gather their thoughts and their courage in order to contribute. I needed to remember this lesson: if my focus was really on process, I had to allow enough time for everyone to work through a process. I had expected to be reflective in my role as a researcher, but the success of that early attempt with students made me see that this practice should be a part of all we did together.

That day I began to ask students to be truly reflective, even if they thought it might hurt my feelings. I knew that many had already formed a bond with me that might prevent them from being entirely honest, so I talked with them about it. Together we learned that this early model of honest reflection and criticism would help each of us help each other become better teachers *and* learners.

At the end of the next week, another "best of times" brought me closer to understanding the importance of modeling. Although students had usually left my classes as readers, I knew that I had not always done a great job of modeling a process of reading. That had been one of my goals for the year, but I still had not moved entirely away from being a secondary teacher who gave an assignment and expected that everyone would complete it. Previously, those completed assignments, the products, were always examples of whatever the students had brought to the assignments. They were not a combination of what the students had brought plus what they had learned from my intervention. On this Thursday in September, I finally forced myself to come to terms with modeling a process for my students before I expected them to adopt or adapt the process for themselves.

We were into our third day of a shared reading of Cusick's *Teacher's Pet* (1990). Several students had missed bits and pieces of our reading, and I thought that perhaps one way to get everyone to the same point was to retell what had already happened. I asked students to take their academic journals and retell what had happened and what they had learned so far in *Teacher's Pet*, and make a prediction about the upcoming events in the book. There was mass confusion.

"I don't understand."

"Do we start from the beginning?"

"I can't remember anything."

"Just ask us questions and we'll answer them."

"This is too hard."

My immediate reaction was anger. How could they not remember anything? I had read it out loud. They had followed in their books. We had talked about the events and the characters. They *liked* the book! Fortunately, working through those negative feelings gave me time to remember my goal. I started again.

"If a teacher asked me to do this, I'd probably say, 'There was a girl named Kate who got chosen to go to a writing camp.' Oh, wait, it would probably be important to include how she got chosen. I guess I'd go back and insert after camp 'because she had the best story in a writing contest.' That would be important for someone who had not read the book. Then I'd say, 'When she got there, she met these two people who worked in the kitchen—a guy named Denzil and a dizzy blonde named Tawney.'"

The kids erupted in laughter, but then quickly took their academic journals and began writing, stopping only to ask questions about whether they should make immediate predictions or predictions for the whole book. All they had needed was a model. The word *retelling* was unfamiliar to them and if I wanted them to see the process a reader goes through in order to choose important points in a story, I had to show them. I had modeled getting started, choosing significant events, revising, and writing in natural language, and students had accepted that model. It had worked, or so I thought until I read their journal responses that night. I realized then that many students had taken this as a story starter exercise since eleven of the fifteen entries began much like that of Tori.

> There is this girl named Kate who got a chance to go to a writing camp. When she got there she meant this boy named Denzil and a dizzie blond named Tawney.

Fortunately, unlike many of the others, Tori had been able to go on from there.

> They were all writers. Tawney wrote poems and Denzil wrote plays and Kate wrote horror stories. Well, they all became friends. They went to a bonfire and when Kate got to her camp she keep hearing somebody whisper her name behind the trees. She got scared and ran in her cabin and locked the windows and the doors. Well, the next day she had her first lecture day so she went instead of William Drewe his brother Gideon was teaching. He kept staring at Kate. Well, he asked her to stay after so he could talk to her about her storie. Well, when she left she walked the path and she seen pet with a glove it was stiff when she looked at it there was meet hanging from the open glove.

In other years, I might have left the assignment there. I had given the assignment, and everyone had produced something. After all, wasn't that enough? As I reflected on our activity, I knew that I could no longer stop with these surface goals if I wanted students to examine and develop strategies for independent learning. This was one of the first times I had ever really considered how many terminal exercises we ask students to do. These exercises are never used again; sometimes students do not even see them again. No wonder students who hate English complain, "We do the same thing every year." Vowing that I would try to change my practice, I decided to use the academic journal responses to look at how they had decided what was important in the text and how they could examine the author's clues to help them predict future events.

"Okay, let's get out our academic journals from yesterday so we can talk about them before we start reading today." There was an almost immediate change in body language. They hesitated, lingering around their seats and not moving toward the storage area where their journals were kept. Again, I forced myself to wait, but this time it didn't move them. Finally, it occurred to me that perhaps I should *ask the students* what was going on. I think perhaps it is our "teachers as answer givers" syndrome that makes us think we should know what is happening. In just a few weeks as a researcher, I had already established the habit of going back to the students for their interpretations and understandings. Now, I needed to incorporate that practice more fully into my teaching. "What's wrong? Why aren't you getting your journals?"

"We don't want to read them out loud." Jennifer and Anne had given words to the fears of the others.

There was visible relief when I said, "You don't have to. We're just going to use them as a reference for what we're doing today. I read them last night and everyone had such good ideas that I thought we could put them all together." Taking a magnetic board, since there were so many books in front of our chalkboard that it was inaccessible, I asked students to tell me one thing they had written in their journals that was important to understanding *Teacher's Pet*. Students participated willingly, seeming proud to see the growing list as I recorded their responses on the board. When I asked them about it later, they said, "Saying the line isn't the same thing as reading out loud."

The point of the list was to demonstrate the ways we can ask questions of the author, the text, and ourselves.

"Since everyone, including me, thought it was important to say that Tawney was a dizzy blonde, one of the things I have to ask myself is why the author would stress these characteristics for Tawney. Did anyone else wonder that?"

"No, but I wondered why he switched the brothers. That made me think there was going to be something funny going on there."

"When the author put the glove with the hand in it, I knew the book was weird."

"Have there been any other clues about the book's suspense qualities? What else has the author done to create a suspenseful tone?"

As students commented on the isolated setting, the strange events in class, the black cat, the bonfire, and the whispers, we were able to look at some of the characteristics of the horror/suspense genre. I was once again reminded of how much more valuable it is to let students come to their own conclusions, to build their own content frameworks, than for me to give them a list of characteristics or definitions. Time, resources, and support are the framework for all of our learning.

Given the positive book experiences we had established on the first day of school, it wasn't surprising to me that many of our "best of times" were related to our encounters with books. After one of her visits to our class, Barb Frick had commented that she wasn't surprised that students just started reading in our room because it "literally invited reading." Although I was pleased that the environment was so conducive to reading, I knew that it would take a lot more than books to turn these fifteen students into independent readers.

At this point most of them depended on me for motivation, resources, and reading. By mid-September, when the students came into the room saying, "Can we read our own books today?" I knew we were on our way. However, as exciting as it was to see students reading, I was also beginning to see beneath the surface to some of the overwhelming problems. The "worst of times" had begun to creep even into the days when things seemed to be going well. Indeed, the extremes of both the best and the worst were often represented within one ninety-minute period. The following journal notes from our independent reading period and writing in the computer room indicate just how ephemeral success could be.

Tanya, one of my very reluctant readers, came into class saying, "I'm at a good part in my book and I don't want to stop." Jennifer had broken up with her boyfriend so she seemed really sad. I thought perhaps she wouldn't want to read, but instead she seemed really engrossed in her reading; in fact, it felt as though she was using reading to escape. She has started reading My Darling, My Hamburger and has finally started to get into it. Mac has finally started reading! He got Christine from the library and read over the weekend. He proudly told me that he was on page 34. I would never have chosen that book for him because of the difficulty, but he has decided that he is a Stephen King fan and so he *is* reading it. Melvin was restless, almost upset, that Mac was reading. They have bonded in the worst sense of the word and they bring out the younger, silly stuff in each other. The girls view their antics with disdain and that makes them even worse. Melvin finally settled with The Man Who Ate the Car and seemed to enjoy that but felt it was a book for sharing, and Mark didn't want to be interrupted.

All the girls, including Tammy, are reading. They were so excited with all of the new horror novels that I think they would read indefinitely. Last week I talked with them again about why our class is the way it is—we learn to become better readers by reading—and most seemed to have accepted that. Derek said, "I never heard that before." It didn't surprise me.

Wayne has a book and is showing reading behavior but I think he's not really reading . . . I need to do a running record with him on his book but it would be demoralizing for him to do that at the moment; in fact, he'd refuse. That's certainly a difference I have to keep in mind. Running records with elementary students might seem normal, but older students with lots of failure baggage see that process as intimidating. It will take them a while to see that as a normal part of their reading class. For now, it's okay, I think, that he has picked a book and seems invested in his choice. But we will both need to look at what's going on.

Dean is reading quietly—alone. He seems to really enjoy this aspect of the class but it's hard to tell, since he barely talks and almost refuses to write. On the plus side, he's reading!

At face value, those notes recorded some very positive behaviors. Students were reading books they had selected. Some were even choosing to read at home! During the second half of our class, however, we went to the computer room for the third time. Here it was a different story.
"When do I put my disk in?"
"What's this *a:* mean?"
"Where's my story from last time?"
"Melvin is erasing my story!"
"Somebody erased my disk. I can't find anything."
Before we left the classroom I had asked students if they had any questions about how to access the writing on their disks. Tammy's words had shattered any possibility of a refresher. "Let's just go. You say the same boring stuff over and over again. Do you think we're stupid or what?" Now her questions could be heard over everyone else in the computer room. The problem was that now I had fifteen students all asking questions at once. Some students were smiling, perhaps thinking of snappy comebacks they would have liked to have made to Tammy if they hadn't been intimidated by her.
I decided to tease the group at large about all the problems we had each time we came into the computer room. "What is wrong with you guys? I could teach chimps how to do this easier than I can teach you!" As cruel as that sounds out of context, it had a special meaning for us. One of my students from Directed Study had said those words to me as he fixed the VCR one day, and they had quickly become a class joke. As I went from student to student showing them the same thing I had shown them three days before, I asked myself over and over again what was wrong. Finally, it hit me.
As I looked at the menu with one student, I said, "What does 'file' mean?" To another I said, "What does 'existing' mean?" When I got to Melvin I said, "What is a 'document'?" My assumptions had once again managed to get in the way of my teaching. I had assumed that the students knew the menu language, when they didn't. They had been trying to do the almost impossible task of remembering the steps while not under-standing the language. Each was trying to remember to put in the disk and then hit numbers in a certain sequence. As amazing as it was to me that I didn't see their inability to do this as a lack of language for the task, it was equally telling that not one student had ever asked what any of those words meant. They had just blindly tried to follow directions. As I walked around conferring with individual students, I tried to figure out what to do. I knew that if I tried to give them the information, they would just tune me out.

Years of being lectured at had made them masters at that. Then, I had an idea. I would have them write a letter to students who have never been in the computer room explaining how to use the computers. That would give me some idea of what it was that had been missing for each of them. There was no sense wasting everyone's time; I would work this through individually. This was a good lesson for me: to make sure that students understood the language of the task.

At the time, an observer in my class commented on how quickly the students had changed, but I knew that there were many problems just beneath the surface. My personality and the way I dealt with students had always made my classroom a favorite place for most students. To most observers it seemed that I had already miraculously turned these students into readers and writers. But I knew that wasn't the case. This year, when I was trying to look more closely at our work together, my reflections helped me realize that one of the things that had made my classroom a safe place in the past was that I did not challenge students. Most of the time I simply let them work at their own comfort level while I took the risks. If I planned challenging reading, I made sure that I gave them all the answers. All they had to do was listen and enjoy.

My journal entry on October 9 reflected my difficulties in trying to support students as they took on more challenging tasks. "Help! I feel like I'm losing my kids. It would be so easy to slip into letting them do their own thing . . . they're quieter, less angry, seemingly more motivated. When I try to challenge them to move up the scale with what they're attempting, they resist—not in an angry way, but still resistant. There's more note writing (perhaps I need to build on that) and more irrelevant (?) chatter." In spite of that, I knew that these students had taken a first step; most of them were now involved in reading and writing. The challenge would come as I tried to support each of them to move beyond where they were in order to become more strategic and independent learners.

Listening and Learning

There's a line in the Angelou (1990) poem "Me and My Work" that I have always thought described my teaching life: "My story ain't news and it ain't all sad" (p. 22). Our days together were not filled with noteworthy, earth-shattering events; rather, they were filled with many things that, taken individually, seemed insignificant. One of the lessons that permeated all my journal notes was the one Tammy taught me: In spite of all your efforts. there may be students with whom you feel you have failed. Tammy was that student for me (and my feelings echoed Gibran's words about being ungrateful to those who teach you such lessons).

In spite of Tammy's boisterous entrance at the beginning of the year, we did not start the year in conflict. Tammy's older sister had been one of my students when I first returned from graduate school, and her stories of sibling abuse, fighting, and abandonment had softened my attitude toward Tammy even before I met her. That did not, however, diminish the negative impact of her presence in the classroom. She took particular delight in getting Tanya, Tori, and Trisha to join her in tormenting Jennifer and Anne. She saw them as preps, since they were on the basketball team, were involved in school activities, and had not traditionally been in special classes. She made fun of their clothes, started constant rumors about them and their boyfriends, and taunted them during our reading and discussions. Jennifer was her special target because her father was the principal of the middle school Tammy had attended. In addition, Tammy was louder than any of the other students and able to respond more quickly in most verbal situations. This intimidated almost everyone in the room. On the positive side—and there were times when it became difficult for me to see a positive side—she was lively, enjoyed reading aloud, and could be counted on to complete almost every task. On the negative side, she was lively, wanted to be the *only* one reading aloud, and had no concern for how a task was completed. The only requirement was that it should move off her desk and onto mine.

In spite of all that, we managed to keep some semblance of peace for the first few weeks of school. I recognized that Tammy needed extra attention and gave it to her as often as I could. I asked her to read orally, invited her to take class notes, encouraged her to be recorder for group discussions, and interviewed her individually several times. Her journal entries were usually filled with talk about boyfriends and school and it seemed she was hopeful that this year would be different for her.

> Mrs. Allan,
> Hi, what's up? Not to much here I guess. I feel so bad for Trisha she is so sick. But I hope she stays for the end of 3rd period. I'm going to try to get an A+ in this class for my next semester. But an 85 so far is not bad at all for me. But I could do alot better than that. I got an 82 so far in math. That's good for me to. I hope I do good in science and gym. Well I'm going to start reading now.
> Bye.

The beginning of the end occurred just after we returned from our harvest break.

Tammy had been coming to my classroom during her study hall period so that she could get books, be interviewed, confer about her writing, and work on the computer. Just before the break, however, she had started taking advantage of that time to wander in the halls, tease the boys in their vocational classes, and disrupt other academic classes. Since her study period was my department chair period, I couldn't always be in the room for the entire time she was there. She had begun to use this as her opportunity to go to the store or cause a commotion.

I had decided that it wasn't fair to me or to the other students I wanted to work with during that time to have her dominate seventh period each day. I told her that she could only come down to the room on days when I gave her a pass. If she had problems she needed to talk about or work she wanted to do, she was welcome to come; however, once there, she had to stay for the entire period and work on whatever it was that had brought her to the room. I thought we had reached an agreement until she said that she wanted to come down to be interviewed *today*. When I told her that we had already done two interviews and I needed to begin doing them with other students, she exploded. "I hate you. This is a stupid class and you're a stupid teacher." Tammy was not the first angry student in my twenty years of teaching and I thought that by talking with her alone, we would be able to resolve the problems. Tammy, however, was not like any of the other angry students. From that point on, things only got worse. In fact, her idea for a class project became our first major class problem.

After we had read a play together one day, Tammy suggested that we ought to work on our own play. Actually, what she said was, "Mrs. Allen, we should act out a play!" While some students moaned, others seemed to agree that this was a good idea. As I thought of trying to use the PC viewer to write a play together, I realized that the possibilities for learning were endless. However, I also should have considered that the potential for chaos was also endless. My journal became the vehicle through which I clarified my purpose and worked out a plan for this cooperative language experience activity.

October 10, 1991
Learning can't be neat and quiet all the time!

- Get PC viewer hooked up.
- Practice.
- Read a few more plays.
- Do dialogue with them.
- Note "play traits."
- Discuss purpose of a narrator.
- "What constitutes a scene?"

I'd better do a DRTA [Directed Reading Thinking Activity] with kids to see what they already know. Once again, I'm slipping back into the "What do I need to *tell* them before we can do this?" mode. I need to figure out how to structure the class so kids can work together to figure out what they need to know. What am I hoping will happen?

1. Certainly kids should learn new words if I type in a language experience activity.
2. Cooperation.
3. Importance of dialogue—show, don't tell.
4. Stretch the imagination.
5. Importance of "right" word.
   Maybe we should do it.

There were many times over the next few weeks when I reread that entry trying to remember why we had ever started this project. The girls gathered close to the PC viewer, yelling to get their individual lines heard.

The boys saw the darkened room as an opportunity to do other things—they wanted nothing to do with this play. All the anger and animosity that had been kept just below the surface by my somewhat inventive grouping and activities came out in the dialogue of the play. Tammy, who could think faster, yell louder, and knew how to be cruel saw this activity as her personal playground. In fact, I had to stop the play twice on the first day and shift the dialogue back to the play and away from personal confrontation. At the end of the first day, I was exhausted; Tammy was ecstatic with all of the shots she had managed to get in; Jennifer and Anne's feelings were hurt; the boys were confused and restless.

The commotion during play writing wasn't enough for Tammy. She had started the practice of beginning every class with a series of loud, whining complaints. "I forgot my homework. I forgot my notebook. I forgot my journal." One day Dean, who seldom said a word in class, mimicked her, "I forgot my brain." It was priceless. She was so shocked by the fact that he could and did talk, that she settled down for a few days.

For her next performance she waited until everyone was involved in silent reading and then started screaming until I took her out of the room. During writing, she began taking a page, scribbling all over it, ripping it out of her journal, and throwing it on my desk. My journal started having a common theme: "Great class today. Tammy was absent. It's so quiet when Tammy is gone. She subtly (not always subtly) disrupts. Everything we do takes twice as long and is twice as complicated when she is here."

By November students were coming to me to complain that although they liked me, they couldn't do their work with Tammy screaming all the time. When there was a substitute teacher, Tammy was kicked out with office referrals that read, "Called me names—made pig noises—left the room without permission—rude to other kids." On days when I was there, I tried talking to her quietly, and she would say, "Are you finished?" and stare over my shoulder at the wall. Finally her disruptions were so constant that I had to start sending her to the office.

Since Tammy was on a monitoring status, her constant referrals prompted the LD teacher to do a series of observations in our class. I had told this specialist that I thought Tammy had been misplaced in this class, but her stance had been that Tammy's standardized test scores and grades indicated that she needed the special help. After observing her for a few days, she was shocked by her behavior and her abilities. After my many complaints, on these days Tammy was a model student, raising her hand and volunteering to read, and then reading better than many students in a college preparatory course. Tammy's behavior and refusal to cooperate on tests had managed to get her assigned to special classes for years, but my assessment of her had proven to be true. She didn't need a "special" class, at least not for the same academic reasons the other students needed it. The question then was whether it would help or hurt Tammy to change her class. By the end of January, she had become such a constant disruption, I was concerned that she would hold up the progress of all the other students if she wasn't transferred, and I was more concerned with that than I was about the impact of a change on her. In early February, she was moved from my class to a General English class.

The disruptions stopped except for those occasional days when Tammy would pound on our door or yell in to one of the students. The remaining students quickly began to make progress. We began taking trips to bookstores and visiting other classes. Tammy, on the other hand, was missing school constantly. She failed all of her classes. She spent her days hanging out behind the store across from our school. I have asked myself a hundred times what I might have done differently. How could I have avoided that first conflict? How could someone with so much potential become lost so quickly? She had become a reader and a writer, but she had learned to use those words to hurt before someone could hurt her. I had lost the opportunity to share the joy of learning with Tammy, and our class had lost the opportunity of learning from Tammy. In spite of the fact that all of the other students were able to thrive in a safe environment after she left, I never got over the feelings of failure whenever I saw her. Our class had been one more negative place in her already long life.

Yet Another New Beginning

"The river of our perceptions continues to flow, but now, in the sunlight of our awareness, it flows peacefully and we are serene." The words of Hanh (1993), a Vietnamese writer, describe the atmosphere of our days after Tammy, at least most of them. It was as if the students were making up for all the days when we felt we were losing ground. Our room was once again a peaceful place where it was safe to take risks. I could change the direction of the class without fearing a fight. The students could ask questions and not worry about being called stupid. One day in December I had written in my journal, "It was one of those days when I wished I could have given them a quiet place, a blanket, a snack and let them rest. For all their talk of sex, drinking, and fighting, today they just seem vulnerable." I had truly forgotten how much I usually enjoyed my students. In this more peaceful environment, those who had barely spoken all year began to develop as readers, writers, and learners.

One day, during our reading of *The Lottery Rose* (Hunt, 1976), Peter came in before class started and said to me, "Do you know the name of that book that Georgie liked?" When I told him that I didn't but wondered why he wanted to know, he replied, "I just wanted to look at it—it sounds good." Once it began, this kind of book connection seemed to be happening for each of the students on a regular basis. For example, as we continued reading *The Lottery Rose*, Georgie became friends with a retarded boy named Robin, which prompted the following response in Derek's journal:

> I know that these kids are different and slow but there also very loving. My brother is Down Syndrome. This is like retarded but not so severe. My brother is a lot smarter than most kids with his disese because he

talks and counts, sings and whistles and he plays and doesn't go in the road. He is stronger than most kids his age. He loves to go in the barn and help do chores.

In fact, one day in class Jennifer raised her hand while I was reading and asked, "When you read, do you put yourself in the book?" The students responses were now more genuine, and their attitudes toward reading evolving, as they saw a place for themselves within the pages of the books.

As they became more involved, they also began to see themselves as qualified to analyze the writing and question the intentions of the authors they encountered. One day Wayne came in with a long explanation about why he thought Hinton should have written *That Was Then, This Is Now* (1971) before *The Outsiders* (1967). After the author Sanford Phippen came to our class, Trisha wrote about why she thought his writing might have caused family problems.

> I thought that Sandy was very out spoken, he's like me, if there's something on his mind about something or someone, he lets you know about it. I liked him very much. I think alot of the reasons why he acts the way he does is because of the people he grew up with, the way they acted, said their words, dressed and so on. Theres really not much more to say about Sandy Phippen, he's a nice person and when he talks about his family in rude ways, I think maybe he's trying to give them a hint on how he sees them and everybody else around them. And thats his way of showing them, that's how I see it. Now his family won't talk to him because he's put them down.

I have always been surprised when students discuss an author's intentions. Although I had made that common practice for our discussions of books, I could still remember my own adolescent feelings—that an author's words were sacred and the idea that he or she might have chosen some other word, character, or ending seemed profane somehow. Not so with these students. Many had not only become readers, they had become critical readers.

They also started seeing oral reading as a way to give another perspective to the writer's words. Just before we began a new unit, students wanted a day to make up work they had missed, since many had been out with the flu. Initially it was chaotic, and I wondered if this had been such a good idea. Within minutes, however, the students had grouped themselves according to the work they needed to complete. As I went to each group to get them to stop talking, I realized that they were reading out loud to each other. In one group, Trisha was reading a short story they had all missed. In another, students were reading drafts of short stories. A student in the third group was reading the directions for a writing assignment. It was heartening to see reading begin to make so much sense for these students. It was also interesting that they had adopted the practice of oral reading— their most hated middle school activity.

The Spring of Hope

Once students became this involved in their reading, they were less interested in causing problems in class. When I could stop spending all of my time focusing on group problems, I could begin to look at individual literacy problems, whether in terms of motivation or strategies. I filled my monitoring book during that time with notes documenting individual student progress and questioning my practice with various individuals as well as with the group. Late one evening I began to reflect in my writing on the changes I was experiencing. Once again I was beginning to feel the peacefulness that my classroom had represented for me at the end of the previous school year. Parent conferences had just ended and the experience had been unusual: I seldom have any parents for these conferences, but this evening Tori's, Peter's, Dean's, and Mac's parents, as well as Derek's brother, had been in to visit and talk about the progress of these students. After everyone had left, I sat alone in my classroom, thinking about my students.

> Sitting quietly, alone now
> usual computer/human noises gone (for this time)
> Books a jumble—
> Writing wall gleaming in the parking lot light
> Desk amazingly neat (but drawers crammed)
> The room feels special
>   —perhaps all the print
>   —perhaps the reminders of kids
> Time to reflect, take stock
> Hard to remember
> Change does happen—
>   one person at a time.

Although I had started to keep these notes as a way to give substance to the students' progress, they had come to chronicle my own questioning and change process. These changes became the "spring of hope" for each of us.

Observation: Independent Reading (1/27/92)
Tanya is still having a difficult time settling into her reading. In my gut I feel that she can read—she's a nonreader because she won't read—what a difference! I wonder what might make the difference for her? I need to know more about her still . . . that's the problem.

Tori—Once I get Tori together *with* her book and *away* from distractions, she will read. When that happens, she actually seems to enjoy reading and to love writing. In the meantime, though, she is easily taken away from those activities by other students' craziness.

Peter has really become a reader! Last week he asked if we could have extra reading days each week. Certainly music to my ears, but there was an uproar from the other kids. I'm starting to despair that things are ever going to click for these kids. I guess what happens is that change really does take place one person at a time. I need to remember that. Rejoice in the changes; support those who need to change.

Anne—Watching her read today makes me sad. She wants so much to be in College English but she reads so slowly. She does really get into her reading, but I worry that she can't possibly keep up in a College English class. I'm wondering what modifications could be made so that she could be part of that class *and* succeed. One thing is certain—nothing will change in Anne's literacy until she starts reading on her own. She always reads for the entire period, but that's it. She doesn't pick up her book again until the next reading day.

Jennifer—I think Jennifer is finally clicking. Today she has moved a stool to the front of the room and is totally engrossed in her reading. She read an entire book last weekend as she traveled on the bus to basketball games.

My notes told me I needed to work with Tanya to connect reading to her life, to allow Peter more time for independent reading, to find ways to give Tori uninterrupted reading time, to convince Anne to become an active reader, and to support Jennifer in her newly acquired reading habit. During our next literacy exploration time, sat down with Tanya, and together we created a web of ways that she could connect language arts to her three stated interests: boys, sex, and love (see Figure 9-1). This not only

Figure 9-1. Web

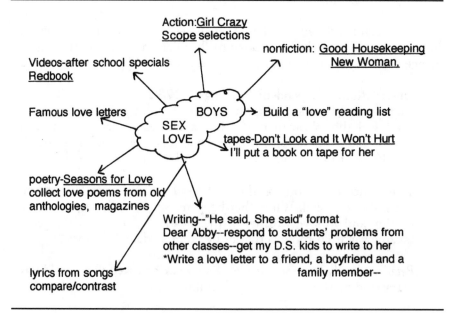

WHO?	DID WHAT?	TO/FOR WHOM?	FOR WHAT REASONS?	OUTCOME?

Figure 9-2. Chart for keeping difficult text straight

helped Tanya see that she could be in control of her learning, it also established the importance of connecting literature to life (see Figure 9-1).

Focusing on individual needs in this way also seemed to make me more responsive to the students' group needs. For example, when most of the students were having difficulty seeing the big picture in Stevenson's *Kidnapped*, I stopped and asked them what *they* thought their problem might be. Although some simply said, "I can't keep everything straight," others were more specific, noting that "they couldn't remember who did what to whom." This gave me an opportunity to think aloud a process I used for keeping complex plots straight.

"You know, everybody reads things that are difficult for them—even me. When I find that I'm getting lost in the plot—the action of the story—I stop and make myself some kind of organizer to keep it all straight (see Figure 9-2). I think you've been able to see what's really not working for you, and maybe together we can figure out a way to keep it all straight. Let's see if this helps."

The simple chart I introduced not only helped them organize their thoughts for this work, it also helped them develop a strategy they could use independently (see Figure 9-2). As with all the graphic organizers we created, I made copies they could use in their academic journals when they chose.

By March, this focus on the individual as well as the group had started to make a difference. My journal notes on 3/11/92 indicate the extent to which everyone had changed during that time.

> The whole atmosphere has now changed. Tanya came in today and said, "I've been doing really good lately. I read to page 64 in *Ransom* (Duncan, 1966)—that's a good book. Do you think I'm better?"

> Derek said, "Can we make making maple syrup have something to do with English?" When I responded positively, we went on. The kids asked to read *Ransom* in spite of my awful voice (cold). Some of the girls (Anne, Terri, Jennifer, and Trisha) decided to read their own novel (*The Face on the Milk Carton*, Cooney, 1990), so I let them go into the English Center to read. They took the tape to record their

sharing at the end. I'm anxious to see/hear how that goes since they have yet to be effective with that in a large group setting.

Tori, Tanya, and the boys did an LEA [language experience activity] at the end so they could put responses in their journals. All participated except Dean. I need to pull him in more. They felt their responses should have characters and setting first. I wrote on the PC viewer exactly what they said. They gathered around the PC viewer and really were actively involved.

Ransom, Lois Duncan
CHARACTERS: The Kidnappers

1. Juan—the person who killed the bus driver.
2. Buck—Rita's boyfriend, nonviolent, friendly sometimes.
3. Rita—Buck's girlfriend, she's ugly, she's just doing this for the money.

The Kidnapped

1. Glenn Kirtland—strong, captain of the football team, handsome, not caring for anybody else, popular in school, he's probably the one who hit the little boy (Miller).
2. Bruce Kirtland—Glenn's younger brother, scared, worried about Jesse, cares about people, little shy, wears glasses.
3. Marianne Paget—(parents Mr. and Mrs. Rod Donovan) talks about her parents' divorce all the time, acts as though her parents were the only ones who ever got a divorce. Doesn't talk with her stepfather very often because he can't get through to her. Doesn't talk to her real father very often because he lives too far away and he doesn't pay attention to her.
4. Dexter—lives with his uncle Mark Crete, very rich, never pays attention to Dexter, away on trips. Maybe Dexter has a disease because he refuses to take his shirt off; could have been beaten.
5. Jesse French—living in Valley Gardens in a rented house. Father is in the military. She doesn't talk very much, keeps to herself. She's the one who gets the key to the storeroom where the boys are locked up.

SETTING: Albuquerque, New Mexico—Valley Gardens, rich neighborhood, cabin in the mountains

My journal notes for the day reflect my ongoing attempt to come to know these fifteen individuals.

It's interesting to note the dynamics of the class when those who are problems are gone. But then, that's the issue, isn't it? We need to figure out how to get kids involved so they are all part of what's happening.

With juniors and seniors in my Directed Study class, there just isn't the hitting, yelling, and commotion that often accompanies grade 9 students. It's almost like their bodies are out of control. They're volatile, emotional, moody, needing affection and time, wanting independence, what a mix! This, added to the literacy problems they experience, is almost insurmountable some days.

Our shared reading of *Ransom* was excellent. Wayne noted that the author "puts extra space after the paragraph when the setting changes from one house to another." Derek pointed out "that Bruce thinks Glenn is a God, but he's really a jerk." This is the first time that I've felt that these kids are really developing their sense of story and actively constructing meaning. I'm reminded of the New Zealand phrase "ten book child" referring to a child entering school with the experience of hearing 10 or fewer books read to him/her. I wonder if that's what's happening here. It seems like all of a sudden books are making sense.

Hope took lots of different forms that spring. There was the day Derek said he wanted to read on his own, not listen to tapes, so that "he could put more feeling into it." There was the day Melvin started following the text during our shared reading of *Of Mice and Men* (Steinbeck, 1937) and asked when we finished, "What book are we reading next?" There was the day that Wayne just scribbled on his paper when we were trying guided imagery, and I in anger ripped it up and then apologized to him and to the class: "No one deserves to have his paper taken away from him—it was his." There was the day Rachel noted that when she was talking, she "didn't know where those words were coming from. I guess I just read all the time, and now those words are mine." Tori wrote a short story that she volunteered to read aloud and Dean wrote a poem. I learned to create assessment tools that looked at process as well as product and allowed for a variety of responses (see Appendix C).

As the students became more involved in literacy activities, our options expanded. We went to bookstores in a neighboring community and students were allowed to choose books for the classroom and for their own personal reading (see Appendix D). They visited another class of students, interviewed them about their reading attitudes using a survey they had constructed, and then wrote to the teacher giving her teaching suggestions based on the results of their survey (see Appendix D). They critiqued the student-written plays read by students in the school's Playwriters' group. They found the courage to leave the classroom to work on their book projects in the art room with the Art II students. Finally, after reading many children's books and discussing reading strategies, they started going to a near by elementary school to read and write with the first graders in a paired literacy experience.

My journal entry on 5/29/92 began, "What an incredible day so far!" That certainly doesn't sound like the same teacher who had lost hope that "these students would ever change." It wasn't. Did they change because my teaching changed or did my teaching change in response to their changes?

I guess we all changed in response to each other: The students had learned to reflect on their learning and my teaching, and I had learned to do the same. One day's journal entry (3/3/92) examined my definition of success:

1. Students want to read.
2. Students like to read.
3. Students do read.
4. The classroom atmosphere has purposeful activity.
5. Students see the room (and me) as a safe place.
6. Students feel confident in setting goals and choosing work.

In addition, I made a list of challenges needing further reflection:

1. Do the kids really know how to learn?
2. Are they strategic?
3. Do I do too much *for* them?
4. Do the kids really feel ownership of their learning? I think most of my Directed Studies students do, but are many of my R/W Workshop students too confused to know how to take a next step?
5. How much time am I directing this learning?
6. How dependent are the students on me?
7. How well do I listen to what they're telling me?
8. How patient am I with really accepting where they are—and who they are?
9. Does my classroom, my teaching, and our learning fit the conditions for learning: immersion, demonstration, approximation, etc.

We were all learners that year, in part because of reflections like this one, and I echoed Tori's journal entry of 6/2/92, "I wish we had more times like this."

When our year together was over, I knew I wouldn't quickly forget the feeling of pride I had when the students asked if they could have a reading day on our last day together. Nor would I forget the tears in Tori's eyes when she walked into the empty room and said, "You've packed away all the magic." I also knew I wouldn't forget Mac's words—or my own tears—when he finally had to return to his special needs class because of his uncontrolled behavior: "You mean I won't be here to read—I'll just do nouns and stuff?" I knew too that I would never get over the sense of failure I felt whenever I heard someone recount Tammy's latest exploits.

When I look back, I see many scenes I would like to relive to make them turn out differently. But I can only take with me the memories of all those students and the lessons they taught me. For each of us, those days will eventually meld together, turning Mrs. Allen and Room 130 into a larger memory that becomes ninth grade, then high school days, and then life.

For me, however, there will always be one student who will never blend in with all the others. Rachel was the constant that gave me my "spring of hope" that year. Each time I felt like giving up, she reminded me of the importance of always being ready to make a difference.

10
"That One Wonder of a Child . . ."

*"Arly," I heared her whisper to my ear, "let me tell you again
. . . you're my morning of life . . . that one wonder of a child
that every teacher dreams of discovering. And there you were,
ready to blossom . . ."*   Robert Newton Peck, *Arly*

I don't think I'll ever forget Rachel's face on that first day of school
two years ago. The others had entered the room in their typically, boisterous, ninth-grade manner, but Rachel walked in quietly and sat in the corner.
Although her long, black hair nearly covered her face, the defeat in her
eyes stopped any casual first-day comments I might have planned. Her entire
body seemed to scream her hopelessness at the prospect of ninety minutes
of English every day for a year. If I had misjudged her body language, her
written reflections about her previous English classes left no doubt in my mind.

English to me is not fun. Homework every night. Once or three times
is OK, but every night. Come on. You first get in the door and they

137

would slap you with worksheets, writing. Then if you didn't finish, bring it home, plus home work. Monday we would get voc. Not bad. Then we are saposed to memorise them. Not trying to be cocky, but why did we write them down in the first place so we won't forget. 30 words on that. And on Friday a test. Thursday, a pretest. It's OK but it lost my interest. Hopefully it will change.

Rachel had encountered little joy in her previous literacy experiences. She had been selected for Reading and Writing Workshop based on her grades in reading and English (Cs and Ds) and her low standardized test scores (Nelson-Denny grade equivalent 5.3, Mane Educational Assessment [MEA] Reading 24 percentile, and MEA Writing 21 percentile). As always, it was difficult to ascertain Rachel's background from these numbers. I knew her self-report data would tell me much more.

According to Rachel, she was not read to as a child. Although her parents had certainly cared for her, leaving the city to move to rural Maine so that she would not grow up as a "weird child," literacy activities had not been a part of her childhood experience. This lack of early literacy experiences caused Rachel to feel behind the others from the beginning of her school years.

When I first started kindergarten all I can remember is that I was always fighting with people. I kept falling further and further behind and after a while I was really discouraged. It was like I was a year behind what I was supposed to be or something. So, I had to stay back a year.

Interestingly enough, however, although Rachel was not doing well in school, her standardized test scores did not indicate that she "was behind everyone else." Her Science Research Associates (SRA) comprehension scores for grades 1 to 3 were as follows: grade 1, 85 percentile; grade 2, 86 percentile; and grade 3, 74 percentile. Her reading scores continued to drop slightly after that, but they were never consistent with Rachel's own perception that "all through my school years, my spelling and English and Reading, that whole situation wasn't very good for me. I wasn't the best student in school!"

Rachel had become convinced that she couldn't read or write very well in spite of standardized test scores that seemed to indicate otherwise. Her grade 4 (MEA) reading score was in the 66 percentile, and her writing score was in the 91 percentile. Yet Rachel continued to remain in the "low reading group," where she could never finish her work and was forced to read aloud.

One teacher who was like that for me was my 4th grade teacher. Up to that point, school was just school. I mean I would try to do the work. In all my memories, she's the one I remember holding on to and hoping—I mean I always wanted to read, I wanted to write, I wanted to be good and everything. But, then we would read out loud and I wanted to be able to, but I couldn't. There was a restraint holding me back.

It was apparent to me that classroom practice, coupled with the lack of literacy activities at home, was a large factor in reinforcing Rachel's negative image of herself as a reader and writer.

> They [her parents] would buy me books and stuff, but you know I never really took interest in it [reading]. I never saw reading as exciting. Like instead of reading, I'd go out and play. That's why my grades have always been low and my spelling isn't good. When I was in grade school and they would have us read out loud, I would stumble on the words. I didn't finish a certain story (the stories were *rather* boring) and I felt like I had no reading or spelling skills and I just lost interest. I hated to read a book. I thought, "What's so interesting about books?"

Rachel's middle school years continued to elicit the same question, "What's so interesting about books?" In fact, not only did she find the books "not interesting," but she was now required to get up in front of the class to talk about them.

> We'd read silently a lot. Like I'd be halfway through the story and the rest of the kids were done and that's where I got messed up on most of my reading work, because I didn't know the whole story so I only got half the questions right. They gave us reading assignments, things like you have so long to read this book and then you have a report on it. They gave us this thick book (somebody rated it a good book, you know) and she gave us three weeks to read it and I didn't get too far. I couldn't finish the book and I felt pretty bad about it. I think that giving a time limit on reading was really bad for me because it takes me a while to read a book but I get through it.

Rachel's silent reading and her oral reading were both problematic for her. In addition, she reported that she was very seldom read to in her elementary years. When she finally did encounter a read aloud in middle school, the book chosen only reinforced her conclusion that books just weren't "very interesting."

> I remember we read *Tom Sawyer* (1962) or something like that and we would have to follow along and I would never follow along because I didn't think it was exciting. I guess maybe it was the book; I was really confused with *Tom Sawyer*. I guess it just didn't catch my interest.

My puzzlement continued as I began to see Rachel's responses to my questions and read samples of her writing. From her responses to a sentence completion that all students did during the first week, I learned that she was not one of those students who had no goals; rather, she simply did not see herself as a reader and a writer. In fact, she regarded it as a distinct possibility that her lack of ability in reading and writing might get in the way of achieving her goals: "I want to go to an oceanography college, but I wish someone would help me understand things better. I often worry about what will happen to me. I'd read more if I could." When I read her completed fall survey, I was struck by the incongruity of her responses. She reported that she saw herself as a below-average reader, yet she said her favorite book had been *Pet Sematary* (King, 1983). Many above-average adolescent readers would have difficulty following King's text, yet Rachel reported that this book was special because of the "intense feeling, the feeling of wonder and the fear." Those words did not seem to fit with someone who saw herself as a below-average reader and writer. When responding to questions about previous reading/English classes, Rachel found fault with the fact that there was "no exsitment, no chills or thrills, to boring for books and the teachers were too stiff." She felt the classes could have been better if the "teachers did not act surperer—be somewhat like the students." Although her spelling was definitely unconventional, her ideas and expressions were as puzzling to me as the class checklist of activities she said she would enjoy doing. Of the fifteen items, the only ones she didn't check were reading orally, listening to cassettes, doing vocabulary, and writing. In response to the question about reading she would like to explore, she indicated plays, fiction, poetry, magazines and historical fiction. These responses didn't seem in keeping with someone who hated English. At least, they didn't until I read more of her journal and spent time interviewing her.

Rachel told me that in the past, she had seen "books as evil." Her memories of days in low reading groups, never having time to finish her reading, and being forced to read orally had told her that she was not a reader and could not read very well. As I listened to her recount those days, it did not surprise me that she considered books and reading evil. Instinctively, I knew that if I were going to help her become a reader and a writer, I needed to show her that reading and writing were enjoyable and then give her the time and the support to experience that joy for herself. As I had learned, if reading is not accessible for students, it is difficult for them to see the value in books. Likewise, students who do not see books as a resource lose many of their options as searchers and researchers. Whatever had been done with Rachel in the past hadn't worked. I needed to rebuild her belief that she could and would learn to read.

A New Beginning

In those days together, some students in the class who were attentive while others stared off into space. Rachel, on the other hand, seemed mesmerized when I said that everyone in the room would indeed become a reader and a writer. I explained that it was my belief that doing worksheets and workbooks would probably never make them better, but I knew what would—reading and writing—and we were going to do that every day! My words received mixed reactions, but Rachel was visibly affected by those words. Perhaps her interest came from the note of authority in my voice, or perhaps it was hearing for the first time that she could become a reader by reading. As I handed each student a copy of a text, I said, "The name of this book is *The Lottery Rose* (Hunt, 1976), and the author's name is right here—Irene Hunt. Let's take a couple of minutes and let each person make some predictions about the book based on this cover. What's a prediction? Can anyone in here help us figure out what that word might mean?"

I also gave each student two journals early in the year: an academic journal in which they could record their actions and reactions in class and a personal journal in which we could carry on a dialogue in order to know each other better.

"How many pages do we have to write?"

"How long does each one have to be?"

"Do we have to do this every day?"

When I said, "Why don't we just start with today and see how it goes," most seemed relieved. The thought of filling both of those notebooks was overwhelming to some, but Rachel immediately became involved in her writing.

"Can we write anything in our personal journals?"

"Anything you choose."

"Who reads it?"

"I do. You'll leave it here in my desk drawer so that I'm the only one who will read it."

As I look back, I think Rachel became a writer that day. When she finished and handed me her journal, she said, "I hope you can read this. I can't spell very well." Her entry began:

Today it is wet and gray. it would make a sad person bluer than blue. But not me. I feel very happy today. And I don't know why.

Rachel filled a page with details about a new boyfriend, her desire to look and dance like Janet Jackson, and joining the school's Flag and Drill Team. I wrote back to her:

Rachel,
Today's weather certainly is as yucky as yesterday and it doesn't make me smile! I was interested to read your journal because last night at home I thought, "Rachel seemed happy today." I really hope to get to know you better through this journal. Since you're not a troublemaker, I seem to have less time for you—that's unfair to both of us!

How is school for you? Have you joined any clubs? How are your classes? Where did you meet your boyfriend? Hope you are having another good day today. Mrs. Allen

Rachel began taking her journal home so she could write more, and that affected her writing in class. Her first responses to independent reading indicated to me her lack of writing background as well as personal involve-ment with the text.

> 17 of Aug
> I read *Degrassi JR High-Exit Stage Left* (Pasnak, 1987). I started on page16, where I left off, and got to page 35. What basickly happened is that everyone but L.D. is nervous abut the auditions. LD thinks her father is going to die.

As I continued reading *The Lottery Rose* (Hunt, 1976) aloud, however, I could see that Rachel was becoming more and more a part of the book. Unfortunately, I missed the next couple weeks of school because I was hospitalized. When I returned, Rachel seemed to have withdrawn again. In a later interview I found that my reading of her body language was accurate.

> When I first came here I was alone in the class. I didn't talk to anybody or anything. But when the substitute was here, I felt bad for her because Raymond and all the guys in the class would give her a hard time. I kind of got attached to her and then she left. Mrs. Allen came back and I was sitting there near Tracy and she said, "Rachel, you're so quiet." It took me by surprise because I had kind of gone back inside myself. I read my book and when she asked who did homework and I told her, the excitement just filled her face. It was like WOW and it was a strange feeling because I hadn't wanted to be there.

By the time I had finished reading *The Lottery Rose* aloud, Rachel's somewhat lifeless responses yielded to the wonder that accompanies the reading of a good book.

> I was so angry with you today when you stopped reading. I just didn't want that book to end. As you read, I could feel Georgie's hand clutching that rosebush. My heart was beating fast and my mind was racing—trying to figure out what Georgie wuld do, but also trying to figure out what I would do. I could feel a lump in my throat—a lump that wouldn't go away—at least not until I (whoops, Georgie) made his decision.

Neither Rachel nor I had to wonder any longer whether she was now engaged with reading. She needed no worksheets, no oral book reports. She had become a reader in those moments when she first learned that she could put herself inside the book. Her response to *Teacher's Pet* told me that she had indeed learned how to do that.

> "Teacher's Pet" is an outstanding book. The book kept me on the edge. Just when I figured it out, it would change. I wished I was in Kate's place. I found it so interesting. A handsom man in love with her. A mystery behind every corner. The suspense was wild. The adventures that Kate went through is what I always wished for. Love, horror, fun,

running from someone, Putting little puzzle pieces together. I really enjoyed the book.

I felt as if I had been given the gift of watching this young woman turn into the person she had only dreamed she might be. Rachel reminded me of Haroun in Rushdie's *Haroun and the Sea of Stories* when he is told by Iff, "A person may choose what he cannot see" (1990, p. 63). As I watched her rapid improvement in and out of class, I often wondered what was causing it. Then I realized that she was finally getting what she needed in order to develop fluency: time, support, and resources. Rachel had finally found her way to a classroom where reading and writing were valued, where many resources were available to support reading and writing, and where she had time to practice her newly discovered talents. Rachel had even read a whole book.

> I like reading now. I never thought I would, but it's better now. After reading *The Lottery Rose*, I realized I liked to read. I thought it was pretty neat. Most books I read, you know like the ones they always give you in school that are *great literature* like *Tom Sawyer*, were boring. The books you give us to read, they're more what I can deal with—abuse or drugs—something like we have to deal with today. I liked when you were reading the book out loud and you'd be reading and we'd stop and I'd want you to read more. I'd be dying for the next day to come so you would read. When we wouldn't have reading periods, I would just sit there and stare at the books and think, "I want to read some more." Since I've been in high school in your classes, maybe it's the book or something, but I've paid right attention to them.

In spite of the success she was enjoying, I knew it was important that she continue to change and that I needed to support her as she took those next learning steps, so she could begin taking risks without feeling she was losing what she had gained. When Rachel chose her first book, she didn't make a very satisfying choice. The book wasn't interesting, but she didn't quite know how to get out of it. When I saw that her reading was slowing down, I talked with her about the book. "It's just not very interesting, but I should finish it." I told her that I started books all the time and then picked new ones if I wasn't interested, and she seemed shocked. I told her that good readers know when a book isn't right for them and choose a new one. "Well, I guess I'm starting to be a good reader then." With great relief she abandoned the book and chose *Island of the Blue Dolphins* (O'Dell, 1960).

Supporting Rachel also meant finding ways to get her to contribute in class and even to read aloud without feeling self-conscious. So many of her feelings of failure were tied to those early oral reading requirements, and I knew she would eventually have to read out loud in order to feel really successful. I decided to start that process by asking her to communicate in writing with someone besides me. When John and I both read *The Snowman* (Stine, 1991) just after Rachel had read it, I asked her to respond to his writing.

Dear John and Mrs. Allen,
When I read this book, I couldn't stop. I wasn't even half done, but
I told myself that I would only read 2 or 3 chapters. That book was
so good, I read the whole thing. You both are in for a good surprise.
Enjoy.

Another successful communication activity was inviting Rachel to
begin using the tape recorder to record her thoughts about books. Then,
she and another student, who had just finished the same book, took the
tape recorder and went off to discuss the book together. The shy Rachel
was gone: "Today is April 9, 1991, and Raymond and myself are going to
talk about *Taming the Star Runner* [Hinton, 1988]. Raymond, do you know
what your favorite part was?"

After a few successes with reading, Rachel started taking risks with
her writing. She often read poetry during her free time and began writing
her own. She wrote a short story with a lead that would have gripped the
most reluctant reader: "I could feel the excruciating pain penetrate through
my mind as my head hit the wall and I plummeted to the floor." The strong
female characters she found in *Island of the Blue Dolphins* (O'Dell, 1960)
and Greek mythology prompted her satirical essay, "Boys are better than
girls in every way." Rachel's reading had helped her find her writing voice.
She explained why in a self-evaluation she did at the end of the year:

> My thoughts run deeper than before. It seems to me that the more I
> know, the more I think. And the more I think, the more good ideas
> I come up with. And the more ideas I come up with, the better my
> writing is. One way to put things is like this. All, well most, of my
> skills come from reading. To have one, you have to have the other.
> No matter what. I think that my skills will show up in my writing and
> my talking. It does now. It can only get better. I hope that my spelling
> gets better too. To me, my skills are all related. They will improve as
> I improve.

Making Up for Lost Time

Stanovich's research (1986) has shown us that students who are behind
their peers need an enriched program if they are ever going to catch up. If
they continue to receive the same fare as the others, they will never be able
to make up for the time and experience that have been lost. As Rachel
said, "When I think about how I feel about reading now and not reading
as a child, I feel cheated. I really was cheated." With this in mind, I tried
to make sure that Rachel, and the others in the class, were part of a larger
literacy picture. We went to plays, visited museums, and saw a mime
perform. We watched videos, created artistic masterpieces, and did computer explorations. We read and wrote and then we read and wrote some
more. I read to them, they read to each other, and they read independently
several times a week. And, underlying it all was talk. We talked about our

books and we talked about life. We told jokes and we told ghost stories. We conducted interviews, and we talked with authors. I often repeated a Wendell Berry line, "Life is large and surprising and mysterious, and we don't know what we need to know" (1988, p. 75). For Rachel this was the first time, at least in an English class, that life had been "large and surprising and mysterious." Her classes in the past had been very predictable, but now she never knew what to expect. She embraced the change with a vigor and a tenacity that I had seldom seen in my twenty years of teaching.

After many weeks of planning, two of my colleagues in the English Department and I had found the funds to take the Honors English I, Honors English III, and Reading/Writing Workshop students to Portland to see a play. Students had worked together studying the artists who would be displayed at the museum, the Italian play we would see, and areas of interest they could choose to visit. As the day for our trip approached, Rachel became more and more excited. On the morning we were to leave, the students were milling around, anxious not only about the trip but also about being with those "Honors kids." As I walked down the hall to make sure everything was set, I met Rachel. She had no luggage and looked as though she had been crying. When I asked her what was going on, she said, "I can't go. I didn't bring any stuff." The principal was there, and I asked him to go out and hold the bus while we got this straightened out. It took several minutes for me to pry out of Rachel that her mother thought she shouldn't go because she didn't have any nice clothes to wear. I said to her, "If we get you clothes in Portland, do you want to go?" The look on her face answered my question. A call to her mother to tell her our plans, a stop in the classroom to get books because Rachel couldn't go "without something to read," and we were on the bus. Our schedule was messed up, and the students were unsettled after having to wait, but we were on our way. When I read Rachel's journal following our trip, it gave me a glimpse of the impact of that experience on her life. It also told me what a crime it would have been to have left her behind.

> I was overwhelmed by what I saw on our trip to Portland. Our first stop in Augusta was the State House. There, we were somewhat exposed to what went on there. In classes you learn how the state is run, but it is nothing like being there. The museum by the State House. I was so enthused by the explicit details. I almost protested when we were leaving. That place was magnificent. You can read about Maine's history, see the pictures, but there is no substitute for what I and many others have experienced. After leaving the museum, we went to the Blaine House, the governor's home, which is also like a museum. There was a lot of remodeling. Most of it went back to what it was first like when the house was given away by a sea captain. He was so fascinated by orentil artafacts, that he mostly had his home set up in such a manner.
>
> We departed for Portland and went to our hotel and the Maine Mall. Boy, you could get lost there. The following day we went to the Performing Arts Center in Portland. Mirandolina was the name of the

play. The actors portrayed their parts very well. Mirandolina's father had just died and she was left to tend the inn. She missed used her fine beauty and soft voice. Men would come to the inn just to see her, shower her with gifts, kind words and love. Her fathers last wish was that Mirandolina marry her servant. A man came to the inn, not to see this love goddess, but to rest . . .

Rachel's entire language and thinking processes seemed to be changing. As I sat alone reading her writing, it was hard for me to imagine the withdrawn, defeated young woman who had entered my class in the fall. I could still see the look of pleasure on her face when she was the only student in our combined Honors and Reading/Writing Workshop group to recognize the sculpture of Medusa. When the museum curator asked her if she could tell the others about this myth, Rachel launched into the story without hesitation. Her dreaded oral book reports belonged to another lifetime and another person. On the bus ride to and from Portland, the other chaperones were in awe listening to our conversation.

"What's a *toll booth*? Where does the word come from?"

"Wait until after we go through it and tell me where you think it might come from."

"How much further to Portland?"

"It will take about another hour and a half. Have you ever heard the term 'delayed gratification?'"

"I know what delayed means. What's gratification?"

As the other students stared out the windows listening to music on their tape players, Rachel was noticing everything, commenting on the things she recognized, and asking questions about the unfamiliar. She was like a sponge, not only with her questions on this trip, but also with her reading.

She was reading everything she could as if making up for lost time. One day as I recorded notes about each student in my monitoring book, I noted that Rachel looked as if she were in another time and place. When I asked her to evaluate the class and her role within it, one of her comments corroborated my observations: "The only problem with this class is the end. The bell rings and I sit there kind of stunned, hating to bring myself back to this time, this place, and the rest of school." From *Island of the Blue Dolphins* (O'Dell, 1960) to *Of Mice and Men* (Steinbeck, 1937), Rachel became part of them all. With each new book, her vision of herself as a reader and a writer changed:

I wish I was there, full of courage and all. She reminds me of me, in a sense. Brave, independent, courageous, not afraid. It made me think about this—that I can make it on my own . . . I really liked *Of Mice and Men*. You made it so alive. I could see Lenny, George and everyone. My favorite part was when Lenny cracked Curly's hand. He had it coming to him. Curly's wife—Boy what a tart. She deserved what she got. She should have let Lenny alone. She did all the trouble. I mean the dream. That dream was the key to happiness and freedom for three, old, lonely men. I wish that they wouldn't have been so mean to Crooks. When she threatened (Curly's wife) him and called him a nigger, I wanted to slap her face off. Gee, I liked the way George killed Lenny. I wished he didn't have to but he did. Lenny left a happy man. Right before he did that, when they were talking, I think George told Lenny, in a sense, that he loved him.

Shortly after reading these two books, Rachel wrote this poem:

"Free"
> free . . .
> If I was a bird
in the sky, that's where I'd be.
Far from the words that hurt me.
Up where no one could bring me down
I could soar in the clouds
> and never be found.
But, when I open my eyes,
I'm back to all the worries
> and the lies.
> Why? I ask
won't people let me be.
> > > Why . . .
Why can't I be
> free?

Although Rachel never complained, I often had the feeling that she felt as though she no longer fit anywhere. She would comment that her friends teased her because she was reading all the time, and when she asked them if they knew what certain words meant, they would make fun of her. On the other hand, she didn't "fit" with the students in the college preparatory classes. After years of being in "low groups" and spending her time doing worksheets and workbooks, Rachel did not have the verbal skills to contribute in their discussions, or at least, she didn't believe she did. Rachel's personal history was also a stumbling block for her. As loving and supportive as her parents were, her socioeconomic status was lower than most of the students in the more advanced classes. In our school, those lines could often be very clearly drawn, and Rachel found herself on the "wrong" side.

In spite of all this, Rachel never complained and continued to be an avid reader, a habit that extended far beyond the classroom. She started taking books home and spending her study hall time in my classroom completing her assignments for other classes, reading, working on the computer, and writing. Instead of sitting quietly in her hopelessness as she did at the beginning of the year, she ran into the room each day twirling and laughing. "There are so many books to read and I've got to make up for all the years I missed," she said one day, handing me a folded note as she left. (See Figure 10-1.)

Wait! Wait!
Please wait for me. I can catch up.
Just give me a chance.

No! No!
Don't leave me behind. Please . . .
I want to be like the others.
I'm no different. Please . . .
Don't make me different.

I don't want to be left behind.
All I want to do
is read.
Please . . .
Help me!

Dear Mrs. Allen,
This is, or was, my silent prayer to the reading teachers before you.
Without telling you, *you* did wait, *you* did give me a chance, *you* did
help me. What you gave me, there is no way I can pay you back or
tell you how much I thank you. You gave me the gift of reading.
Reading is not just a gift, it's a power within itself. I owe you my life
and my mind. You've opened so many doors for me. May God bless
you.

Love, Rachel

For Rachel, reading had taken on a life of its own; it had indeed become a
"power" in her life. Whether reading mythology or a love story, poetry or
Romeo and Juliet, she had left rural Maine for the places she had chosen
long before she was able to see them.

Shortly after this, however, Rachel's mood began to change. Still
pleasant and hard-working, she seemed to have lost her vision of herself as
independent and capable of changing her life. All too soon I understood why.

Dear Mrs. Allen,
I'm sorry I can't tell you this in person. I haven't told many people,
but I had to tell you. Over the past months I've come very close to
you. I owe you everything. You are one of the people who made me
want to do something with myself. Well, I hope you won't think any
less of me. I'm going to have a baby. I'm finishing this year, a month
of next year and then six weeks of tutoring. I'm sorry I let you down.
With the greatest respect, Rachel

Rachel had just started to see herself as someone who could go on to college
and lead an independent life, in spite of the fact that no one in her family
had ever finished high school, and now she was confronted with a problem
that was making her see all of those hopes go down the drain. I have always

believed that life and literacy were too finely connected to be treated as separate entities; Rachel was reinforcing that belief.

Helping Rachel see that she could continue to make the same strides in her literacy and still make her dreams come true was not easy. For one thing, even I lost hope for a few days. Rachel's morning sickness had caused her to be absent for the first time all year, and I wondered if she would get so discouraged that she would follow the path of least resistance and quit. I was more disillusioned than I should have been because it seemed that, no matter what I tried to do as a teacher, her background and her frame of experience constantly pulled her back from the changes she was trying to make. Then I remembered one important difference. Now Rachel could read. She saw herself as a learner and knew the importance of learning. She had dreamed her dreams and she would not easily forget them. Just as I had supported her as a reader, I now needed to support her in hanging on, at least until she could start climbing again.

As our year together came to an end, we talked and decided that she should stay in my class for another year. I knew she was capable of going on to college preparatory English, but she didn't want to begin that program while she was pregnant and needing to miss school. We decided that she would come into my Directed Studies in English class for one period so that she would be with a heterogeneous group of students, and also come back into my Reading and Writing Workshop for one period. In addition, she would take a Publications class that was comprised of all Honors and College students. Although she thought the class and the clique would be difficult for her, I knew that it was important that she see herself as capable of working with that group and being a part of it.

Rachel had added another layer of meaning to the origin of the word *remedial*, "to heal again." She believed she needed the time in my classroom to heal again, both literally and figuratively, before she moved on to other challenges. I agreed. Life itself had been challenging enough for one year. Rachel had received the coveted Gold Cat Card for making the honor roll, a first in her life, independently read seventeen books, become a writer, established goals for her life, and signed up for her first college preparatory class. She needed time and a place to continue the transformation she had begun, a place that made her feel successful and safe. An Argus poster on our wall displaying a quote by William Shedd seemed to chide us: "A ship in harbour is safe, but that is not what ships are built for." Both Rachel and I knew that she couldn't stay in this safe harbor forever, but we also knew it wouldn't serve any purpose to send her out to sea in the middle of a storm.

Beginning Again, Again

That's how Rachel became part of my Reading and Writing Workshop again in the 1991–92 school year, the year I decided to do a research study in my classroom. When Rachel completed her fall survey this time, she put reading at the top of her list of favorite subjects. Equally as telling was the question mark she put under the question asking for least favorite subjects. She now saw reading and writing as extremely important in her life and herself as an average reader and writer. In response to my question about what I could do to help her become a better reader, she responded, "Let me read." Rachel might have decided that she had limited her options with her pregnancy, but she knew that now she was reading for two people, which made it even more important to her.

Rachel's world, however, had become immeasurably more complicated than it should have been. Her pregnancy made her feel uncomfortable, both physically and socially. At this point reading really had become an escape for her. "I find I want to read more and make my mind expand with the world by reading. I know that I will never leave my home to go on trips to India or other places like that, but I can read about them and I can really feel like I'm there." Rachel's mother suggested night school as an alternative for her, but Rachel didn't want to leave my classes or her new Publications class. I knew that if we were going to keep her in school, we needed to remind her of the options that were here for her. She needed to see that her dreams were still achievable. Fortunately, several things occurred during that fall to make Rachel believe in herself again.

First, she got her driver's license. That seemed to validate for her that she had taken a step toward becoming the independent woman she dreamed of being. Then she read a book I recommended, *The Longest Weekend* (Arundel, 1969). This story of a young woman who had a baby and decided to raise the child alone had a great impact on Rachel. She broke up with the baby's father because she knew she "would have all I can do to pull myself and my baby up in life. He doesn't have an education and won't get a job. I want more than that for my baby, and me." She started visiting the theater as we rehearsed *The Crucible* (Miller, 1955) and fell in love with the idea of being on stage. When I asked her why she had never tried out for a play before, her words broke my heart. "I thought I could never be in a play because I couldn't read. But, now that I can read, I can do anything." The language of the play began appearing in Rachel's writing. As she told me about a new romantic attraction, she admitted that she "thought softly of him" but "only the two of us hold the story."

One of Rachel's poems was published in our school literary magazine, and she joined a group of students who critiqued plays written by the Playwriters' group. To add to these interests, an exchange student from Poland joined our class. Speaking limited English, she often turned to Rachel for help, and Rachel gladly accommodated. Rachel found herself in the role of teacher, and that was addicting. They read out loud to each other, looked at magazines, and talked about cultures. Rachel had found someone who had traveled to the places she had only imagined, and the Polish student had found someone who was patient enough to help her learn English. A friendship was born. At the end of the first semester, Rachel's journal read: "You won't believe it! I made high honors!" She had continued to read and write, to expand her world knowledge, to survive her pregnancy and childbirth, and to make high honors for the first time in her life. Once again it felt that even Rachel believed she could be a success.

As she evaluated herself at the end of the year, we were both somewhat overwhelmed by the changes we had experienced in our two years together.

> I find now that I'm a more daring reader. I'm not afraid to read and I'm not afraid to read aloud. My reading itself is much better. I'm reading more often and I'm reading thick books. Most of all, when I'm reading, I'm lost from reality and I find myself in a jungle or fighting the evil dark side of the Force or in the arms of Hans Solo. Whether running from a killer or feeling the fangs of a vampire sinking into my warm and milky flesh, I really do envy my books. I get angry at myself for being real.
>
> My thinking has changed a great deal by my reading. When I read before, I liked a book or I didn't. Usually I didn't. But, that was it. There would be no emotion. I couldn't get inside the people in the book. I couldn't feel the book. I think my reading has improved a lot. I was reading out loud to Jonathan [her baby] and I was reading smoothly only stumbling once or twice and that was mostly on names that I never saw before. And if it wasn't, I could basically figure what was trying to be said. I might not know what the word exactly means, but I can figure out what the sentence means. By this, my vocabulary has grown. When I talk now, I can express myself better than speaking like a fifth grader would.

Rachel had become a reader: She read for enjoyment and information. She had developed strategies that allowed her to attempt new and increasingly difficult texts on her own. Rachel had become a writer: She wrote short stories, essays, and poetry. She wrote letters and critiques. In fact, she even wrote in her journal minutes after she came out of the labor room. Rachel had become a searcher and a learner. She knew how to find answers to her questions and how to get help with her problems. She knew how to celebrate her successes and determine her next learning steps. As part of her final exam for our Reading and Writing Workshop, she wrote the following poem to describe her growth as a reader:

> I never liked to read when I was small
> I would rather play with my Barbie doll
> Ride a bike or play Frozen Tag
> To me, reading was nothing but a drag.
> Then one day, she opened the door,
> And there were my Barbie dolls and so much more
> I walked inside to take a quick look
> I never expected that I would get hooked
> I would find myself in a meadow sometimes
> Or sitting in a beautiful garden listening to windchimes.
> Reading has done a lot for me

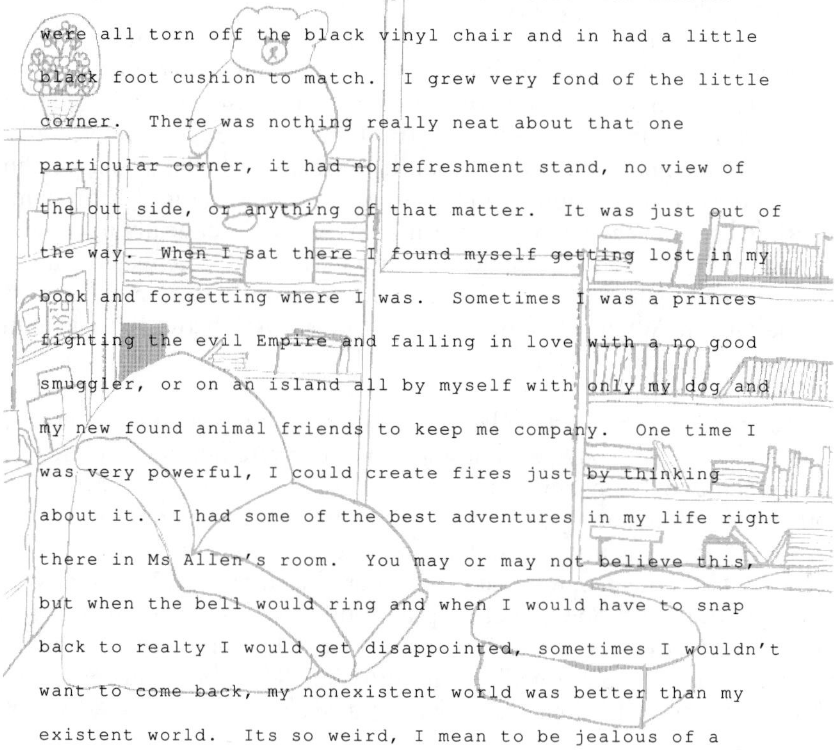

My Interpretation of the Corner

In the corner of the room is where I sat my sophomore and most of my junior year, well till I had a hard time getting out of the chair ha ha. The chair was well broke in the when you sat in it you were almost sitting on the floor, but it was still very comfortable. To sit in the chair you had to be talented, if you sat in it the wrong way you would slide off the chair and end up on the floor. The buttons were all torn off the black vinyl chair and in had a little black foot cushion to match. I grew very fond of the little corner. There was nothing really neat about that one particular corner, it had no refreshment stand, no view of the out side, or anything of that matter. It was just out of the way. When I sat there I found myself getting lost in my book and forgetting where I was. Sometimes I was a princes fighting the evil Empire and falling in love with a no good smuggler, or on an island all by myself with only my dog and my new found animal friends to keep me company. One time I was very powerful, I could create fires just by thinking about it. I had some of the best adventures in my life right there in Ms Allen's room. You may or may not believe this, but when the bell would ring and when I would have to snap back to realty I would get disappointed, sometimes I wouldn't want to come back, my nonexistent world was better than my existent world. Its so weird, I mean to be jealous of a person in a book. I had a lot of good and bad times in that corner. So that corner had a lot of my memories and I would guess the memories of others as well. I guess that is way I drew a picture of that corner, the meaning and the memories that it held for me. Now when I would look at where most of my day dreams began, it is all gone, there is no old warn chair and no little black stool to go with it, just another corner of empty dreams.

Figure 10-1. Rachel's Interpretation of "Corner"

Expanding my mind and setting it free.
I no longer want to play out in the sand
All I need to do is settle down with a book in my hand.
My book will take me to wherever I want to be
Dear Mrs. Allen,
this is the best gift you could have given to me.

Rachel truly was for me "that one wonder of a child that every teacher dreams of finding."

11

Living a Meaningful Life

I decided, early in my journey, to attempt to listen very carefully to children and, whenever possible, to let their voices and their judgments and their longings find a place within this book.
Jonathan Kozol, *Savage Inequalities*

As I packed to leave my high school teaching job, I was overwhelmed by the jumble of mementos I couldn't bear to throw away. Packing often came to a halt as a painted rock, a folded note, or a dried flower reminded me of a person and a time I knew I would always want to remember. This book has been built around many of the stories connected to those gifts. Sometimes the gifts were left on my desk or in my mailbox, to be newly discovered on a day when I particularly needed to know that I was living a useful life. Writing about them now has made me relive that year, those students, and the gifts they gave me. In doing that, I have once again struggled with the meaning beneath the surface of our time together.

Meaning is such a subjective term that it is almost always difficult to define. Meaning to whom, for whom, under what conditions, and in what context are questions I keep before me as I analyze anything. Therefore, to ask myself what a year as complex as this meant unsettles me. But that's good. We never really learn anything without experiencing unsettled thoughts. If that is true, I no longer have to wonder why this year of almost constant disequilibrium was the most significant learning experience in my life.

This was not a study with significant numbers of subjects: sixteen teachers and learners and one classroom. It was, however, a study of significant events in the lives of those teachers and learners. Nehring (1992) says that "one voice has been noticeably absent from the chorus of school-reform literature: students. We hear from scholars and policy makers, task forces and think tanks, sometimes even teachers. But what about kids?" (p. 129). In contrast, this is a study of voices—the students and mine. My claims in this book have been their claims.

As I read through the transcripts of the tapes and videos, as I looked again at the samples of students' writing and sorted through hundreds of photographs, I heard those voices again and again. The more I tried to take a somewhat scholarly approach and put our year into the larger picture of educational research, the more the voices brought me back to its personal significance. For the first time, I really knew that I wasn't searching for significance in statistical terms; rather, I was discovering significance in the dictionary terms of important, notable, and meaningful.

In the first chapter, I used the term, "epiphanies of the ordinary" (Meek, 1991) to describe those seemingly insignificant events that lead to unexpected "ah-ha's." There were so many of these powerful events during the year, I wondered how I could choose one over the rest. As I struggled with this notion I thought, "Surely everything wasn't equally enlightening?" And then one evening, while sitting in a movie theater, my question received at least the beginning of an answer.

Anthony Hopkins, playing the English writer and university don C. S. Lewis in *Shadowlands* (1993), was questioning one of his students, and the young man said, "We read to know that we're not alone." It struck me that when all the curriculum guides, writing assignments, state mandates, and school rules are taken away, it is those students who discover the power and joy in reading who take something lasting away from our time together. I smoothed out my butter-stained napkin and jotted down the words to save for my reflection and writing.

Once again, I began looking at and listening to students' voices. This time, however, I did it through the "reading to know we're not alone" lens. Sure enough, their words showed me many ways in which reading had changed their perceptions of themselves and their lives.

Reading Supports a Changing Role for Students

Johnston and Winograd (1985) argue that "many of the problems evidenced by poor readers stem from, or are compounded by, the fact that they are passive, helpless participants in what is fundamentally an interactive process—reading" (p. 279). It is this very passivity, at least in terms of academics, that I have found often characterizes students in special programs or resource classes. They wait for work. They wait for something to happen. They wait to get out of school. As passive nonreaders, they wait for reading to happen to them, not knowing that reading doesn't work that way.

Students in this class were certainly products of a society and an educational system that had helped them see the reading failure as theirs. Jennifer's words echoed in my head, "I learned all the sounds and it still didn't make sense to me." In spite of their attempts to participate in the acquisition of reading skills, they were essentially nonreaders. Jennifer and the other students in the class often referred to this failure as *their* problem.

Most were quick to say that it wasn't the fault of the teachers. "I guess I've always been what you'd call a slow learner. It wasn't anybody's fault, I guess, that's just the way I am."

These students had fallen into the trap Johnston and Winograd describe as a sure way to produce passive failure: "The most debilitatingly effective way to produce passive failure is to have the learner attribute failure to ability, an attribution which is global, internal, uncontrollable, stable, and long-term" (p. 284). As an antidote they suggest that we "treat passive failure as a state rather than a trait" (p. 290). When I began the year by saying that everyone in the room would become readers and writers and that I knew what we all had to do to achieve that goal, I had in essence given students control over this temporary state. I had shown them a glimmer at the end of the tunnel of failure they had experienced.

Previously, these students had no reason to be motivated. Weiner (1979) cites his claim that "in our culture two sources of motivation are most dominant: achievement and social recognition" (p. 21). These students could not tell me of any times they had felt successful or received social recognition for their academic achievements. In fact, for years they had been characterized, and characterized themselves, as "failures, slow learners, learning disabled, special ed, remedial and resource." These characterizations, and their accompanying traits, had edged these students into a state that Seligman (1975) terms "learned helplessness." They had entered my classroom last August expecting nothing.

Challenging students to set goals for themselves as individuals and as a class, to evaluate and describe our progress in meeting those goals, to see mistakes as a necessary step in the process of learning, to understand that they were the critical element in their own learning and changing, and to see that they were indeed capable of change, drew students away from that passive role. In every case, they progressed significantly when they began to see the locus of control as within themselves and not in standardized test scores, textbooks, curriculum guides, or PET recommendations. They internalized the messages of honest praise I gave them so that eventually they could give themselves that same encouragement.

Butkowsky and Willows (1980) conclude that "by modifying what poor readers say to themselves about their performance, we may potentially effect increases in their motivation, persistence, and expectancies of success in reading" (p. 421). My constant belief in students' abilities and my praise of their accomplishments gave them the scaffold they needed to internalize the messages they gave to themselves.

> **Derek:** Whenever we'd read just a little bit, she'd always praise us for reading. Boy, that was so great. I mean even if you'd only read two or three pages. And then you'd want to impress her. It makes you feel good when somebody is telling you how good you are. She was always so positive.
>
> **Stan:** You knew she wanted you to learn so you felt like you'd please her if you learned—if you read—because she put so much effort into trying to help us.

Anne: She always compliments us.
Derek: We've done a lot of the work but it's just so much easier when you have a teacher—I mean she'll go 99 percent of the way if you'll go the other 1 percent. I mean if you're just there . . .
Rachel: If you just try . . .

In spite of almost insurmountable years of "failure," these students were capable of changing their expectations, their roles, and their achievements. This made me wonder how many other students in our general or college preparatory tracts, who have not experienced such severe failure or have perhaps learned to play school more effectively, are also playing passive roles—waiting for work, for learning, for life to happen to them. They are perhaps less noticeable but in my mind no less at-risk in the broad sense of the term than the students represented in this study.

My students learned that when we wait for someone else to motivate us or challenge us, we always run the risk of being bored or frustrated. Conversely, when they began to see learning as their right and their responsibility, when they understood where to go and how to ask for answers, and when they had strategies to support their next steps, they become independent learners. Derek's words indicated to me that he had become not only an active reader but also an active learner:

> You learn from asking questions—no question is a stupid question. You've got to ask questions if you're not learning. You've got to get out and talk. You've got to say, "Hey, wait a minute. I don't understand what we're doing here. You're going too fast. Just because he understands that don't mean that I understand." You've got to tell them.

In our classroom, one of the clearest examples of carryover from a changing role in reading to a changing role as a learner was the enthusiasm with which students accepted my invitation to become coresearchers in understanding what helps or hinders someone from becoming a lifelong reader. In their roles as researchers, students interviewed other students in our class and developed a series of survey questions based on the information they obtained in those interviews. They then went into another English class and interviewed students there. On the basis of that research, they made recommendations to the English teacher about her classroom practice and the resources she needed to support her students' learning (see Appendix D).

Within the context of this research project, students took on many active roles. They had to interview, write, discuss, collaborate, revise, edit, interview again, analyze data, and report their information. During that process, they began to examine their own literacy and the impact of the learning environment upon that literacy. The results of their research, a group letter to the teacher, conveys a newly found voice for these students (see Figure 11-1). Positive feelings, increased literacy, and new roles within a school community were all results of this class research project.

Mrs. Piper   April 17, 1992

_____

_____

RE: Reading Research

Dear Mrs. Piper:

We have finished analyzing the reading interviews which we did with your students. Based on those interviews, we came to the following conclusions:

1. The majority of your students don't read very often.
2. The majority of your students prefer realistic fiction and mystery/suspense.
3. There is a large variety of books which your students like to read.
4. Most of your students think they can read good. The students who don't think they can read well give the following reasons for thinking that:
      a. They don't read much and
      b. They stumble too much.
5. Most of your students remember being read to as a child.
6. Most of your students read their books became they want to. Examples of those favorite books are:
      a. Nine Mile Bridge   h. The Lottery Rose
      b. Ace Hits the Big Time   i. Christine
      c. Stir Crazy   j. Murphy's Gold
      d. Babysitter   k. Master of the Game
      e. Weekend   l. Island of the Blue
      f. Grapes of Wrath   Dolphins
      g. The Accident   m. Waldo
8. Most of your students have favorite authors. Examples of their favorite authors are Wycoff, King, R. L. Stine, Hemingway, Paulsen, Sheldon and O'Dell.
9. In the past, most of your students have had Mrs. Allen who would read to them.
10. Most of your students think Mrs. Allen is the best reader they know.
11. Your students think that if you read a lot, you can become a better reader.
12. Most of your students would like to be better readers.

Figure 11-1. Letter to Mrs. Piper

Reading to Know We're Not Alone

Reading gave many students the impetus to become more active readers, writers, and learners. It also gave them hope that there were others who had experienced problems similar to theirs. Their books, in a sense, became their mentors. The need for mentors is not a new concept. In early Greece, we find Odysseus leaving behind in Ithaca his wise old friend Mentor as a counselor for his wife and a tutor for his son: "Mentor, friend and comrade of the excellent Odysseus, to whom Odysseus had entrusted his whole house when he sailed away; they were to obey the old man, and he was to keep all safe" (Homer, trans. Rouse, 1937, p. 27). In a society where many traditional mentors—grandparents, parents, trusted family friends and rela-

13. Most of your students think that women are better readers than men.
14. Your class was equally divided between students who prefer long stories and students who prefer short stories.
15. Most of your students like to read magazines.
16. Most of your students like comedy movies best.
17. When students were asked to give a comment about reading that hadn't been asked, their comments were:
    a. Reading should be an activity for everybody.
    b. Reading gives me something to do when bored.
    c. Reading is very important in life.
    d. I never started reading on my own until I was in Mrs. Allen's room.
    e. I like to read so I can become smarter like Mrs. Piper.
    f. I don't like to read.

Based on our research, we can make the following recommendations for you as you teach this English class:

a. Your students will read if they are given a variety of books and time to read them. You should give them books and time.
b. Your students believe that reading is important and they want to become better readers so you should give them a chance to do that.
c. You should have a variety of books, magazines and authors in your calssroom.
d. Realistic fiction and mystery/suspense are two favorite types of reading so you should have lots of those books in your room.
e. Since most of your students think women are better readers than men, you should help the men become better readers.
f. Since most of your students enjoy being read to, you should continue to do that.

Sincerely,

Mrs. Allen's students

Figure 11-1. Letter to Mrs. Piper (*continued*)

tives—have been lost for many children, where do these troubled young people find the wise person who is friend and tutor, who makes them feel safe?

Brendtro, Brokenleg, and Van Bockern use the terms "alienated and troubled to emphasize what it feels like to be alone and in conflict" (1990, p. 2). Many of my students had indeed been alienated by a society that had become too busy or too confused to mentor its children into adulthood. Quality time with adults who care for them is a precious—and rare—commodity for our children. My students, like many others, suffered because of it.

Many of the "troubled" students in my Reading and Writing Workshop and in my other two classes certainly fit this category. They not only lacked the supportive family I'd had as a child, they also lacked the "second family" I had acquired through my books. They couldn't or didn't read and therefore often turned to direct experiences that were unsafe to find answers to their questions or to feel less alone. Their stories are testimony to my belief that reading can help each of us feel less alone and less alienated as we make our life transitions. Their stories demonstrate the significant life we lead when we connect children and books—books that help them know they are never alone.

Books as Mentors Who Share Our Secrets

The class was quiet and all the students had found comfortable reading places in the room on the day Kendra came in and handed me a reading response in a sealed envelope. I gave her a puzzled look and she replied, "You'll understand when you read the response. Don't read it now." Kendra had spent the last two days reading *Visions* (Gallo, 1987) and I wondered what there could have been in that adolescent short story collection that would prompt a response in a sealed envelope. As requested, I put her letter in my "To Read" basket. Alone later that afternoon, I once again picked up the envelope and settled down to read her response.

The Good Girls, Fran Arrick

I had a hard time understanding where this story was leading to. I understood that this might have been an abusive story and a sexual abuse story.

I know that it was hard growing up with this secret. I kept my secret for twelve years. I just thought it was a game that we use to play over and over again. It all starts out by wrestling around. I didn't realize what was happening to me until I was in the six grade, and I did a project on Sexual Child Abuse. That's where I learned all about it. As I was getting my sources and reading more about it, I would say to myself, "that sounds as if I wrote the story myself." I didn't dare to tell anyone, because at that time I was twelve years old, and I thought that NO one would really believe me. And at that time my father was very ill and to bring up something of this nature was quite unreal.

So last year my secret slipped out. My mother was shocked to hear it, and didn't at first believe me, until I started telling her some of the incidents and how I never wanted to be left alone again with him. Then things started to turn around, and we sat down and talked about it. She asked, "Why didn't you tell me sooner?" It really was a rotten time to tell her then, since my father has only been gone for five months.

I know this story is real and it doesn't hurt for me to talk about it, because it is real and can happen to anyone, and I would want to help anyone else who has gone through this.

Fran Arrick's story, in which a teenage dance instructor helps a young girl who is being sexually abused talk about her pain, had given Kendra the courage to share her story with me. Sadly, Kendra's secret life was not unique in my classroom, nor is it unique in any classroom in this country. Krueger (1993) cites statistics reporting that 27 percent of girls and 16 percent of boys are sexually abused before they are eighteen years of age. In fact, during that same year, three other students shared similar stories after reading

Chinese Handcuffs (Crutcher, 1991); *Abby, My Love* (Irwin, 1985); and *Secrets Not Meant to Be Kept* (Miklowitz, 1989). In every case, students talked about the relief they felt when they read someone else's story that "was just like mine." In all four of these students' lives, these books had been the mentors who told them that it was okay to be honest and that there were others who had experienced similar pain and yet survived to lead valuable lives.

Books Help Us Explore Our Life Questions

Charlotte Huck says that, "Literature has the power to take us out of ourselves and return us to ourselves, a changed self" (1987, p. 69). As students responded to their reading, it was evident that many of the books were helping them find information, develop opinions, and explore diverse options in terms of the questions they had about life. Sometimes the line between information and opinion blurred, but in every case there was evidence of a "changed self" in their thinking and writing.

Questions about love, sex, and relationships are almost always critical to teenagers, and my students were no exception. As they read, thought, and wrote about the various relationships they were experiencing vicariously, they began to articulate their own beliefs about the puzzling events in their own and others' relationships. Jane's initial reading of Blume's *Forever* (1975) was connected to her interest in famous banned books. (I did wonder if she left the reading with more than information about book banning!)

> I did like this book, even though it had too much sex in it and really went into detail. I guess it made me want to continue reading the book. It kept me on the edge of my seat. I really haven't read a book like this one, but I do wish to continue to find another one like it. I thought, "I can see why this book was banned!"

Lee's reading of a historical fiction series (Sunfire, Scholastic) in which the main character is a young woman struggling to establish her identify, find love, and deal with the period in which the book was set, caused her to think about her own notion of marriage:

> Sabrina was caught between a war and two men. She had no idea her life was going to change so drastically.
>
> *Sabrina* (Ransom, 1989)

> Renee is determined to make something of her life. She was *not* going to be one of those women who would become a teacher or get married and take care of her husband for the rest of her life. Well, she did want a husband, but not unless he understood what she wanted out of life.
>
> *Renee* (Schurfranz, 1989)

Nathan's response after reading *The Truth About Alex* (Snyder, 1987) showed his current thinking about the topic of homosexuality:

> The way I look at homosexual relationships is this. I personally don't believe that members of the same sex should love each other or have sexual feelings for each other. I think the main reason I feel this way is because I live in northern Maine. And the gay population is not very dense up here. So basically I'm just not used to it. I understand other peoples point of views too.
>
> I firmly believe that if God wanted people to be gay then he would have put more than one man one woman on the earth to begin all of the creating process with, instead he would have put 3 or 4 men and women on the earth at the same time and say, "Take your pick."
>
> That theory is of course if you believe in God. Which I do.

Nathan's thinking could probably still use some further reading, which would cause him even more uneasiness, but allowing any room for "others point of views" was a quantum leap from where this young man was before he read this novel.

It is a popular misconception that teenagers are only interested in love and sex. It may be all many of them talk about, but actually I found that students shared the same range of interests my adult friends discussed. For example, I was pleasantly surprised to find that many students still chose to read Richard Bach's *Jonathan Livingston Seagull* (1970). I was also pleased to see that it still had the impact it first had for me when I read the book in the early seventies. For Graham, it affected not only his thinking about life, but also his seeing himself as a possible writer:

> Jonathan Livingston Seagull, a story I have now finished, was an uplifting book. This book kind of explained to me how it is getting by in the world if your not like everybody else.
>
> As I think to write this response I find my self saying that if there was a new book, a book to follow this one, one could call it Jonathan Livingston Seagull, the teacher. In this follow up one could progress further and expand on the ideas that are already here. I might tell the battels of teaching and maybe have a part about a kid that tries to be one of the outcast but ends up going back to its group. Or it might lead up to the separation of the groups in a war or hate like in Germany or a country that divides itself because of different ideas and then finaly having it reunite.
>
> Reading this book, I enjoyed it and thought that only if my parents could read this and see it the same way I do. Oh, well, a day will come when I won't need anybody to pass judgment on me for what I think and do.

Jane found that the Bach books she read had a similarly profound impact on her thinking and she, like Graham, connected Bach's writing to her own writing. Although her reading of *Illusions* (1977) and *Jonathan*

Livingston Seagull (1970) happened somewhat by chance, I believe that Jane will keep the words and images with her for a long time.

> Although this book [Illusions] is old and is not on the bestseller list anymore, I decided to read a book that would give a whole new outlook on life. Well, really it didn't happen that way. I had actually taken the book from inhouse detention by mistake, and found it some time ago mixed up with a bunch of books that can be found all over my room. I showed it to my mom who in turn told me the writer was a good one and that she had read a previous novel of his back in the sixties—Jonathan Livingston Seagull. I read the book. At first I was bitterly confused, what kind of book is this, and how did he think up this topic, were questions that ran through my head. After, I felt like a new person. Like I was living up to my infamous poem that you have, and had really learned from the book. About life and how we take it. There should be more writers like Richard Bach. He is almost like a Messiah, and I am forever his follower.

When Brenda read this book, her religious background helped her make many connections between Jonathan and Jesus. She saw the "Son of the Great Seagull" as having the kind of impact on his world that Jesus had with his disciples and followers. In addition to the critical reading connection, she also had a personal response to the text that reflected an impact similar to both Nathan's and Jane's.

> Jonathan Livingston Seagull made me take a closer look at my life and see that I needed to learn to try to fly in different ways. I also began to feel guilty for not living my life to the fullest. I began to see that I have a lot of wasted time. I could be learning new things with this extra time. I could be applying myself more in school. (Please don't hold your breath for that to happen.) I even liked the pictures. I've learned a lot about human nature, and a lot about myself, from a seagull.

From Stephen King to Charles Dickens, from Nikki Giovanni to Emily Dickinson, my students explored their questions through reading. They actively pursued books whose characters lived lives very different from yet very similar to their own. They read books that confirmed and validated beliefs they had already established. They read about the mysterious: unicorns, the occult, the Black Hole, and Vietnam. They read about loss: dying, broken homes, and shattered lives. They read about contemporary social issues: AIDS, drugs, kidnapping, homelessness, and aging. Eventually, my students realized that whatever they were reading, they were reading about themselves. John Donne's familiar "no man is an island, entire of itself" became a reality for my students as they saw themselves and their lives reflected over and over again in the books they read.

As students became connected to the larger world, they began to feel more control over their own world. They began to finish their books with the belief that they could make the world better, and many believed that one place to start that process was by reexamining their roles as readers and writers and how our English curriculum could best support those roles.

Books Give Voice to Making Schools Different

As I read with my students during this year, it did not surprise me that so many young adult books were set in high schools and had teachers as main characters. School and teachers take up much of students' time and energy, sometimes in unproductive ways. My students read a wide variety of school/teacher-related books that year: *Killing Mr. Griffin* (Duncan, 1978); *Winning* (Brancato, 1988); *Chinese Handcuffs* (Crutcher, 1991); *Arly* (Peck, 1989); *The Pigman* (Zindel, 1968); *The Effect of Gamma Rays on Main-in-the-Moon Marigolds* (Zindel, 1970); *Nothing but the Truth* (Avi, 1991); *Jemmy* (Hassler, 1980); and all of the Torey Hayden and Mary MacCracken books about children with special needs. These books helped them talk about the ways in which schools and teachers could have been different for the children in those books. This naturally led to their finding public voices to express the ways English classrooms could be different for students at our school.

> If a teacher is boring, then the class is boring.   —Ray

> If I had my way on how I wanted the English classes, I would have 3 years of regular English classes and senior year a direct study class so that the kids that didn't get any reading in those first three years, they would have to read in their last year to get an understanding of reading a book.   —April

> When a teacher tells students a big writing assignment is due on Monday, most students make up their minds right there not to do it. If English teachers would look back at when they were in school and remember what it was like to be told what to do and if you didn't do it you failed, they would probably be a lot easier on students.   —Phil

> Sometimes a teacher can hinder a student's love for literature with too much forced reading.   —Amber

> If a teacher wants his/her students to become writers, helping them to read will benefit the students immensely. When a person reads, they will constantly be expanding their vocabulary. By hearing the words used in context, they tend to remember them and use them in everyday conversation.   —Chris

> A good English class is when you can come to the class and know you don't have to work your brains out on nouns, pronouns, adjectives and verbs. That rots to high heaven. I like to come into class, sit down, and read a book.   —James

People don't realize how boring a reading-writing class can be when you have a teacher that lets the other kids read out loud. Sometimes you can't hear them and other times they read so fast you can't understand a word they're saying. Also, teachers don't take the time necessary for kids to do things. They don't spend enough time individually with their kids.   —John

I know why Dewey [*I Never Loved Your Mind* (Zindel, 1970)] dropped out of school. He dropped out because he did not suffer from scholasticism of the brain.   —David

What would make kids readers? A lot more reading and a hell of a lot less writing! If you could just go to class without the teacher telling you what to do, just let you read. There is never enough time to read, always doing other work.   —Raymond

These students, like their counterparts in the books they read, felt compelled to speak out in their writing about how learning could have been more effective for them. They came to see the power of words to influence others and wanted to use their words to change one aspect of their world they thought needed changing. They had found the "incredible thing" that Ralph Fletcher describes in *What a Writer Needs*: "What an incredible thing, to be able to affect adults and children, total strangers, people in other countries, with nothing but words, words forged out of your own experience, your own heart, your own imagination!" (1993, p. 12). My students spoke for the characters in their books who couldn't or wouldn't speak; they spoke for students in our school who hadn't yet found their voices and those who would listen.

Books Help Us Go On With Our Lives

The year was over, yet I didn't want the students' voices to become silent with the closing of school in June. Listening to those voices had made me keenly aware that many of the answers to our educational questions have been sitting quietly, or perhaps yelling loudly, in classrooms all over America. We haven't needed outside experts to give us the answers. Perhaps we have been looking in the wrong place. Traditionally, we have looked outside our classrooms, but the answers have been inside our classrooms just waiting for someone to ask the questions.

I recently heard a principal of a large inner-city high school talk about the changes they had made at their school. The audience was overwhelmed by the statistics of success, and one questioner finally gave voice to what many were thinking: "How can we do that here?" For me, her response said it all, "You start where we all start—you start where you are and roll up your sleeves and get in there and work" (Beck, 1993, personal communication). Illiteracy and aliteracy did not happen overnight, and this year of teaching certainly taught me that any positive changes will take time, energy, and resources committed to change.

Part of my belief is tied to what Fullan calls the "moral purpose" of education: "The moral purpose is to make a difference in the lives of students regardless of background" (1993, p. 4). I have come to believe that we can continue to change curriculum and add new resources, but until we have teachers who believe that *all* their students can ask purposeful questions, communicate through reading and writing, and lead meaningful lives, we will have no systemic changes in the lives of many of our students. I recently heard Clinton Bunke, (1993) say, "We have had all kinds of paradigm shifts, but we don't have the mind shifts to go with them." We definitely need a "mind shift" when it comes to having high expectations for *all* our students.

As I read Jennifer's neatly word-processed letter, I saw anew what happens when we really believe that *all* children can and will read and write.

Mrs. Allen,
Hi how are you? I begin with a THANKS for being there for me when I needed you the most. (even though this could have happened to me a long time ago) I owe you so much! I feel like a different person. Not one of the dumb kids in the low classes.

I can't believe that your leaving. After you brought me up three grade levels in reading. What am I going to do next year when I don't have you to fall back on. I will be lost. I am so *Glad* I took this class this year even though I thought I didn't need it at the beginning. I was really *embarrassed* to let anyone know how low I was. Do you realize that was past tense. Now at least I don't have to say that. I know that I have improved, thanks to you!!!!!!!!!!!!

I will always remember the teacher who taught me to read and be proud of who I am not the class I am in. I would like to make this up to you but I just don't know how. You mean the world to me because you changed my life by making me realize I was smart and not to let anyone tell me different.

Not only me but through the years you have taught people like me but they just don't always appreciate the things you do for us. Well you can say that I do! I love you from the bottom of my heart and I wish you the best in the years to come.

Sincerely,
Jennifer

Before I left, I wanted to find a book that would help students go on with their lives in the positive ways they had already begun. Derek said he would continue reading because he knew that "she will always be proud of me." For others, I feared my leaving might affect their newly established confidence. In my search for a book that would make a difference, I was reminded of some of the books I had read in the past few years that made a difference in my life. There had been many. Mary MacCracken's *Turnabout Children* (1987) pushed me to return to graduate school. Kate Chopin's,

"The Story of an Hour" (1991), helped me look at my protected life. Ralph Fletcher's *Walking Trees* (1991) helped me see the significance of writing. Gloria Houston's *My Great Aunt Arizona* (1992) confirmed my belief that we give children a gift when we connect them to books. Although I see the basic truth in Ralph Fletcher's comment that "our classrooms are filled with students desperate for adults who care about writing and books as much as they do" (1993, p. 10), my students needed someone who cared about writing and books *more* than they did. They had already spent too much time with teachers who cared *as much* as they did. My students needed to know that as a reader and a writer I turn to books, pens, and computers when I'm searching for ways to heal pain, to solve problems, to find answers to questions, and to give voice to my desire to make schools and classrooms better.

I could tell from Jennifer's letter that for those who tied their success in school to my physical presence, it was going to be a difficult separation. Rachel, like Jennifer, had made incredible changes in her life and her literacy in our two years together, and I knew that leaving her was not going to easy for either one of us. As I tried to think which book might help the Jennifers and Rachels, I remembered the impact of *Lovey* on students who had read it when I left for graduate school. I handed Rachel my tattered copy of *Lovey* (MacCracken, 1976) with the words, "Maybe this will help."

Tears filled my eyes as I saw her curled up in her favorite reading chair finishing the book. She felt my glance, looked up and smiled, and then left for the computer room.

> I read 'Lovey' and I understand what the message is. I will miss you very much. It didn't hit me right away but I know what the book was saying. I can't use you as a leaning pole and I can't have the feeling that I need you to be there for me all the time, like I have been. It was wrong for me to be selfish when there are others out there that are in need of the gift you have given me. I call it a gift because that is what it is. And I am the luckiest person in the world to have this gift. To think that there are other people out there that know nothing of this gift, it makes me sad. And, I believe that is why you were here when I came. It wasn't luck that put us together, someone planned it to be that way. Then once I'm on the right path, you are sent out to find others that are in trouble. And if you think that you are not doing your job, think about this. You, not somebody's reading books or worksheets, but you made a difference in a person's life, my life. You helped give me a better life. Just as things were falling down on me, you gave me the confidence I needed. Now because of you, I have a chance in life to be somebody, not just anybody, but someone special and I can pass that gift on to my son.

Although I was leaving, I didn't need to worry about my students. I didn't need to wonder where they would find the wise person who could be the friend and tutor, the one who would make them feel safe. That person was there for all of them in the thousands of books lining the walls of classrooms, libraries, and bookstores.

Although I have written about just one teacher's experience in one school in rural Maine, I know it was a significant year. I don't think I'll ever forget the message in Rachel's words: "Now that I can read, I can do anything." Her words remind me of *Parade Magazine* editor Walter Anderson's (1994) words:

> I could open a book, and I could be anything. I could be anywhere. I could be anyone. My friends, I read myself out of poverty long before I worked myself out of poverty.

There were not many material things I could give my students, but if I helped even one to acquire the tools to read him/herself out of poverty, my days had been well-spent.

In *Dead Poet's Society* (Schulman, 1989), Mr. Keating says to his students: "Life is a powerful play that goes on and you may contribute a verse. What will your verse be?" This year of teaching, researching, and learning with these students was my verse. When we connect books and children we live meaningful lives and we show children how they can live meaningful lives. It is never too late to make those connections. With each memory of a positive reading experience, we give the generative gift that lasts for lifetimes. We give them friends, wisdom, answers, and hope. We give them mentors—mentors who will be there long after we are gone.

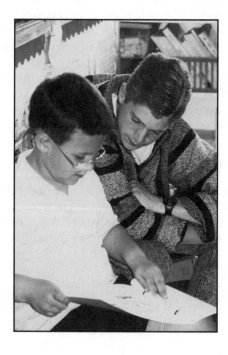

Appendix A: Research Methodology

Although I taught four classes each day, for my research I chose to focus on the students in the Reading and Writing Workshop. My study was designed to investigate the impact of a whole language literacy program in a secondary remedial reading class. Assuming the dual role of teacher and researcher, I would collect data for an entire school year in order to see changes over time. I had no doubt that at times these roles would be impossible to keep separate. I also had no doubt that being a researcher would make me a better teacher and being a teacher would make me a better researcher. While I was struggling with the issue of objectivity in my dual role, Eisner (1991) put the issue into perspective for me: "Ontological objectivity cannot, in principle, provide what we hope for and procedural objectivity proves less than we think" (p. 43). Accepting this, I chose to build on the benefits that subjectivity, and thus familiarity, provided in the hope that the dual teacher-research role would help me discover the needs of my learners. I liked how Hubbard and Power (1993) characterize a teacher-researcher: "an artist at work."

Research Site

My study took place at a high school located in northern Maine. The school district, comprising five elementary schools, two middle schools, and a high school (grades 9–12) is located in a rural area where the economy is largely dependent on agriculture, forestry, and agribusiness. This dependence on agriculture has created a rather unusual school calendar: school begins in mid-August, stops in mid-September to allow students to work in the potato harvest, and resumes in early October. In 1991, the district's School and Community Committee cited the occupations of the students' parents as 5 percent military, 34 percent professional, 36 percent skilled workers, 5 percent farmers, 11 percent self-employed, and 9 percent unemployed. Only 26 percent reported completing college with 9 percent having advanced degrees (1992 School Accreditation Report). Unlike many schools across the nation, the enrollment at this school has been declining since the 1970s. Since that time the student population has decreased from 1,300 or more to 730 in 1991. In spite of the declining enrollment and failing economy, the district has maintained high academic standards for the students. Students who have not experienced academic success in their K–8 years are a priority for administrators and many staff members at the high school. Given that priority, programs that focus on innovative approaches for improving the attitudes and knowledge bases of these students are encouraged and supported, both financially and professionally.

Gaining Access

Since the population chosen for this new class and for the research met the broad definition of "at risk," the proposal for both the class and the research was met with enthusiastic support. Letters outlining the rationale for the research were sent to the superintendent of schools and the principal. Both the superintendent and principal met with me to discuss the research and granted approval for me to conduct the study.

The parents of the students enrolled in the class were notified in writing that I was conducting this research and invited to come in to discuss the program and their child's participation in it. Parents were told that classroom procedures would follow the standard methodology any teacher would employ in teaching a secondary reading class and that the research would only document what occurred in the class. The research was also discussed with the students, who were given permission letters so that samples of their writing, taped interviews, and photographs could be included in the book. All parents and students agreed to allow those artifacts to be collected and used for any professional purposes.

Theoretical Base

The theoretical base for the methodology of the class was designed to establish a literacy program that was not based on the diagnosis of deficiencies. Johnston and Allington (1991) and Stanovich (1986) have characterized this kind of instruction as overemphasizing decontextualized skills; providing little time in real reading events; allowing only small amounts of teacher-student interaction other than monitoring; lacking in opportunities for learner independence; producing little improvement in either reading attitude or competency; and thus resulting in an ever-widening gap between low progress and high progress readers. The class was based on several key ideas. I believed that students would learn if a classroom environment could be established in keeping with Cambourne's (1988) conditions for learning: immersion, demonstration, engagement, approximation, use, response, and feedback (p. 33). In terms of classroom context, these conditions for learning require several necessary elements within a classroom. The first, and I believe most important, area for all students is immersion. Students must be surrounded by texts of all kinds. This would happen in a variety of ways: read alouds, shared reading, language experience, guided reading, independent reading and writing, and a print-rich environment. Demonstrations would occur as students participated in developing a knowledge of how texts are constructed by using their own and other published writing. Demonstration and immersion are only effective if students are engaged with the literature and the task, and this engagement can only occur if students see that texts are accessible to them and that they are capable of creating their own meaning and texts within the context of a relatively risk-free environment. With at-risk students, it is initially difficult to build the trust necessary for them to engage in literacy activities. For most of these students, literacy has been an area filled with failure—failure they would not willingly experience again. In order to support this engagement, I knew I had to find ways to make literacy rewarding.

Making literacy events meaningful and rewarding would begin with my high expectations that everyone in the class would become readers and writers. Given that these students did not perceive themselves to be readers and writers, I would have to have high enough expectations to carry them until they could set these standards for themselves. I do believe that students can learn to have high expectations, even when they have not experienced them in the past, if supportive systems are in place. In my class, those supports would involve giving students the responsibility of making decisions for themselves about their own learning. Sharing this responsibility—and then providing multiple opportunities for them to achieve success—moves the locus of control for their lives away from others and within themselves. The key to this shared decision making would lie in allowing students multiple opportunities to hear and use language and learning in situations where they could be successful. If their approximations of language use could occur in ways that allowed me to reward their "mistakes" as valuable tools for learning and their questions as more important than answers, they would feel free to take ever-increasing risks. Given my commitment to those strategies, my response to students' attempts needed to be nonthreatening, honest, personal, and timely. In part, I anticipated that it would be necessary for students to move through an initial stage of dependence in order to take on a role so different from their experience, one that would require them to be questioners, decision makers, monitors, collaborators, teachers, and learners.

Context of the Class

Since 1971 some form of reading instruction had been offered at our high school, in addition to the tracked English classes, for students reading below grade level. This program had diminished from one that served one hundred and fifty students each year to one that served approximately forty students. (This was due in part to the increased options available to students and the changes in methodology that reduced the number of students in the class.) Although some students elected to take the class in addition to their other English classes, many were required to take it because of low test scores. This took the place of an elective and, in most cases, did little to turn students into lifelong readers. Except for reading day, students completed *Reader's Digest* stories with questions from the teacher's guide, read the newspaper, and completed the workbooks that accompanied a Jamestown testing program. In fact, by December of the 1990–1991 school year, students enrolled in these reading classes—designed to "improve their attitude toward and skill in reading" (1990 Curriculum) had yet to read a single novel either individually or together.

In February 1991, in anticipation of this study, I requested permission to teach one section of this class. In addition, I received permission to have the fifteen students enrolled in Basic English I who would also be required to take Efficiency Reading scheduled for my class of Efficiency Reading. Students' schedules were done manually to ensure that all students would be assigned to both classes, giving us a total of ninety minutes. The principal and I decided to change the name of the class at that time to help alleviate the stigma of the term Basic English and also to differentiate this class from the remaining section of reading. Thus, the Reading and Writing Workshop was offered to students for the first time in 1991–92. The student handbook listing programs of study described the course as follows: "This two-period course is required of ninth-grade students who are reading and writing significantly below grade level and recommended by the English Department Chairperson. Students will be involved in a literature-based program designed to improve reading, writing, and thinking skills. Enrichment activities include field trips, arts activities, computer explorations, and independent learning programs."

Selection of the Participants

Students were selected for participation in the program based on several indicators that categorized them as at-risk in terms of literacy. An initial screening of all eighth-grade students in March 1991 indicated that thirty-two had test scores so low they would be potential candidates for the class. Those students' test scores and grades in middle school English and Reading classes were used as initial indicators to place them in a reading class, either Efficiency Reading or Reading and Writing Workshop. A team of people met to decide which class placement might best meet the needs of each individual student: the Director of Special Education, the teachers for students with Learning Disabilities and Behavioral Disturbances from both middle schools, the middle school English and Reading teachers, and the English Department Chairperson, who would be the teacher and researcher in this study. Since class size was limited to fifteen students, the group decided not to enroll those students who would receive additional services from other sources as already prescribed within the Pupil Evaluation Team (PET) process (for example, Special Education or Learning Disabilities). These meetings produced the names of the fifteen students who would be recommended for the program pending the approval of their parents. All parents approved the committee recommendation except one, a district middle school principal who did not want his daughter enrolled in the class. He was told that she would either have to be enrolled in this class or take General English and Efficiency Reading because her test scores and grades indicated that she would not be able to succeed in the College English program. Neither he, nor his daughter, agreed with the placement recommendations, but in the end he chose to place her in the class, at least temporarily. Prior to the beginning of the class in the fall of 1991, another student was taken from his home and placed in the state's detention facility;

therefore, there were only fourteen students enrolled when the study began in the fall of 1991. Although statistical analyses were not used to document the progress of students within the program, the following ranges of test scores were represented by the students chosen for the program: Maine Educational Assessment (MEA) Total Reading range 5–24 percentile; Science Research Associates (SRA) Total Reading range 13–74 percentile; and Differential Aptitude Test (DAT) Verbal range 10–75 percentile. Variations in test scores aside, all students displayed many behaviors typical of those at-risk in literacy: disliking reading and writing, not seeing themselves as "good" at reading and writing, lacking in knowledge of what makes a good reader and writer, lacking independence in literacy, low self-esteem, and a previous history of little or no success in reading/English classes.

Research Methodology

In choosing a research methodology, I discovered Patton's (1990) discussion of when applied research is appropriate: "The purpose of applied research and evaluation is to inform action, enhance decision making, and apply knowledge to solve human and societal problems" (p. 12). Given that the purpose of my research was to implement an alternative literacy program for students who had previously experienced academic failure in literacy classes, a qualitative design fit the purpose of the study because "qualitative methods permit the evaluator to study selected issues in depth and detail" (Patton, 1990, p. 13). Illustrating this point further, Eisner (1991) posits that "teaching is a form of qualitative inquiry . . . a form of qualitative inquiry that is called educational connoisseurship" (p. 6). Since the research design should be based on one's questions and the best methodology for finding the answers to those questions, it was important to make clear my broad questions at the beginning. It was also important to remember Lincoln and Guba's (1985) statement: "design in the naturalistic sense . . . means planning for certain broad contingencies without, however, indicating exactly what will be done in relation to each" (p. 226).

Goals and Questions

In his discussion of the importance of design flexibility, Patton (1990) makes clear that "qualitative inquiry designs cannot be completely specified in advance of fieldwork . . . the 'design' will specify an initial focus, plans for observations and interviews, and primary questions to be explored . . . A qualitative design unfolds as fieldwork unfolds" (p. 61). In keeping with that framework, I chose to pose broad questions, what Eisner (1991) calls "the intentional dimension," which he explains as the "aims or goals that are explicitly advocated and publicly announced as well as those that are actually employed in the classroom" (p. 73). These goals and questions were formed to frame my data collection and analysis in order to "produc[e] educational knowledge" (Hoffke, 1989, p. 27).

Theoretical Concerns

1. Can an instructional model based on whole language philosophy be developed at the secondary level?
2. Will an instructional model based on whole language philosophy help improve the attitudes toward reading for readers who have negative attitudes?
3. What new meanings does the role of teacher take on in a classroom model based on a whole language philosophy?
4. Will an instructional model based on whole language philosophy help develop the confidence and strategies needed to support lifelong, independent reading behaviors?

Pedagogical Concerns

1. What are some effective ways of knowing the students as learners?
2. What resources are necessary for creating a literacy-rich environment that allows all learners to be successful?
3. What instructional approaches are most effective in changing the syndrome of reading failure?
4. Is it possible to move students away from the worksheet response and toward authentic response?

Teacher-as-Researcher Concerns

1. How does the role of teacher-researcher affect the role of teacher and the role of researcher?
2. Can students share in the role of classroom research, and if so, what impact will their participation in this activity have on their literacy?

Bias

Patton (1990) advises researchers to "carefully reflect on, deal with, and report potential sources of bias" (p. 56). With that admonition in mind, I must be frank and state that a source of bias for me in terms of this study was my previous experience with students who were at-risk in literacy. Having taught for seventeen years, I had already dealt with many students who fit this category. Experiencing some success in those classes meant that I had already developed insights into the methodologies and philosophy that seemed particularly appropriate to this population. Though I had never actually documented my teaching, with its successes and failures, in any organized manner, I had developed what might be termed a "gut instinct." I was not a new teacher who had never worked with this specific population; rather, I was an experienced teacher who had received commendations for working with students who fit this population. Thus, my goals centered on two broad areas: structuring the methodology, which had been somewhat laissez-faire in my previous teaching, and carefully documenting student reactions to the program.

Another biasing factor was my knowledge of current professional literature and practice related to whole language in the classroom. In addition to the literature search I conducted for this study, I have been reading, observing, and conducting workshops related to whole language for several years. This knowledge led me to sort through the literature with a perspective that might be termed purist as I categorically eliminated reports not grounded in a pure whole language philosophical base. Newkirk's (1990) point that "for most teachers, decisions about how to teach and what to teach are rooted in personal philosophies about teaching, and these in turn are often rooted in our own experiences as learners" (p. 59) certainly fit my practice.

The third bias lay in the area of qualitative methodology and reminded me of Patton's (1990) humorous story that "all too often the methods choices made by evaluators are like the bear's decision to like honey" (p. 198). I agreed with Patton that "qualitative methods typically produce a wealth of detailed information about a much smaller number of people and cases" (p. 14); in fact, it was this very "wealth of detailed information" that I sought. Thus, although I didn't design a study that would fit my preference for qualitative research, I really believed that qualitative research would result in the best documentation and information about the population under investigation. As Allen et al. (1988) have stated, "Designing and conducting research became a new way of reflecting on children, change, and themselves" (p. 380) and that was what I wanted to accomplish. During my twenty years as a public school teacher, I have been amazed at how little impact scholarly research has had on most classrooms. Warawa's (1988) comments on the reasons for this gap made sense to me: "Because of our defensive claims that research is done by scholars who know nothing of the real life in the classroom, we ignore conclusions drawn by researchers, we resist change arising from findings, and we avoid reading articles that describe various investigations" (p. 30). It was my goal to narrow this gap between research and practice in my individual classroom and in my school. I wanted to join the group characterized by Atwell (1989) as "teachers who came out from behind our big desks and hodgepodge programs in order to move around among our students, to follow their leads, observe their learning, ask them genuine questions, and revise our behavior as teachers" (p. 1).

Finally, I knew that the interconnected roles of teacher and researcher had the potential for bias in both areas—teaching and researching. As a teacher, I would have to decide what was best for my students in that place and at that time without considering its research implications. As a researcher, I would have to stand apart from my personal involvement with the students in order to gain alternative perspectives. Yet it was important to keep in mind Patton's (1990) comment that "closeness does not make bias and loss of perspective inevitable; distance is no guarantee of objectivity" (p. 48). This interconnectedness is not only unavoidable, but desirable. It is within this dual role that one learns to listen and to see in a new way. As Queenan (1987) notes, "You will listen to your students and teach a new curriculum: the one to which your listening leads you" (p. 88).

Data Collection Procedures

One way to counter bias and strengthen a study is through triangulation. The type of triangulation that I chose to employ was "data triangulation" (Patton, 1990, p. 187), in which a variety of data sources is used in order to corroborate the findings. Eisner (1991) likens this to "structural corroboration," which he defines as "a means through which multiple types of data are related to each other to support or contradict the interpretation and evaluation of a state of affairs" (p. 110). Thus, I had fourteen sources of data in my study: students' academic journals, students' personal journals, my field notes, transcriptions of interviews with each student, samples of student writing, samples of class assignments, photographs, multiple surveys, class records, standardized testing data, transcriptions of several classes, first-grade pen pal documentation, end-of-the-year debriefing videos, and students' reflections on their growth and change.

In an effort to establish "investigator triangulation," wherein several different researchers would be involved, I invited a teaching colleague to share in observing and participating in the study at various points during the year. Initially, she observed the class, although not on any regular or frequent basis but rather as time permitted within her own teaching schedule. Several times during the year, she worked with the students on creative dramatics, discussion of theater events, and their writing while I became the observer. At the end of the year, she also conducted interviews for one of the debriefing videos.

Data Triangulation

Academic Journals

Students were required to keep academic journals as part of their literacy program. Typical entries in these journals might include characters, vocabulary, and summaries of texts being read in class; responses to independent reading; predictions about novels being read; graphic models to aid in following a story line. These academic journals were used as a source of information for the students during their writing and testing.

Personal Journals

Students also kept personal journals on a fairly regular basis at the beginning of the school year. As the year progressed and students felt more comfortable in sharing through class talk, the entries in the personal journals stopped. At that time, many students started writing letters to me on a fairly frequent basis, which seemed to fill the same need and purpose as the personal journals. Initially, these journals were a rich source of information because students discussed not only their personal problems but their feelings and opinions about the class and school in general.

My Field Notes

Although I attempted to take field notes on a regular basis, there were times when the commitments of school precluded it. In anticipation of this problem, I used a quiet detention duty period directly following the two-period class under study as a time to record notes. I also kept field notes in an ongoing monitoring journal whenever possible during class. These field notes, jotted down as I observed students working in groups on projects, doing independent research, reading, or watching videos often gave a more detailed perspective because of their immediacy and focus. The following excerpt, which I recorded while students were viewing a video about a teenage alcoholic (11/13/91), illustrates the realism that can be documented in field notes as students participate in an activity.

Mac: She's so ugly.
Anne: Shut up!
Mac: Now she's really drunk.
Johnna: No, she's not.
Mac: Then why is she talking to a dead cat?

In all, I compiled six notebooks of field notes during the span of the study.

Transcriptions of Interviews with Students

During the course of the year, I interviewed all the students except one about their reading histories, their attitudes toward literacy events, and their understandings about literacy. In addition, I taped samples of their reading of a selected text. I interviewed several students more than once (depending on time allowances and students' willingness to be interviewed). Although all the tapes contain some questions that are similar or identical, each interview also included questions and discussions relevant to the particular learner being interviewed. These questions often came out of and were built on students' own responses or questions. Excerpt 4/25/92:

J.A: Tell me anything that sticks out in your mind from your previous school years, especially those things that have to do with reading and writing.
Peter: Well, I had to go to the resource room.
J.A: And what was that like for you?
Peter: I didn't like it.
J.A: How come?
Peter: Because I would rather be with my friends.
J.A: Did they talk with you about why you were in the resource room?
Peter: Yeah, but—
J.A: What did they tell you?
Peter: That it was a good reason and that I'm no different from anyone else, but it still felt bad.

Although the question "Tell me anything that sticks out in your mind . . ." was asked of nearly all the students, the direction of the interview was specific only to Peter.

Samples of Student Writing

Samples of students' writing, including writing done on both the first and the last day of class, were collected during various points of the year. In addition, these samples include various writing genres: short story, poetry, group play writing, expository prose, narrative, and response to specific writing prompts.

Samples of Class Assignments

Class assignments took several forms: tests, essays, writings, sentence completions, and so on. Samples of students' responses on these various items were collected and saved to gain perspective on the students that might not emerge from independent reading and writing challenges.

Photographs

From the first day of school and throughout the year, photographs were taken in the classroom and on various field trips. Although I often took these photographs to illustrate the context of the classroom, the activities occurring at given points, or the methodologies being employed, the students were allowed to take photographs of people, events, and classroom materials that had significance for them (for example, their art, bulletin boards, and work they did with a group of first-grade students, which were excellent indicators of what students valued.)

Multiple Surveys

During the course of the year, students were given several surveys to complete in order to elicit information about their attitudes, previous experiences, understandings of course content or literacy instruction, and knowledge of bookstores and books. These surveys became valuable tools, which informed my teaching practice as well as my research. Students worked together, for example, to devise a survey that would give information about someone's attitude toward and understanding of reading. Students experienced real ownership of the class as they worked together to develop surveys and interview techniques and then administered their surveys to students in other classes. From a researcher's perspective, I gained valuable knowledge about their ability to ask questions, about group interactions, and about their independent, responsible behavior. As a teacher, I gained in those areas as well as in my understanding of my literacy.

Class Records

Class records offered the study a variety of information. Status of the class (Atwell, 1987) records students' documented book choices, the amount and type of reading, and their selection-of-book behaviors. Attendance, tardiness, disciplinary actions, and school-related absences offered another perspective on students' success in school.

Standardized Testing

Standardized testing records were available for each student in the program, since these tests were used in the selection criteria. Standardized tests had been administered to the students in this program at least once a year each year in grades 1 to 9. These included the Differential Aptitude Test (grade 8), Maine Educational Assessment Test (grades 4 and 8), Science Research Associates (grades 1–7), and the Nelson-Denny Test of Reading (grade 8).

Transcriptions of Classes

At several times during the year, I put a cassette recorder out to record a class in session. Although this was quite ineffective for the most part (it either picked up too much surface noise or it distorted sound for those not close to the recorder), pieces of the transcription give information about those who managed to "make themselves heard" in the classroom.

Pen Pal Information

Near the end of the year when the students felt more confident about their literacy abilities, we began corresponding with a local first-grade class in an elementary building within walking distance of our school. Artifacts collected during that time include not only the pen pal letters, but also photographs, videos, and surveys administered to the students. These offer rich documentation of students' understandings of literacy as well as of their levels of confidence and self-esteem.

Debriefing Videos

At the end of the year, we made two debriefing videos. One session was conducted by a teaching colleague with whom the students had had contact at several points during the year. During the taping, I left the room and students discussed their year with the interviewer. This video included discussion by all the members of the class remaining at the end of the year.

The second video was also made at the end of the year. This interview, conducted by an elementary teacher, focused on three students who wanted to discuss the literacy program at greater length.

Student Reflection

In keeping with my belief that reflective practice is one of the keys to active learning, students were often asked to reflect on their own learning, our classroom practice, and their understanding of their literacy development. Samples of those reflections were kept in order to establish the students' perceptions over time and to document the impact of reflection on students' roles within the classroom. As Kutz (1992) reminds us, "It is not enough for us, as teacher-researchers, to do research *about* our students and their learning. We must do research *with* our students, working together to discover answers to the questions that arise in our classrooms" (p. 196).

Investigator Triangulation

As mentioned previously, I attempted to incorporate investigator triangulation into the study by soliciting help from a colleague. This research assistance took the form of participant observation in which she would observe and interact with the students and with me if she felt it would lead to a better understanding of the context. The times when she was actually available to participate in this way offered an excellent opportunity for collaboration or contradiction of what I was observing.

Several events conflicted with the biweekly schedule we originally hoped to adhere to: changes in her duty and teaching schedules, administrative conflicts in terms of scheduling meetings, and her own teaching commitments. In spite of those drawbacks, she did manage to come in at least once a month during the entire year. During that time, she was able to observe students in the classroom context during a read aloud time, working on book projects, writing in the computer room, and participating in a class discussion. In addition, she was able to work with the students, while discussing their learning, in the following contexts: a creative dramatics session, a discussion of viewing a play, a discussion with actors following the presentation of a play, writing a student-generated group play, and conducting the debriefing video at the end of the year.

Data Analysis

As Patton (1990) points out, data collection is the easy task when compared to data analysis: "The challenge is to make sense of massive amounts of data, reduce the volume of information, identify significant patterns, and construct a framework for communicating the essence of what the data reveal" (p. 371). My plan for the analysis of the data is modeled after Graves's (1981). In this model Graves supports a pyramid design in which several levels of data collection and analysis occur: Level 4, School Data; Level 3, Class Data; Level 2, Small Sample of Children; Level 4, One Child. Since students were assigned to my class from the larger context of all the students in grade nine, and my class was the only one offered to these students, there was no narrowing process to choose the right teacher or the right class in which to conduct the research. This level does exist in the sense that the class level was marked out from the broader context through a series of meetings, analysis of standardized test data, students' previous reading and English grades, and recommendations from administrators and teachers. The other levels of Graves's model work well in a study like this because they lend themselves to what Glaser and Straus (1967) describe as "constant comparison."

At Level 3, class data will be collected and analyzed for all the students assigned to Reading and Writing Workshop during the school year 1991–92. Goetz and LeCompte (1981) stress that "researchers generally use a variety of overlapping techniques rather than relying on a single approach" (p. 56). That will certainly be the case for this larger population at Level 3. Various methods of data collection will be employed, reflective of my initial goals and questions and responsive to the evolving nature of naturalistic research. Graves (1981) indicates that "Level 3 data come from the entire class in which Level 1 and 2 children reside. Some informal observations are taken from them but all of their products are classified for examination" (p. 204). He suggests that this process should span at least an entire year so that the full context can be seen, his rationale being that "data gathered in such depth usually point the way to discovering new variables not seen in the larger data gathering" (p. 205).

Students chosen for Level 2 give information on the process of the classroom in a more in-depth manner than is possible for an entire class. Graves's model suggests five students at this level from a typical class of twenty-five. Given my student population of fifteen, three students at this level would seem to be analogous. These students will be selected according to their ability to articulate the literacy changes they are experiencing to "illustrate the value of detailed, descriptive data in deepening our understanding of individual variation" (Patton, 1990, p. 17). Although the decision about which students will provide that information could be based on several possibilities, I plan to choose them in keeping with what Patton has defined as "critical case sampling." In this instance, "critical cases are those that can make a point quite dramatically or are, for some reason, particularly important in the scheme of things" (p. 174).

The final stage, Level 1, will be a student who best gives a picture of the broadly-defined questions and goals of the study. Embedded in that picture will be that student's ability to articulate what is happening for him or her within the context of this study, the context of the classroom, and the context of literacy acquisition. This aspect of the study is extremely important. As Diesing observes, "an informant's account of an activity can be compared with direct observation or participation in the activity, and with the written report or the written instructions, or even with a videotape of an activity" (1983, p. 3). This student will be chosen based on the data gathered from written samples, interviews, and reflections. This final level will take the form of a case study of an individual student. Bissex (1987) notes that "when they [researchers] closely observe individual students in their classrooms, they come to appreciate the many resources students utilize in learning, including but not limited to instruction" (p. 16). Although the student chosen for the individual case study could be selected for any one of several reasons, Patton (1990) mentions the possibility of using unusual successes, failures, or dropouts. I plan to choose a student who has been successful, since that is in keeping with my philosophical stance that my classroom be built on the strengths and successes of students and not on their weaknesses or failures. Case study research allows the researcher to collect an immense amount of data on one individual and then look for themes within that data. With the intensity of that focus, I will be able to look at this student's transition over time as he or she engages in literate behaviors. I use practice here in Armstrong's (1982) sense: "as the sustained exercise of skill, judgment and imagination in successive intellectual tasks" (p. 55).

Case studies do not offer educators large samples in which we might find generalizable patterns. Case studies do, however, provide us with the in-depth look at one individual within his or her school, family, community, and cultural context. Bissex (1987) supports this when she states: "While case studies do not provide the generalizability of large numbers or of experiments that can be readily duplicated, they are more true to life in their revelation of individuals in action and their reflection of the complexities of those individuals and actions" (p. 11). It is this capability that I will seek in the individual chosen for the case study—an individual who will be able to reflect upon both personal and academic changes explored during the course of this study. Although there are those who would see a case study as too narrowly focused, Harste's (1987) point is well-taken: "A good model, now don't you agree, ought to at least be able to explain the behavior of one child before it gets implemented" (p. 12).

Bruton (1985) successfully implemented this design model in her dissertation, "Toward Defining Written Fluency: Connecting Process and Product." She demonstrated the strength of the data collection in this model with this information: "At the conclusion of Level 4 . . . students had been observed throughout the present study for a total of 160 hours" (p. 139). My research study will have that same wealth of information gathered from prolonged, in-depth observation of a small sample of students, what Geertz (1973) would call "thick description."

Appendix B: Surveys

Fall Survey

1. Has anyone ever talked with you individually about the following:

   a. your writing   no   yes

   b. a book you've read   no   yes

   c. your journal   no   yes

   d. your goals/future plans   no   yes

   e. your classes   no   yes

   f. you as a person   no   yes

2. What are your favorite classes in school?

3. What are your least favorite classes?

4. What do you think the most important qualities are for a teacher?

5. What books have you read in the past few years?

6. What is your favorite book?

   What makes this book special?
   Do you have a favorite author? If so, what makes this person
   a good author?

7. What have you disliked about previous reading/English classes?

   What could have made the class better?

8. What have you enjoyed about previous English classes?

9. How important do you consider reading to be in your life?

   not very important   important   extremely important

10. How important do you consider writing to be in your life?

    not very important   important   extremely important

11. How would you rate yourself as a reader?

    below average   average   above average

12. How would you rate yourself as a writer?

    below average   average   above average

13. Do you consider yourself (a) a better reader than writer (b) a better writer than reader (c) equally good in both reading and writing.

14. Who do you know that is a good reader?

15. What do you think has made this person a good reader?

16. What does this person do that makes you think he or she is a good reader?

17. Which of these remarks comes closest to the way you feel about reading?

    a. "I hate reading."

    b. "Reading is something you do if someone makes you, but I don't enjoy it."

    c. "Reading is okay. Sometimes I pick things up to read."

    d. "I like to read but have a hard time with it."

    e. "I really enjoy reading and often read when I have free time."

18. Please check all that you like to read.

    _____ plays

    _____ young adult novels

    _____ best-sellers

    _____ nonfiction

    _____ fiction

    _____ poetry

    _____ newspapers

    _____ magazines

    _____ westerns

    _____ romances

    _____ historical fiction

    _____ biographies

19. Which of the following have you written in the past six months?

    a. a letter to a friend

    b. a business letter

    c. a request for something

    d. a personal journal or diary

    e. an academic journal

    f. a poem

    g. a short story

    h. an essay

    i. lyrics for a song

20. What do you think I could do to help you become a better reader?

21. What could you do to become a better reader?

22. What could I do to help you become a better writer?

23. What could you do to become a better writer?

24. What is your favorite movie and what did you particularly like about this movie?

25. What magazines do you like to read?

26. What are your favorite television shows?

Classroom Activities

Please check those you would enjoy doing.

_____ reading silently

_____ reading orally (plays, quotations, etc.)

_____ having someone read to you

_____ writing in journals

_____ watching movies

_____ listening to cassettes (stories, poetry)

_____ working as a whole class

_____ working alone

_____ completing worksheets, workbooks

_____ doing vocabulary, dictionary work

_____ class discussions

_____ writing

_____ publishing your writing (classroom magazine)

Beginning-of-the-Year Sentence Completion

1. Today I feel
2. When I have to read, I
3. I get angry when
4. To be grown up
5. My idea of a good time
6. I wish my parents knew
7. School is
8. I can't understand why
9. I feel bad when
10. I wish teachers
11. I wish my mother
12. Going to college
13. To me, books
14. People think I
15. I like to read about
16. On weekends, I
17. I don't know how
18. To me, homework
19. I hope I'll never
20. I wish people wouldn't
21. When I finish high school
22. I'm afraid
23. Comic books
24. When I take my report card home
25. I am at my best when
26. Most brothers and sisters
27. I'd rather read than
28. When I read math
29. The future looks
30. I feel proud when
31. I wish my father
32. I like to read when
33. I would like to be
34. For me, studying
35. I often worry about
36. I wish I could
37. Reading science
38. I look forward to
39. I wish someone would help me
40. I'd read more if

Midyear/End-of-Year Sentence Completion

1. When someone assigns a book for me to read, I

2. When I'm asked to write in a journal, I

3. When I think of school, I think of __, __, __ and __.

4. If someone asked me if I were a good reader, my response would be

5. When I am asked to write on any topic I choose, the process I use to decide what to write about is

6. The way I choose a book to read for independent reading is

7. If I were asked to summarize my past reading experiences, I would say

8. The things I think I do well as a reader are

9. The biggest problem for me when I try to read is

10. The hardest type of reading for me is

11. Given my future plans, I feel that reading and writing

12. Some believe that writing is a gift; others believe that everyone can be a good writer. In my opinion,

13. I think that what would make me a better reader is

Reading Attitude Survey

N=No, almost never   S=Sometimes   A=Almost Always

1. Do you like to hear and use new words?   N S A

2. Do you enjoy making up new words or playing games with words you already know?   N S A

3. Do you enjoy listening to stories or poems which are read to you?   N S A

4. When you start to read a book, do you expect the book to be fun and/or exciting?   N S A

5. Do you expect reading to make sense to you?   N S A

6. Do you enjoy reading books that you have read before?   N S A

7. Do you want to read?   N S A

8. Do you enjoy responding in some way to your reading?   N S A

9. Do you see yourself as a reader?   N S A

10. Do you feel comfortable attempting to pronounce a word even if you are unsure of the word?   N   S   A

11. Does it bother you to receive feedback from other people about the way you read?   N   S   A

12. Are you eager to read increasingly longer stories/books?   N   S   A

13. Do you expect to get meaning from the texts (books) you read?   N   S   A

14. Are you willing to work at getting the meaning?   N   S   A

15. Do you see reading as more than just being able to say the words printed on the page?   N   S   A

16. Are you confident in taking risks because you see this as a way to learn?   N   S   A

17. Do you feel comfortable sharing your ideas, thoughts, and feelings about what you read?   N   S   A

18. Are you eager to build on reading success by reading a new book?   N   S   A

19. Are you eager to read aloud to others?   N   S   A

20. Do you ask for feedback (help) with your reading?   N   S   A

21. Do you expect to take an active part in your reading by trying to understand and add your own meaning to the author's message?   N   S   A

22. Do you expect reading to be challenging but you're confident that you can overcome the challenges?   N   S   A

23. Do you expect to get something new out of a book each time you read it?   N   S   A

24. Are you eager to choose books on your own, perhaps choosing books on new subjects or by new authors?   N   S   A

25. Do you respond to books either by writing or talking about the books, without someone asking you to do so?   N   S   A

26. Do you expect to agree with everything that you read?   N   S   A

27. Do you see books as a way of finding answers to some of your questions?   N   S   A

28. Do you expect books to be part of your daily
    life?   N   S   A

29. Do you try to find time or make time to read?   N   S   A

Expanding Our View of Available Books

Before Arriving at the Bookstore

1. Do you have any books already in mind that you would like to
   purchase?   Yes   No

   If yes, what types of books or specific authors do you already know
   you would be interested in?

2. Have you ever been to a bookstore before?   Yes   No

   If yes, which bookstore(s) have you visited?

3. Think back to the books we have read together this year. Which
   books did you like well enough to buy another similar book?

   Think of the books you've read during independent reading. Which
   books or authors have you enjoyed so much that you would like to
   extend your reading through similar books or books by the same
   author?

During the Bookstore Visit

1. Name the two bookstores we visited today.

   a.

   b.

2. In order to learn about as many new books as possible and really find
   books that you will make a commitment to read, I'm asking you to
   find books of each of the following types and then list a book/author
   for each type (genre). I'm hoping that as you do this you might find
   new books you never would have thought of reading.

   a. HISTORICAL FICTION

   b. REALISTIC FICTION

   c. BIOGRAPHY/AUTOBIOGRAPHY

   d. ADVENTURE/WAR

   e. FANTASY

   f. NONFICTION

   g. MYSTERY/SUSPENSE

h. WESTERNS

i. COLLECTIONS OF POETRY OR SHORT STORIES

j. BOOKS FROM MOVIES OR BASED ON MOVIES

After the Bookstore Visit

3. When you were deciding on books to buy/read, what things affected your decision? (CIRCLE ALL THAT APPLY.)

   a. cover

   b. back of book

   c. title

   d. length of book

   e. an author you've read and enjoyed

   f. a book someone recommended

   g. type of book in which you know you have an interest

   h. size of the print/type

4. Which bookstore did you prefer? Why?

5. List below the three books/authors you purchased today.

   BOOK   AUTHOR

   a.

   b.

   c.

6. Interview two of your friends or people in the class about the bookstore experience. Record in writing the highlights of your interviews (what they liked/disliked; kinds of books they bought; books they purchased that you might like to read, etc.)

Appendix C: Assessment
Samples of Assessment/Evaluation Prompts

Personal Writing

A whole semester has gone by with your spending two periods every day doing activities that relate to language arts: reading, writing, discussing, listening, working together, working alone, and thinking. What have you learned about yourself as a learner, a reader, and a writer? How has this class been different from the other Reading/English classes you have had? What are we doing that you like and what are we doing that you dislike? How have you changed during this time? What have you contributed to the class so far and what could you do to get the most out of the time that we have left? What could I do to make things better for you and what could you do to make things better for me and the rest of the class?

Final Writing Prompt

All of you have been in English/Reading classes for many years now. In terms of your growth as a reader, writer, and learner, what makes a good Reading/English class? Compare this class to other classes you've had K–8 and tell me what advice you would give to the person who teaches this class next year about the kinds of things they should do in class and what the kids should know by the time they finish the class.

Independent, Lifelong Readers and Writers

If my goal is that I would like to help you become independent, lifelong readers and writers, what am I doing right? What could I do differently that would help me achieve this goal?

Success

The reason I have been successful as a reader this year is . . .

Please address the following activities by telling what you liked and/or disliked about each one and what you learned from each one.

1. Sanford Phippen
2. Paul Janeczko
3. working with the students at elementary school
4. reading novels out loud
5. going to see plays

6. watching videos that relate to the theme of our read aloud

7. interviews about reading (interviewing each other, Mrs. P's students, elementary students, and my interviews with you)

8. the final discussion (with Miss Frick) of your growth as a reader and writer

9. writing in your academic journal

10. independent reading days

11. visits to the bookstores

12. working with me and with each other to plan for things (visits, time with substitute teachers, parties, etc.)

Discussing Reading Strategies

1. In your opinion, what things can each one of us do to become better readers?

2. When we're reading a novel and there is a space between passages, what might that tell you that would help you as a reader?

3. Why do people often have trouble with the beginnings of novels?

   If you were having trouble at the beginning of a novel, what could you do to help?

4. When you're reading and some of the words are in italics, what might that tell you about those words?

5. We've talked about the word composition as it relates to writing and as it relates to art. In your opinion, what does it mean to have good composition in both a piece of writing and in a picture?

6. Why do I ask you to take responsibility for choosing your own reading two days each week?

7. In what way could making a diagram or writing a character list help you in reading a novel or a play?

Appendix D: Students as Researchers Student-generated Reading Interview Survey

*Group 1: Reading Survey**

1. How often do you read books?
2. WHAT DO YOU LIKE TO READ?
3. Do you like comics?
4. What books have you read this year?
5. What kind of books do you like to read?
6. How good do you read?
7. Do you have any previous reading experience?
8. What was the last book you read?
9. What's the best book you ever read?
10. Who is you're reading teacher?
11. Who is you're favorite author?
12. Do you watch TV?
13. Does anyone ever read to you?
14. Are you male or female?
15. Who is the best reader you know?
16. What makes this person a good reader?
17. Would you like to be able to be a good reader?
18. Who do you think reads better, male or female?

* Unedited survey questions submitted by groups.

Group 2:Reading Survey*

Do you consider yourself a good reader?
If so what makes you a good reader?

Do you read a lot in your spare time?
Did you like to read books when you were a young kid?

What kind of books do you like to read?

Did your family ever read to you when you were little?

Do you injoy reading or looking at the pictures?

How many books did you read when you were younger?

What kind of children's books do you like?

Do you like to read horror books?

How many books per day do you read or per month?

Do you like personal books?

Do you like to read thick or thin books?
If so, why?

Do you have your journal or not?

Do you like to write or read books?
Why?

Who is your favorite horror book aurther?
Why do you like this person so much?

Do you read in school a lot?
If so what kind of books do you read?

* Unedited survey questions submitted by groups.

Group 3: Reading Survey*

1. What types of books do you like to read?

2. What is your favorite book?

3. How many books have you read?

4. Do you like long or short stories?

5. Do you remember being read to as a child?

6. What is your favorite movie?

7. Do you like scary or comedy books?

8. Do you like fiction or nonfiction books?

9. What things do you like to read?

   ___magazines   ___newspaper

   ___short stories   ___novels

   ___comic books   ___other

10. What kind of movies do you like?

    ___scary   ___comedy

    ___non-fiction   ___romance

    ___mystery   ___other

11. Do you remember the first book ever read to you?

12. What was the last book you read?

* Unedited survey questions submitted by groups.

Final Version of Reading Survey**

Male   Female   Age

1. How often do you read?

2. What types of books have you read this year?

   __horror   __romance   __realistic fiction

   __westerns   __comedy   __mystery/suspense

3. What kind of books do you like to read?

4. Do you consider yourself a good reader? Why/why not?

5. Have you had any good previous reading experiences? For example, do you remember being read to as a child or do you remember the first book you ever read? Please describe these experiences.

6. What was the last book you read?

7. Was the book you listed in #6 assigned to you or did you read it just because you wanted to read?

8. What is the best book you have ever read?

9. Who is your favorite author?

10. Does anyone ever read to you? If so, who, and what do they read?

11. Who is the best reader you know?

12. What do you think makes this person a good reader?

13. Would you like to be able to be a good reader?

14. Who do you think reads better, men or women? Give a reason to support your answer.

15. Do you like long or short stories?

16. What things do you like to read?

    __magazines   __short stories

    __comic books   __newspaper

    __novels   __other

17. What kind of movies do you like?

    __scary   __nonfiction

    __mystery   __comedy

    __other   __romance

18. Tell me something about reading that I haven't asked in any of the first 17 questions.

**Edited as part of a whole group, language experience activity.

Page 1 of Analysis of Interview Data*

1. How often do you read?

> Not often
> Three times a weeks
> Every day
> Once a month
> Whenever I get a chance
> Five days a week
> Two times a week
> Once in a while
> Fairly often
> **Conclusion: The majority of your students don't read very often.**

2. What types of books have you read this year?

> Horror
> Western
> Romance
> Comedy
> Realisitc Fiction
> Mystery/Suspense
> Non-fiction
> **Conclusion: The majority of your students prefer: realistic fiction and mystery/suspense.**

3. What kind of books do you like to read?

> Native
> Strong female character
> Action
> Modern fiction
> **Conclusion: There is a large variety of books your students like to read.**

4. Do you consider yourself a good reader? Why/why not?

> yes
> no
> fair/ok
> yes and no
> **Conclusion: Most of your students think they can read. For the students who don't think they can read well their reasons are don't read much and stumbles too much.**

* **Unedited responses submitted and generated by students.**

References

Adams, D., and C. Cerqui. 1989. *Effective Vocabulary Instruction.* Kirkland, WA: Reading Resources.

Allen, J., J. Combs, M. Hendricks, P. Nash, and S. Wilson. 1988. "Studying Change: Teachers Who Become Researchers." *Language Arts,* 65 (4): 379–387.

Allen, J, Kristo J., Giard, M. 1991. Read Aloud: Prime Time Instruction. New England Journal of Reading.

Allington, R., H. Stuetzel, M. Shake, M. and S. Lamarche. 1986. "What Is Remedial Reading? A Descriptive Study." *Reading Research and Instruction,* 26 (1): 15–30.

Anderson, W. February 1994. Personal Communication, International Reading Association Third North American Conference on Adult and Adolescent Literacy. Washington, D.C.

Armstrong, M. 1982. "A seed's growth." In *What's Going On?*, ed. M. Barr, P. D'Arcy, and M. K. Healy, 52–69. Montclair, NY: Boynton/Cook.

Ashton-Warner, S. 1963. *Teacher.* New York: Simon and Schuster.

Atwell, N. 1984. Writing and Reading Literature from the Inside Out. *Language Arts,* 61 (3): 240–252.

———. 1987. *In the Middle: Writing, Reading, and Learning with Adolescents.* Portsmouth, NH: Boynton/Cook.

———. 1989. "The Thoughtful Practitioner." *Teachers Networking,* 9 (3): 10–12.

———. 1991. "Wonderings to Pursue: The Writing Teacher as Researcher." In *Literacy in Process,* ed. B. M. Power and R. Hubbard, 315–331. Portsmouth, NH: Heinemann.

Barton, B. 1986. *Tell Me Another: Storytelling and Reading Aloud at Home, at School and in the Community.* Portsmouth, NH: Heinemann.

Beck, C. 1993. Personal Communication, University of Central Florida Diversity Conference.

Bissex, G. L. 1987. "What Is a Teacher-Researcher?" In *Seeing for Ourselves: Case-study Research by Teachers of Writing,* ed. G. L. Bissex and R. H. Bullock, 3–5. Portsmouth, NH: Heinemann.

Brendtro, L. K., M. Brokenleg, and S. Van Bockern. 1990. *Reclaiming Youth at Risk.* Bloomington, IN: National Education Service.

Brozo, W. G., and M. L. Simpson. 1991. *Readers, Teachers, Learners: Expanding Literacy in Secondary Schools.* New York: Macmillan.

Bruton, D. L. 1985. "Toward Defining Written Fluency: Connecting Product and Process." Ph.D. University of Georgia, Athens.

Bunke, C. 1993. Personal Communication, Tampa, FL. Middle School Conference.

Burke, C. 1988. "Burke Reading Inventory." In *Whole Language Strategies for Secondary Students*, ed. X. Gilles et al. Katonah, NY: Richard C. Owen.

———. 1991. Personal Communication, Presque Isle, ME. Aroostook Right to Read Conference.

Butkowsky, I. S., and D. M. Willows. 1980. "Cognitive-Motivational Characteristics of Children Varying in Reading Ability: Evidence for Learned Helplessness in Poor Readers." *Journal of Educational Psychology*, 72 (3): 408–422.

Cambourne, B. 1988. *The Whole Story*. New York: Scholastic.

Clay, M. 1979. *The Early Detection of Reading Difficulties*. Portsmouth, NH: Heinemann.

Dewey, J. 1902. *The Child and the Curriculum*. Chicago: University of Chicago Press.

———. 1956. *The Child and the Curriculum*. Chicago: University of of Chicago Press.

Diesing, P. 1983. "Ethnography." *The English Record*, 34 (4): 2–5.

Dodd, A. W. 1973. *Write Now!* New York: Globe.

Duncan, J. 1992. Personal Communication. Richard C. Owen Publishers Whole Language Workshops.

Eisner, E. W. 1991. *The Enlightened Eye*. New York: Macmillan.

Ernst, K. 1993. *Picturing Learning: Artists and Writers in the Classroom*. Portsmouth, NH: Heinemann.

Flavell, J. H. 1979. "Metacognition and Cognitive Monitoring." *American Psychologist*, 34 (10):

Fletcher, R. 1991. *Walking Trees*. Portsmouth, NH: Heinemann.

———. 1993. *What a Writer Needs*. Portsmouth, NH: Heinemann.

Fullan, M. 1993. *Change Forces: Probing the Depths of Educational Reform*. Bristol, PA: Falmer Press.

Geertz, D. 1973. *The Interpretation of Cultures*. New York: Basic Books.

Gillespie, T. 1992. "Teacher-Researcher-Storyteller." In *Workshop: The Teacher as Researcher*, ed. T. Newkirk, 13–20. Portsmouth, NH: Heinemann.

Glaser, B. G., and A. L. Strauss. 1967. *The Discovery of Grounded Theory: Strategies for Qualitative Research*. Hawthorne, NY: Aldine de Gruyter.

Goetz, J. P., and M. D. LeCompte. 1981. "Ethnographic Research and the Problem of Data Reduction." *Anthropology and Education Quarterly*, 12: 51–70.

Goodman, K. S. 1986a. *What's Whole in Whole Language?* Portsmouth, NH: Heinemann.

———. 1986b. "Basal Readers: A Call for Action." *Language Arts*, 63: 358–363.

———. 1987. "Who Can Be a Whole Language Teacher?" *Teachers Networking*, 1 (1): 1, 10–11.

Goodman, K., and Y. Goodman. 1983. "Reading and Writing Relationships: Pragmatic Functions." *Language Arts*, 60 (5): 590–599.

Goodman, Y. 1992. In *Questions and Answers About Whole Language*, ed. O. Cochrane. Katonah, NY: Richard C. Owen.

Goodman, Y., and C. Burke. 1980. *Reading Strategies: Focus on Comprehension*. New York: Richard C. Owen.

Graves, D. 1981. "Writing Research for the Eighties: What Is Needed." *Language Arts*, 58 (2): 197–206.

———. 1983. *Writing: Teachers and Children at Work*. Portsmouth, NH: Heinemann.

Graves, D., and J. Hansen. 1983. "The Author's Chair." *Language Arts*, 60 (2): 176–183.

Harste, J. 1987. In *Seeing for Ourselves: Case-Study Research by Teachers of Writing*, ed. G. Bissex and R. H. Bullock, 12. Portsmouth, NH: Heinemann.

———. 1992. In *Questions and Answers About Whole Language*, ed. O. Cochrane, 8–11. Katonah, NY: Richard C. Owen.

Hill, W. R. 1979. *Secondary School Reading*. Boston: Allyn and Bacon.

Hoffke, S. E. 1989. "The Social Context of Action Research: A Comparative and Historical Analysis." Paper presented at the annual meeting of the American Educational Research Association, San Francisco, CA.

Hubbard, R., and B. M. Power. 1993. *The Art of Classroom Inquiry*. Portsmouth, NH: Heinemann.

Huck, C. 1977. "Literature as the Content of Reading." *Theory into Practice*, 16 (5): 363–371.

———. 1987. "To Know the Place for the First Time." *The Best of the Bulletin*, 1: 69–71.

Johnston, P. 1992. "The Ethics of Our Work in Teacher Research." In *Workshop by and for teachers: The Teacher as Researcher*, ed. T. Newkirk, 31–40. Portsmouth, NH: Heinemann.

Johnston, P., and R. Allington. 1991. "Remediation." In *Handbook of Read-*

ing Research. Vol. 2, ed. R. Barr, M. L. Kamil, P. Mosenthal, and P. D. Pearson, 984–1002. New York: Longman.

Johnston, P., and P. N. Winograd. 1985. "Passive Failure in Reading." *Journal of Reading Behavior*, 17 (4): 279–301.

Jones, D. May 1992. "The Parking Lot Syndrome." In *Outdoor Photographer*, 26–27.

Kohl, H. 1991. *I Won't Learn From You!* Minneapolis, MN: Milkweed Editions.

Kozol, J. 1985. *Illiterate America*. New York: New American Library.

———. 1991. *Savage Inequalities*. New York: Crown.

Krueger, M. M. 1993. "Everyone Is An Exception: Assumptions to Avoid the Sex Education Classroom." *Phi Delta Kappan*, 74 (7): 569.

Kutz, E. 1992. "Teacher Research: Myths and Realities." *Language Arts*, 69: 193–197.

Lincoln, Y. S., and E. G. Guba. (1985). *Naturalistic Inquiry*. Newbury Park, CA: Sage.

Lynch, P. 1986. *Using Big Books and Predictable Books*. New York: Scholastic.

Martin, N. 1987. "On the move." In *Reclaiming the Classroom: Teacher Research as an Agency for Change* ed. D. Goswami and P. R. Stillman, 20–28. Upper Montclair, NJ: Boynton/Cook.

Matthews, C. E. 1987. "Lap Reading for Teenagers." *Journal of Reading*, February.

Mazer, N. 1992. "The Ice-Cream Syndrome" (aka "Promoting Good Reading habits"). In *Authors' Insights*, ed. D. Gallo, 20–31. Portsmouth, NH: Boynton/Cook Heinemann.

McKenzie, M. 1977. "The Beginnings of Literacy." *Theory into Practice*, 16: 315–324.

Meek, M. 1982. *Learning to Read*. Portsmouth, NH: Heinemann.

———. 1991. *On Becoming Literate*. Portsmouth, NH: Heinemann.

Moffett, J. 1973. *A Student-Centered Language Arts Curriculum, Grades K–13: A Handbook for Teachers*. Boston: Houghton Mifflin.

Mooney, M. 1988. *Developing Life-Long Readers*. Wellington, NZ: Learning Media, Ministry of Education.

———. 1990. *Reading to, with, and by Children*. Katonah, NY: Richard C. Owen.

Murray, D. 1986. *Read to Write*. New York: CBS College Publishing.

———. 1987. *Write to Learn*. New York: Holt, Rinehart and Winston.

Nehring, J. 1992. *The Schools We Have, the Schools We Want*. San Francisco: Jossey-Bass.

Newkirk, T. 1990. "Research Currents: One Teacher, One Classroom." *Language Arts*, 67 (1): 58–69.

O'Brien, Tim. 1990. *The Things They Carried*. New York: Penguin Books.

Patton, M. Q. 1990. *Qualitative Evaluation and Research Methods*, 2nd ed. Newbury Park, CA: Sage.

Peterson, R. 1992. *Life in a Crowded Place*. Portsmouth, NH: Heinemann.

Powell, A. G., E. Farrar, and D. K. Cohen. 1985. *The Shopping Mall High School*. Boston: Houghton Mifflin.

Queenan, M. 1987. "Teachers as Researchers?" *English Journal*, 76 (4): 88–90.

Readence, J. E., T. W. Bean, and R. S. Baldwin. 1985. *Content Area Reading: An Integrated Approach*, 2nd ed. Dubuque, IA: Kendall/Hunt.

Rosenblatt, L. M. 1976. New York: Modern Language Association.

Seligman, M. E. P. 1975. *Helplessness: On Depression, Development and Death*. San Francisco: Freeman.

Simpson, M. 1962. *Reading in Junior Classes*. Katonah, NY: Richard C. Owen.

Sizer, T. R. 1984. *Horace's Compromise*. Boston: Houghton Mifflin.

Smith, F. 1971. *Understanding Reading*. New York: Holt, Rinehart and Winston.

———. 1976. *Comprehension and Learning*. New York: Richard C. Owen.

———. 1986. *Insult to Intelligence*. New York: Arbor House.

Stanovich, K. 1986. "Matthew Effects in Reading: Some Consequences of Individual Differences in the Acquisition of Literacy." *Reading Research Quarterly*, 21: 360–406.

Stephens, D. 1991. *Research on Whole Language*. Katonah, NY: Richard C. Owen.

Trelease, J. 1985. *The Read-Aloud Handbook*. New York: Penguin.

Vacca, J. A., R. T. Vacca, and M. K. Gove. 1987. *Reading and Learning to Read*. Boston: Little, Brown.

Veatch, J. 1968. *How to Teach Reading with Children's Books*. New York: Richard C. Owen.

Vygotsky, L. S. 1962. *Thought and Language*. Cambridge, MA: M. I. T. Press.

Warawa, B. 1988. "Classroom Inquiry: Learning about Learning." *English Journal*, 77 (2): 30–46.

Weaver, C. 1990. *Understanding Whole Language: From Principles to Practice*. Portsmouth, NH: Heinemann.

Weiner, B. 1979. "A Theory of Motivation for Some Classroom Experiences." *Journal of Educational Psychology,* 71 (1): 3–25.

Weinstein, C. E., and Mayer, R. E. 1986. "The Teaching of Learning Strategies." In *Handbook of Research on Teaching,* ed. M. C. Wittrock. New York: MacMillan.

Wells, G. 1986. *The Meaning Makers.* Portsmouth, NH: Heinemann.

Literary References

Adams, Ansel. *The portfolios of Ansel Adams*. 1981. Boston: Little, Brown and Company.

American Friends. *The Wabanakis of Maine and the Maritimes*. 1989. Bath, ME: Maine Indian Program.

Angelou, M. 1989. "No Loser, no Weeper." In *Maya Angelou: Poems* New York: Bantam.

———. 1990. "Me and My Work." In *I Shall Not Be Moved*. 22. New York: Bantam.

Arrick, F. 1987. "The Good Girls." In *Visions: Nineteen Short Stories by Outstanding Writers for Young Adults*, ed. D. Gallo. New York: Dell.

Arundel, H. 1969. *The Longest Weekend*. New York: Tempo Books.

Attenborough, R., Director. 1993. *Shadowlands* [Film]. Screenplay by W. Nicholson. New York: Savoy Pictures.

Avi. 1991. *Nothing but the Truth*. New York: Orchard Books.

Bach, R. 1970. *Jonathan Livingston Seagull*. New York: Macmillan.

———. 1977. *Illusions: Adventures of a Reluctant Messiah*. New York: Delacorte.

Baylor, B. 1974. *Everybody Needs a Rock*. New York: Macmillan.

Berry, W. 1988. In A. M. Kuller *Readings from the Hurricane Island Outward Bound School* 75.

Blume, J. 1975. *Forever*. New York: Bradbury Press.

Brancato, R. 1988. *Winning*. New York: Knopf.

Charlip, R. 1980. *Fortunately, Unfortunately!* New York: Macmillan.

Chopin, K. 1991. "The Story of an Hour." In *A Vocation and a Voice*. New York: Penguin Books.

Chekhov, A. 1989. *The Cherry Orchard*. In *Types of Drama: Plays and Essays*, 5th ed., ed. S. Barnet, M. Berman, and W. Burto, 369–393. New York: HarperCollins. Originally published in 1904.

Clapp, P. 1968. *Constance: The Story of Early Plymouth*. New York: Bantam.

Cooke, A. 1984. *America*. New York: Knopf.

Cooney, C. B. 1990. *The Face on the Milk Carton*. New York: Bantam.

Cormier, R. 1974. *A Chocolate War*. New York: Dell.

Crutcher, C. 1991. *Chinese Handcuffs*. New York: Dell.

Cusick, R. T. 1990. *Teacher's Pet*. New York: Scholastic.

Dahl, R. 1964. *Charlie and the Chocolate Factory*. New York: Bantam.

Danziger, P. 1988. *The Pistachio Prescription*. New York: Dell.

Duncan, L. 1966. *Ransom*. New York: Dell.

———. 1973. *I Know What You Did Last Summer*. New York: Pocket.

———. 1978. *Killing Mr. Griffin*. New York: Dell.

Gallo, D., ed. 1987. *Visions: Nineteen Short Stories by Outstanding Writers for Young Adults*. New York: Dell.

Gardner, J. R. 1980. *Stone Fox*. New York: First Harper Trophy.

Gibran, K. 1986. *The Prophet*. New York: Knopf.

Gilmour, H. B. 1985. *Ask Me if I Care*. New York: Fawcett Juniper.

Hanh, T. N. 1993. None. In *The Soul of the World*, ed. P. Cousineau. San Francisco: HarperSanFrancisco.

Hassler, J. 1980. *Jemmy*. New York: Ballantine.

Hayden, T. L. 1992. *Ghost Girl*. New York: Avon.

Head, A. 1967. *Mr. and Mrs. Bo Jo Jones*. New York: New American Library.

Hinton, S. E. 1967. *The Outsiders*. New York: Dell.

———. 1971. *That Was Then This Is Now*. New York: Dell.

———. 1980. *Tex*. New York: Dell.

———. 1989. *That Was Then, This Is Now*. New York: Dell.

———. 1988. *Taming the Star Runner*. New York: Doubleday.

Hirsch, E. D. 1989. *A First Dictionary of Cultural Literacy*. Boston: Houghton Mifflin.

Hoh, D. 1990. *Funhouse*. New York: Scholastic.

Homer. 1937. *The Odyssey*. Trans. W. H. D. Rouse. New York: A Mentor Book, New American Library.

Houston, G. 1992. *My Great Aunt Arizona*. New York: HarperCollins.

Hunt, I. 1970. *No Promises in the Wind*. New York: Tempo Books.

———. 1976. *The Lottery Rose*. New York: Berkeley.

Irwin, H. 1985. *Abby, My Love*. New York: Atheneum.

King, S. 1983. *Pet Sematary*. New York: Doubleday.

———. 1988. *The Gunslinger*. New York: New Audio Library.

Konigsburg, E. L. 1973. *From the Mixed-Up Files of Mrs. Basil E. Frankweiler*. New York: Atheneum.

Lanes, S. G. 1980. *The Art of Maurice Sendak*. New York: Abrams.

Lopez, B. 1976. *Desert Notes*. New York: Avon.

———. 1990. *Crow and Weasel*. San Francisco: North Point Press.

Macaulay, D. 1988. *The Way Things Work*. Boston: Houghton Mifflin.

MacCracken, M. 1976. *Lovey: A Very Special Child*. New York: New American Library.

———. 1987. *Turnabout Children*. New York: Penguin Books.

Mazer, H. 1978. *The War on Villa Street*. New York: Dell.

———. 1985. *When the Phone Rang*. New York: Scholastic.

Miklowitz, G. 1989. *Secrets Not Meant to Be Kept*. New York: Dell.

Miles, C. 1976. *Christmas Customs and Traditions*. New York: Dover.

Miller, A. 1955. *The Crucible*. New York: Penguin.

Novak, W., and M. Waldoks. 1990. *The Big Book of American Humor*. New York: HarperPerennial.

O'Dell, S. 1960. *Island of the Blue Dolphins*. New York: Dell.

Pasnak, W. 1987. *Degrassi Junior High-Exit Stage Left*. New York: Scholastic.

Paulsen, G. 1977. *Tiltawhirl John*. New York: Puffin.

———. 1978. *The Night the White Deer Died*. New York: Dell.

———. 1983. *Dancing Carl*. New York: Scholastic.

———. 1983. *Popcorn Days and Buttermilk Nights*. New York: Puffin.

———. 1984. *Tracker*. New York: Scholastic.

———. 1985. *Dogsong*. New York: Scholastic.

———. 1986. *Sentries*. New York: Puffin Books.

———. 1987. *The Crossing*. New York: Dell.

———. 1987. *Hatchet*. New York: Bradbury Press.

———. 1987. *Murphy*. New York: Pocket.

———. 1988. *Murphy's Gold*. New York: Pocket.

———. 1989. *The Madonna Stories*. Minnesota: Var Vliet.

———. 1989. *The Winter Room*. New York: Dell.

———. 1990. *Woodsong*. New York: Scholastic Book Services.

———. 1991. *Woodsong*. New York: Bantam Audio.

———. 1991. *The Cook Camp*. New York: Dell Publishers.

———. 1991. *The River*. New York: Delacorte Press.

Peck, R. N. 1972. *A Day No Pigs Would Die*. New York: Dell.

———. 1989. *Arly*. New York: Walker.

Prather, H. 1972. *I Touch the Earth, the Earth Touches Me*. Garden City, NY: Doubleday.

Ransom, C. F. 1989. *Sabrina*. New York: Scholastic.

Rushdie, S. 1990. *Haroun and the Sea of Stories*. New York: Viking.

Schulman, T. 1989. *Dead Poet's Society*. Burbank, CA: Buena-Vista Home Video.

Schurfranz, V. 1989. *Renee*. New York: Scholastic.

Schwartz, A. 1984. *More Scary Stories to Tell in the Dark*. New York: The Trumpet Club.

Segal, E. 1970. *Love Story*. New York: Harper and Row.

Service, R. 1959. *Collected Poems of Robert Service*. New York: Dodd, Meade.

Snyder, A. 1987. *The Truth about Alex*. New York: Signet.

Steinbeck, J. 1937. *Of Mice and Men*. New York: Bantam.

———. 1974. "The Origin of Tularecito," *The pastures of heaven* (1932). In *Look Back in Love*, ed. S. Rosner, 224–237. New York: Scholastic.

Stine, R. L. 1991. *The Snowman*. New York: Scholastic.

———. 1990. *The Boyfriend*. New York: Scholastic.

Swarthout, G. 1967. *Bless the Beasts and the Children*. New York: Bantam.

Theroux, P. 1981. *The Imperial Way by Rail from Peshawar to Chittagong*. Boston: Houghton Mifflin.

Twain, M. 1962. *The Adventures of Tom Sawyer*. New York: Macmillan.

Vance, C. 1991. *If I Had a Hammer*. New York: Harper Collins.

Viorst, J. 1972. *Alexander and the Terrible, Horrible, No Good, Very Bad Day*. New York: Atheneum.

Wallace, B. 1987. *Panther Peak*. New York: Dell.

Weller, T. 1987. *Culture Made Stupid*. Boston: Houghton Mifflin.

Williams, H. 1989. *Whale Nation*. New York: Harmony.

Zindel, P. 1968. *The Pigman*. New York: Bantam.

———. 1970. *The Effect of Gamma Rays on Man-in-the-Moon Marigolds*. New York: Dramatists Play Service.

———. 1970. *I Never Loved Your Mind*. New York: Harper and Row.

Resource References

Action Library. 1971. New York: Scholastic Book Services.

Classic Concentration. 1989. Chandler, AR: Share Data, Inc.

CTBS. Comprehensive Tests of Basic Skills, 4th ed. New York: Macmillan/McGraw-Hill.

DAT. Differential Aptitude Testing. 1982. New York: Psychological Corporation, Harcourt Brace Jovanovich.

English Journal. 1111 W. Kenyon Road, Urbana, IL, 61801: National Council Teachers of English (NCTE).

Jeopardy. 1988. North Miami Beach: Game Tek, Inc.

The Leaflet. P.O. Box 234, Lexington, MA, 02173: New England Association of Teachers of English (NEATE).

Maine Resource Bank Information Exchange. Augusta, ME.

MEA. Maine Education Assessment. Augusta, ME: Department of Education.

MECC. Maine Education Computer Consortium. Augusta, ME.

Microzine. 1989. Jefferson City, MO: Scholastic.

Porter, R. 1984. "Journeys Outward, Journeys In". In *The Reading Road to Writing,* 1–2. New York: Globe.

Potter, R. R., ed. 1976. *Tales of Mystery and Suspense.* Englewood Cliffs, NJ: Globe.

Priven, J. 1984. *Intellectual PSAT/SAT Vocabulary Intellectual Software.* 338 Commerce Drive, Fairfield, CT, 06430: Queue.

Reader's Digest. K. Gilmore, Ed. Pleasantville, NJ.

SRA. Science Research Associates Testing. Chicago, IL.

Warriner, J. E. 1969. *English Grammar and Composition: Complete Course.* New York: Harcourt, Brace Jovanovich.

Index